P9-DUK-556

WHO SPEAKS FOR EUROPE?

Lois Pattison de Ménil

WHO SPEAKS FOR EUROPE?

THE VISION OF CHARLES DE GAULLE

St. Martin's Press
New York

For Jean-Charles, Joy and Benjamin
and For Georges

 For information, write:
St. Martin's Press, Inc., 175 Fifth Avenue, New York, NY 10010

Printed in Great Britain

Library of Congress Catalog Card Number: 77-77137

ISBN 0-312-87025-6

First published in the United States of America in 1978

Contents

Acknowledgments

The completion of this book represents a long journey, with countless debts incurred along the way. My interest in European politics began when, in Paris from 1960 to 1962 as a Fulbright Scholar at l'Institut d'Etudes Politiques, I followed Professor Alfred Grosser's subtle and provocative lectures on Germany. During those years, we lived first-hand the heavy drama of the Algerian war, relieved from time to time by the hope-over-the-horizon of a New Europe that was in the air. Both Alfred Grosser and Jean-Bernard Raimond, then Maître de conférences at la rue Saint-Guillaume, permanently and fundamentally influenced my understanding of European politics and French foreign policy.

As a graduate student at Harvard University subsequently, my interest in European politics was encouraged and deepened by the many lectures, seminars and discussions, both formal and informal with Professors Stanley Hoffmann, and Henry Kissinger. The West European Studies Programme, where I was a Research Fellow, provided a lively forum for discussion of European developments and a refuge for writing the first draft of this manuscript. I also benefited from my association with Harvard's Center for International Affairs.

My research was generously supported by a two-year grant from the Ford Foundation's Foreign Area Fellowship Programme which permitted me to interview many of the participants in the history of the period covered. This included over a hundred interviews with officials at the foreign ministries, military leaders, journalists, and members of parliament. While the confidential nature of these conversations, and the consequent willingness of these participants to speak openly and candidly about events prevents their being identified, I am enormously indebted for their help in filling in where the obvious sources left off.

My debt to Stanley Hoffmann, my teacher, adviser and friend is more than evident throughout this book. His insights have influenced my thinking at every turn.

It is still more difficult to measure the debt owed to friends and colleagues, whose lively interests and curiosity sustain one's own. Guido Goldman, Heinrich Winkler, Josef Joffe, Karl Kaiser and Linda Miller, who were all then at Harvard, were part of an on-going dialogue on European politics. Joe Joffe read the manuscript and offered invaluable criticism. Guido Goldman has shared his vast knowledge of German politics during several trips to Bonn. Beyond that, my personal gratitude for his constant encouragement and support, his apt criticisms and unfailing sense of humour, is inestimable.

While all of these people have contributed to the preparation of this book so generously, responsibility for the facts and conclusions presented is, of course, completely my own.

Finally, I should like to record special thanks to my editor, Linda Osband, and to Jacqueline Jacobs and Rosemarie Granjon, who cheerfully and efficiently typed successive versions of the manuscript. And lastly to my patient husband and young children, who occasionally teach me what deadlines and diplomacy are about.

Lois Pattison de Ménil
Paris, France

Publishers' Acknowledgments

The author and publishers are not only grateful to the people and the firms acknowledged in the text, but also to the following: Quotations from *The Edge of the Sword* by Charles de Gaulle are reprinted by kind permission of Faber and Faber Ltd; passages from *The Complete War Memoirs of Charles de Gaulle Vol. III: Salvation* are reprinted by kind permission of Simon & Schuster Inc., a division of Gulf & Western Corporation; passages from *The New York Times* are © 1966 by *The New York Times* and reprinted by permission; and quotations from *The Army of the Future* by Charles de Gaulle. Translated by Vyvyan Holland. Copyright 1941 by J.B. Lippincott Company. Copyright © renewed 1969 by Mrs Vyvyan B. Holland. Reprinted by permission of J.B. Lippincott Company. The photograph on the back cover is copyright © Martina Franck/Viva.

L'objet politique de cette couronne a été et sera toujours de jouer en Europe le rôle supérieur qui convient à sa grandeur; d'abaisser toute puissance qui tenterait de s'élever au-dessus de la sienne, soit en voulant usurper ses possessions, soit en s'arrogeant une injuste prééminence, soit enfin en cherchant à lui enlever son influence et son crédit dans les affaires générales.

Choiseul, Minister of Louis XV

Introduction

The continent of Europe has been the battleground and stake of three wars in the twentieth century: World War I, which saw the dismantling of the great continental empires; World War II, which resulted in the liquidation of the overseas colonial empires; and the Cold War, which pitted the states of Europe against one another in symmetrical alliance systems dominated by the two superpowers locked in tense competition for global ascendancy. The humiliation of defeat, the political and material dislocations, the economic and moral weakness in the aftermath of World War II put the security and future destiny of the major nation-states of Western Europe in the hands of US diplomacy. Their need for recovery, the common need for security, the common value systems all contributed to a temporary identity of prevailing interests between American and European foreign policy, supported in varying degrees by public opinion and domestic political structures. The case of France was always particularly problematic because of the existence of a strong Communist Party opposed to the Atlantic Alliance and overtly favourable to the foreign policy objectives of the Soviet Union. None the less, so long as the Soviet threat continued to dominate the European political context, it was the pro-American policy that prevailed. The need for security was paramount; it radically simplified the choices. America spoke for Europe.

The American domination of postwar Europe was, none the less, benign. With the massive infusion of capital under the Marshall Plan, Western European economic recovery proceeded at a rapid pace. Franco-German reconciliation was institutionalized in the European Communities. Supported by American policy, the new European institutions promised that both economic and political co-operation would continue, resulting one day in centralized decision-making and federal institutions – a sort of United States of Europe. Security was provided for by the Atlantic Alliance. The enemy states of Germany and Italy were restored to equality: the Federal Republic of Germany, created in 1948, became an equal partner in Nato. Western Europe flourished under the American protectorate born of the cold war.

With the death of Stalin in 1953, and the emergence of Khrushchev as leader in 1956, Soviet policy began to shift away from the gripping confrontations of the cold war toward a more moderate stance of 'peaceful coexistence'. There were, none the less, continued tests of will over Berlin; dramatic episodes of brutal repression, as in Hungary in 1956; head-on superpower confrontations such as the Cuban missile crisis in 1962. But there was also a considerable let-up in tension, a *détente*, compared to the Stalin period.

At the same time, as the states of Western Europe tasted an unprecedented economic affluence and left behind the material and moral scars of the war, more traditional features of their political systems began to reappear. The legacy of history, the political traditions, the 'belief systems' that constitute a nation's sense of its destiny – the psychological underpinnings of policy – all contributed to a reconsideration of the habit of looking to Washington to decide on their destiny. Now that the states of Western Europe were back on their feet, to varying degrees they reasserted their right to be responsible for their own future, even if that meant challenging US policy. There were head-on conflicts, such as the Anglo-French Suez expedition in 1956; and there were chronic conflicts – over colonial policy, for instance – between the US and France – with US diplomacy taking no account of the domestic forces behind its allies' policy. The US continued its rhetoric of common interests, common effort, and the need for Western unity. But it was clear to any close observer of the French political system that a clash of interests was the more likely product of French domestic politics, as perceived interests parted ways.

In regard to Atlantic policy, there was a hard-core resistance to American political domination of the Alliance on the part of the Communists, the Socialists and the Gaullists. Their opposition was in part 'anti-American', but, still more, resistance to having French policy dictated by Washington. They favoured an active, independent 'French' foreign policy, and were not unwilling to entertain neutralism as a possible option. In regard to European policy, there was a 'pro-European' alignment that included part of the Socialists, the centre, the right, and some – but not all – of the Gaullists.[1] Other Gaullists would favour Europe so long as it was nothing more than a vehicle for French leadership of the continent to replace US leadership. What is immediately clear is that a pro-European policy based also on resistance to America would have the support of the Socialists and the Gaullists, and would pull along the centre and right as well – the broadest possible foreign policy coalition, though evidently covering important differences in emphasis.

France would therefore speak for itself. It gave itself the voice it needed in Charles de Gaulle.

Faced with the French demand for accommodation of its desire to resume its traditional diplomatic status, American diplomacy continued to voice the old rhetoric of the common cause, and to dismiss the French bid on the grounds that it originated in an irrational assessment of France's real power, that French power objectives were unattainable and founded on nationalist illusions, that France's determination to steer its own course was contrary to the real interests of Europe, which were amply protected by American policy then as in the past. De Gaulle was denounced as a madman temporarily in charge of the conduct of French policy. No attention was paid to the broad base of support his policy of independence enjoyed domestically, across the spectrum of public opinion and political parties, despite intermittent domestic opposition to specific Gaullist tactics *vis-à-vis* the EEC. No effort was made to accommodate the bid for participation. Instead, US diplomacy stepped up its determination to resist the possible contagion of French attempts at disengagement from the US-dominated Atlantic system, by calling its friends into line in the other European capitals in the name of 'Atlantic Community'. This struggle between French and American diplomacy posed again the question of who was responsible for Europe's destiny: who speaks for Europe?

1. See Stanley Hoffmann, "No Trumps, No Luck, No Will", in James Chace and Earl Ravenel (eds), *Atlantis Lost: U.S.–European Relations after the Cold War*, New York, New York University Press for the Council on Foreign Relations, 1976, p. 13.

De Gaulle staked out France's claim to European leadership in the name of her traditional role as a continental power. Stripped of her former colonial empire, what role, after all, could France play if not one of continental leadership? What other European state could compete for that role? The Habsburg empire had disintegrated after World War I. Italy and Germany were discredited from leadership by their defeat in World War II. Soviet Russia, which had overturned the tsarist regime during World War I, had consolidated for itself both an empire and a sphere of influence in Eastern Europe in the aftermath of World War II. Great Britain appeared more preoccupied with its commonwealth relationships and its reliance on American policy than with assuming leadership of the continent, and only reluctantly moved toward identifying its destiny with Western Europe – moreover with fragile domestic support for that option. France viewed her destiny as European. For French diplomacy to take up the European option was, therefore, both a means for the states of Europe to increase their common weight in international politics, and also a recognition of French identity – her sense of belonging to the peoples of Europe united in a common destiny.

The central problem in Europe was the stalemated superpower confrontation over the postwar political settlement. The question involved frontiers and political ideology. It centred above all on the place and weight of Germany within a European settlement. Divided Germany was the very symbol of the superpower confrontation, of the cold war conflict that resulted in stalemate between the two blocs. Within France, that pattern was reproduced, with partisans of Atlantic policy, partisans of Soviet policy, and a broad spectrum of neutralist opinion ranged in between. Breaking out of the cold war straitjacket would therefore produce a certain *détente* in French domestic politics as well.

Hence, de Gaulle's European policy had its origins, in part, in France's desire to reassert her historical role, and in the pressures of the domestic political context. De Gaulle defined and mobilized those forces of support behind his personal conduct of policy. He galvanized public opinion by the force of rhetoric, orchestrating his diplomatic action and public statements in counterpoint to maximize his influence in the diplomatic bargaining process. Demonstrating French steadfastness in the face of Anglo-

American vacillation during the Berlin crisis, he succeeded in consolidating the Franco-German rapprochement he required as the foundation for his European policy.

But his moves were no match for the sheer weight of the US presence in European politics. He could resist American moves and pose an obstacle to the designs of US diplomacy, since nothing could be accomplished without France, but he could not accomplish his own objectives once the weight of US diplomacy was thrown against them.

De Gaulle was a master statesman. A shrewd observer of history and international politics, he exploited events adroitly to further his objectives, trading astuteness, persuasion, wit and will for the advantages of material power. This study explores the origins, the substance and the conduct of de Gaulle's European policy.

CHAPTER ONE

Roots

Nathanaël, je t'enseignerai la ferveur.
André Gide, *Les Nourritures terrestres*

When Charles de Gaulle first addressed himself to the great issue of diplomacy, he was a relatively obscure professor of military history at the French Army Staff College. Born in 1890, the son of a Catholic intellectual professor of philosophy who had fought in the army of Napoleon III and seen Alsace and Lorraine surrendered in defeat to the Prussians, Charles de Gaulle had been raised in a generation whose historical mission it was to avenge the defeat of 1870. It was a generation whose world view was perforce to be dominated by an obsession with Germany. Nurtured on their fathers' bitter memories of the Franco-Prussian War, they were in their own youth to suffer the terrible toll of another German invasion, only to see their fragile victory shattered in the wake of a third German invasion twenty years later. It was a generation which imbibed the sentimental cult of the soil of Barrès, a generation whose early days were marked by the passions of the Dreyfus affair and the stormy antagonisms opposing Catholics and free thinkers, a generation impregnated with the lofty philosophy of Henri Bergson. And finally, it was a generation that added to the best-seller list the works of Rightist historian Jacques Bainville, whose grandiose tomes on European history viewed through the German prism now collect dust behind elegant bindings on the bookshelves of the French bourgeoisie. In that nationalist context of de Gaulle's early youth, *le problème allemand* – the German question – posed the principal challenge to French policy and defined the realities with which French diplomacy had to contend. It is against this background of the world of his youth, and in the concerns of his early writings, that one recognizes the mainsprings of action of Charles de Gaulle the statesman.

Charles de Gaulle's intellectual debt to the philosopher Henri Bergson, to whom he alludes liberally in his book, *Le Fil de l'épée*,[1] is evident. Bergson's philosophy influenced de Gaulle's understanding of the world profoundly and permanently. Bergson set forth a dynamic philosophy that went beyond the fixed and rigid logical categories widely used to explain reality by stressing the qualities of movement, becoming, flux. Reality – by definition fluid and vibrant – could not be fully comprehended in abstract rational or cognitive categories, but rather through the creative faculties, in the interplay of instinct, intuition and intellect. Bergson's compelling philosophy of *l'élan vital* was a French variant of the growing interest at the turn of the century in the workings of the unconscious. As a philosophy of action, it gave rise to a heroic idealism that sent the young poet Péguy and countless others of his generation fervently forth to the battlefields of World War I. And as an intellectual movement it was perhaps to die there along with them.

Whatever the fate of his philosophy as an intellectual revolution, Bergson's emphasis on the dynamic character of reality, on the forces of instinct and intuition, the fervent passions animating human existence, were lessons not to be lost on the young Charles de Gaulle. Years later, when he came to write his famous treatise on leadership, *Le Fil de l'épée*, de Gaulle credited Bergson for his insight into the nature of reality and the functioning of human intelligence.

> The human mind is so constructed as to deal most easily with the constant, the fixed, the definite; it does its best to avoid the fluid, the unstable, the changeable. Bergson both analyzes and depicts the discomfort felt by the intelligence when it tries to come to grips with a *reality which is forever on the move*.[2]
>
> It is Bergson, also, who has shown that the only way in which the human mind can make direct contact with reality is by intuition. Our intelligence can furnish us with the theoretic, general abstract knowledge of what is, but only instinct can give us the practical, particular

1. Translated as *The Edge of the Sword*, London, Faber and Faber Ltd, 1960; New York, Criterion Books, 1960. Subsequent English quotations are taken from this edition.
2. De Gaulle, *The Edge of the Sword*, p. 16. Emphasis added.

and concrete *feel* of it. Without the cooperation of the intelligence there can be no logical reasoning, no informed judgement. But without the reinforcement of instinct there can be no profundity of perception and no creative urge.[3]

Bergson's reliance on intuition as an essential ingredient in perceiving reality became indeed a cardinal tenet of de Gaulle's personal convictions. It was therefore natural that when he reflected on the nature of leadership, he was to attach especial importance to that unique 'feel for things' which sets the leader apart from the multitudes. Despite the fact that others were later to label him an illusionist and a dreamer, de Gaulle stubbornly clung both to the correctness of his intuitions and to his self-image first and foremost as the realist. To view the world 'as it really is' was always his object and prelude to action – at least, that was *his* view of things.

To those few mortals who could fulfil the stiff requirements of instinct and intelligence as prerequisites to realistic action, de Gaulle addressed his treatise on leadership, *Le Fil de l'épée*. Great diplomacy required a first-rate leader to give it shape – one capable of acting decisively and of rallying men to his support. The question is: what qualities of character and mind are essential to leadership, to the man who would embrace men and events realistically and act autonomously on both? *Le Fil de l'épée* is a remarkable self-portrait.

Broadly speaking, there are three major themes that wind in and out of de Gaulle's recipes for leadership and that constitute the conceptual framework: (1) his vision of human nature, and thus of both men and nations, as characteristically selfish, acquisitive and short-sighted; (2) the chivalric penchant for service of the great statesman or soldier hero – values which set him apart from the selfish masses whose collective good he would serve; and (3) the importance of the radical technical and social changes that have occurred since pre-World War I days, and that form the historical stage for action.

De Gaulle's categorical pronouncements on the behaviour of men and nations echo the austere pessimism of conservative Christianity with its uncompromising insistence on the fallen nature of man – or still more, the grim Hobbesian vision of the selfish struggle for survival in the state of nature. De Gaulle was

3. De Gaulle, *The Edge of the Sword*, p. 20. Emphasis added.

no Wilsonian, still less a disciple of Kant. There is little sympathy for prophetic or utopian visions of history in his concept of human nature. Indeed, he asserts sceptically, men have hoped forever for the reign of peace when swords would be beaten into ploughshares:

> But hope though we may, what reason have we for thinking that passions and self-interest, the root cause of armed conflict in men and in nations, will cease to operate; that anyone will willingly surrender what he has or try not to get what he wants; in short, that human nature will ever be something other than it is? Is it really likely that the present balance of power will remain unchanged so long as the small want to become great, the strong to dominate the weak, the old to live on? How are frontiers to be stabilized, how is power to be controlled if evolution continues along the same lines as hitherto?[4]

Here is de Gaulle-the-sceptic in most naked view. How can frontiers be guaranteed and power limited so long as the age-old forces of history remain unchanged? Only counterforce or constraint will curb the old selfish ambitions. Since conflict and not harmony is the condition natural to men and nations, constraint alone can guarantee a peaceful order. Not that de Gaulle extols this egotism of nations; rather, he claims that this is the raw material, the 'facts' of life. Virtue and harmony do not prevail spontaneously, they must be imposed.

> International agreements will be of little value unless there are troops to prevent their infringements. In whatever direction the world may move, it will never be able to do without the final arbitrament of arms. As for . . . that international order which this age is trying to build up, how is it possible to conceive of such an organization without an armed force to establish it and to guarantee its continued existence?[5]

Constraint is therefore necessary to discipline the natural self-seeking urge of men and nations. In relations between nations, constraint is identified with military power.[6] The overriding preoccupation with the relationship of military power to political goals thus becomes a persistent theme in de Gaulle's statements and policies. It goes far toward explaining his constant equation

4. De Gaulle, *The Edge of the Sword*, p. 9.
5. De Gaulle, *The Edge of the Sword*, p. 75
6. Atomic weapons do not alter this age-old equation – they constitute one more ingredient in the reservoir of power.

of defence policy with all policy, or at least as the *sine qua non* of foreign policy.

In contrast to the intrinsic selfishness of men and nations stands the virtue of the heroic leader, who strides across the canvas of history as a brilliant mixture of the chivalric knight-in-shining-armour and the biblical suffering servant. The leader belongs to a special breed of men. Like the heroes of Stendhal's novels, he is superior in both natural ingenuity and vigour; and like the Nietzschean hero, he is impelled to seek his own self-fulfilment in great feats of self-transcendence. The hero's virtue is at once his self-mastery and his courageous self-sacrifice to a cause higher than himself. Power in itself is not an intrinsically worthy goal. The greatest virtue is the service of a noble cause. Hence, although force is required in order to curb selfish passions and to protect one's interests, power and confrontation afford above all the occasion for valour. De Gaulle's soldier hero combines the Roman and Christian notions of grandeur:

> The self-sacrifice of individuals for the sake of the community, suffering made glorious – those two things which are the basic elements of the profession of arms – respond to both our moral and aesthetic concepts. The noble teachings of philosophy and religion have found no higher ideals. . . .
>
> Only if the philosophy proper to the soldier is restored will an edge be given to the sword. In that philosophy he will find nobility of outlook, pride in his vocation, and a chance to influence the world outside himself. In it, till the day of glory dawns, he will find the sole reward worth considering.[7]

The 'sole reward worth considering' is the valour of public service. Too often overlooked, this theme of service is, in fact, fundamental to de Gaulle's concept of leadership: it forms at all times the complement to a purely self-serving ambition. De Gaulle does not broach the ethical issue raised by the service of an ignoble public policy – in fact, he does not discuss the ends of policy at all, although elsewhere he does exalt lyrically men of history who knew how to disobey, to part with popular course and strike out independently on the strength of their own conviction and character alone.[8] De Gaulle's heroic leader identifies his own reward with the service of the highest interest of the

7. De Gaulle, *The Edge of the Sword*, p. 10.
8. De Gaulle, *The Edge of the Sword*, pp. 44–5.

nation – an interest which may not necessarily correspond to the popular view. That he does not go further to postulate an ideal of service and self-sacrifice to the wider community of men doubtless hinges on two factors: (1) the legacy of the nationalism of his youth – his subjective attachment to France as a kind of enlarged family group; and (2) the peculiarly French propensity, dating back to the universalism of the Revolutionary ideology, to assume as axiomatic the identity of French interests with the universal interests of mankind. This latter concept runs unabashedly all through de Gaulle's writings and public statements, for example his 1968 New Year's message to the French people: 'As for our external activity, we shall pursue it on the basis of our independence. This activity aims at reaching goals, linked among themselves, and which, *because they are French*, serve the interest of mankind.'[9]

In any case, de Gaulle's concern in *Le Fil de l'épée* is obviously not with policy. Rather, the book is a manual on leadership, setting forth the personal qualities and style the superior leader must incarnate – spartan qualities tinged at times with an austere, jansenistic tone:

> Aloofness, character, and the personification of greatness, these qualities it is that surround with prestige those who are prepared to carry a burden which is too heavy for lesser mortals. . . . The degree of suffering involved varies according to the temperament of the individual, but it is bound to be no less tormenting than the hair shirt of the penitent.[10]

The lyrical style of this summation reveals it as a ringing and passionate statement both of de Gaulle's personal ideals and of his own intense desire to play the role of leader.

Perhaps the most remarkable theme expounded in *Le Fil de l'épée* is one which is most often overlooked. It is the emphatic preoccupation with *change*, with the role of the contingent in human affairs. The opening sentence sets the tone for everything that is to follow: 'War is an activity in which the contingent plays an essential part.'[11] It is here that de Gaulle the strategist and de Gaulle the student of Bergson is at his best. De Gaulle's lasting debt to Bergson is perhaps this heightened awareness of reality

9. *Sélection hebdomadaire du Monde, 28 décembre–3 janvier 1968.* Emphasis added.
10. De Gaulle, *The Edge of the Sword*, pp. 65–6.
11. De Gaulle, *The Edge of the Sword*, p. 15.

as constant movement, and consequently of the new 'contingencies' that are constantly altering our perceptions of yesterday and today, forcing us to reappraise our fixed strategies and judgments. He pleads eloquently for a new French military strategy, based on an empirical approach open to the full range of immediate circumstances, and inveighs against the prevailing strategy, based on deductions from abstract *a priori* principles largely derived from the circumstances of the last war. The world has changed radically since 1914, de Gaulle pleads – the technological revolution brought about by the internal combustion engine is the wave of the future and is already in process. He summons all his literary eloquence to the cause, painting in flowing three-part cadences a sensitive portrait of a new generation of Frenchmen:

> The men and women of this generation can only with great effort imagine what life was like before 1914, can barely visualize that era of stability, economy, and prudence; of vested interests, traditional political parties, and solid business concerns; of fixed interest securities, settled rates of pay, and carefully calculated pensions of the three per cents and the sliding scale; of the old-fashioned machinery and equipment, and solid marriage settlements. Competition and improved techniques – an allegoric group symbolizing the new age.
>
> These new conditions of life have strengthened tendencies which were once rare. For a hundred years French society lived in constant dread of everything that seemed risky, remote or changeable. But now a new wind is blowing. Our countrymen have become enterprising, hungry for adventure, eager for renewal. A century ago the Frenchman's ideal was to occupy a safe position in the civil service, to stay at home, to imitate those who had made a success of their lives. Today his taste is for making money, covering great distances, and avoiding living by the rule, in a stereotyped pattern of existence. He feels the need for different criteria of thought and action. He no longer grumbles about expense, but hankers after the 'latest model'; he no longer hesitates to board a liner, with a pocketful of appreciated sterling, and travel the world. There was a time when we canvassed all the wisdom of the ages to help us live unlaborious days. But life has now become an endurance test in which we all go full out.[12]

The surrealists also had their heyday in the restless 1920s. But de Gaulle viewed the changes in society through the eyes of a moralist.

12. De Gaulle, *The Edge of the Sword*, pp. 47–8.

In another early work, *Vers l'armée de métier*,[13] which first appeared in 1934, de Gaulle rehearses this theme of technological and social change still more trenchantly, concluding with one of his characteristically pithy summations: 'Secourable amie de toujours, la machine à présent régit notre destin.' The machine rules our destiny. Charles de Gaulle was later to witness this first-hand: it was by radio from London that he was able to assert his leadership over the Resistance; it was the radio, not the sword, that shaped his own destiny. But de Gaulle's attitude toward change is dispassionate: he espouses neither the Left's exaltation of progress, nor the Right's appeal to tradition. For though times change, human nature does not. The hankering for change of his contemporaries is elsewhere wedded to that deeper pessimism which de Gaulle reserves for his pronouncements on the human condition:

> In three words: 'inconstancy, boredom, anguish', Pascal summed up the human condition, and prophesied the passion for travel that would seize us as soon as the means of transport enabled us to move quickly from place to place. To leave home, to escape one's familiar environment, to seek beyond the horizon a new object in life: such is indeed our impulse nowadays – and perhaps our illusion.[14]

Vers l'armée de métier is the work of a disciple of Auguste Comte, herald of the technocratic age, the age of specialization, the age of professionalism. De Gaulle declared himself advocate of the mechanization of the army. Pitting himself relentlessly against the prevailing strategic theory of the times, the defensive Maginot Line strategy, he called for a professional army of highly mobile, technically skilled and flexible offensive units. The major lesson to be drawn from the past, according to de Gaulle, was the constant change in military tactics accompanying progress in weapons development and technology. To formulate a universal strategy by codifying the experiences of the past war was therefore to court defeat, for a change in any of the conditions of the war would render the strategy obsolete. The key to strategy is manœuvrability – keeping options open to meet varying circumstances. Manœuvrability, secret and surprise – the strategist's

13. De Gaulle, *Vers l'armeé de métier*, Paris, Presses Pocket [no date]. Translated as *The Army of the Future*, London, Hutchinson Publishing Group Ltd, 1940; New York, J.B. Lippincott, 1940.

14. De Gaulle, *The Army of the Future*, p. 98. I have adapted the text somewhat to follow the French text more faithfully.

trinity that has since been elevated to his personal recipe for government. But France did not listen to Charles de Gaulle then. It was ironically the German General Staff who prepared for the war of movement, while France remained tranquillized behind the fortress frontiers of the Maginot Line.

Charles de Gaulle had drawn his own *éducation politique* – his concept of the grandeur and misery of men and states, his admiration for noble acts of heroism, his view of reality as contingent and constantly changing – from his austere Catholic upbringing, his deep love for the characters and episodes of history, from the lessons of Bergson's philosophy. He was, in addition, possessed of that combination of awareness and sensitivity that endows some few men with a sharp insight into the spirit of their times. Alone among his contemporaries, he foresaw the consequences of the dawn of the technical age that we now live in, the crisis in authority, the crumbling of the old and secure way of life of the world he had grown up in. Yet, in concrete terms, what he warned his country against was the menacing resurgence of Germany.

There was, of course, nothing new about the obsession with Germany: Germanophobia had long become the characteristic reflex in French thinking on foreign policy. It was indeed the fetish for security *vis-à-vis* Germany that provided the psychological underpinnings for the mentality symbolized by the Maginot Line. Rightist historian Jacques Bainville's best-seller, *L'Histoire de deux peuples*,[15] had first appeared in 1915, and was reissued in a revised edition in 1933. Bainville's book, a sweeping 250–page synthesis of French history from the Capetian kings to the rise of Hitler, traced the whole history of Europe schematically through the prism of France's relations with her German neighbours. To French schoolboys, accustomed to viewing French history as an epic of intermittent wars with the English, this must have come as a very new perspective on the past. Bainville's book is an historical crusade, animated by Germanophobia and supported by selective analyses of French diplomacy toward the Habsburg empire and Prussia. It is wholly continental in its focus. Bainville's work is important not only because he was so widely read in the interwar years, but more particularly because so

15. Jacques Bainville, *L'Histoire de deux peuples*, Paris, Arthème Fayard (1915), revised ed. 1933, translated by Lois Pattison de Ménil.

many of his key ideas appear only slightly altered in de Gaulle's 1934 book, *Vers l'armée de métier*.

In the introduction to his *L'Histoire de deux peuples*, Bainville sets out immediately the scope of his work:

When one studies France's relations with the rest of Europe, one notes that the greatest task of the French people has been imposed by the fact that the Teuton race is its neighbor. With our other neighbors – English, Spanish, Italian – if there have been conflicts, there have also been enduring periods of peace, long periods of accord, security and confidence. France is the most genial of all peoples [sic]. Indeed, that is attested by the fact that at certain moments – and rather long ones – we have even been in alliance and friendship with Germany itself. To be sure, it was after having defeated her. To be sure, it was only after long effort and hard work that permitted us through political strength to deprive her of destructive means. For the Germans are the only people that has always perforce preoccupied France, that she has always had to keep under her surveillance.[16]

The most immediately evident paradox in this text is the anachronistic use of the term 'l'Allemagne' for 'Germany' with reference to past history. It betrays the bias underlying Bainville's whole analysis. What 'Germany' does he have in mind? The Habsburgs? The Holy Roman Empire? Prussia? Or the mosaic of lesser principalities? Does he refer to a political unit, or rather to a kind of linguistic unity – or again to an ethnic or racial common denominator? What is 'le peuple allemand' of which he speaks? Nor does the subsequent exposition make this much more explicit. At best, 'l'Allemagne' was a kind of national mystique for Bainville, the very symbol of a human force at once ominous, compelling and mysterious – and that mystique was very largely shared by his readers as well.

Bainville's purpose in writing *L'Histoire de deux peuples* is essentially to probe an issue of causality in history. Is Franco-German enmity the work of chance or fate? Wherein does the responsibility lie? His conclusion is hardly encouraging – a combination of geography and history holds the two nations in a predetermined grip, a veritable visiting of the sins of the fathers upon the sons:

How true it is, in Auguste Comte's words, that the living are governed by the dead! By turns, the French have reaped the fruits of

16. Bainville, *L'Histoire de deux peuples*, pp. 7–8.

wisdom of their forebears and suffered from their errors. We do not escape from this law of dependency. Let us at least understand how it operates! Such is the object of this work.[17]

Bainville begins his exposition with the classic linking of geography and destiny – a theme which de Gaulle subsequently took over and expanded in his *Vers l'armée de métier*:

> On five sides of the hexagon, the successors of Hugues Capet had given France its shape and limits. They disappeared before having completed their task. And the work of so many years was indeed threatened, compromised, along that Northeastern frontier where the French nation had so long applied its effort....
>
> France is not safe so long as the weight of neighboring Germany presses upon her, so long as German armies remain at a few days' march from Paris.[18]

In looking back through European history, Bainville finds a law at work in French diplomacy. The French kings, according to Bainville's analysis, sought persistently and zealously to oppose all efforts to unite the Germanic peoples, out of fear of continental hegemony. Thus, French diplomacy skilfully resisted the efforts of the Habsburgs to establish a hereditary empire replacing the electoral system, and consistently favoured the elements of dispersion and parochial interests within the Holy Roman Empire by maintaining a veritable mosaic of clients in an anarchic system. For Bainville, it was indubitably the monarchy of the *ancien régime* that best protected France's interests *vis-à-vis* Germany: from the Revolution on, it had been straight downhill. This was because the Revolution had actually reversed the policy of the last Bourbons. In the middle of the eighteenth century, there had been a spectacular reversal of alliances based

17. Bainville, 'Avant-propos', *L'Histoire de deux peuples*, pp. 8–9.

18. Bainville, *L'Histoire de deux peuples*, p. 12. This theme of France as an incomplete hexagon is a very familiar one to anyone acquainted with French primary school textbooks. It was the Revolution that first popularized the slogan of 'natural borders'. But while it may well satisfy one's sense of geometric balance to fancy that the Rhine frontier would complete the hexagon in faultless symmetry, the facts are unfortunately less impressive than the theory. In fact, the meandering Rhine offers no natural boundary of any consequence: north of Koblenz, its banks are virtually flat, and south of Koblenz, it becomes so narrow as to be illusory as a protective demarcation line. And in any case, even with the Rhine frontier, the German army would still remain only 'a few days' march from Paris'. If the Germans were intent on attacking France, it would not be the Rhine that would dissuade them. But this mystique of the natural borders was a deeply ingrained article of faith in France.

on a new convergence of interests: the Habsburgs were no longer dangerous to France, while Prussia was growing rapidly. Accordingly, the crown had prudently reversed its age-old policy of opposition and had joined in an alliance with Austria to counter the growing Prussian strength. Bainville considered this policy excellent, or, in his highest words of praise, 'manœvrière et novatrice'. But it was an intensely unpopular policy:

> In adapting its system of foreign policy to new conditions, the French monarchy showed itself to be skillful and innovating. But the public at large did not follow it, remained instead lethargically in a rut, attached to a dead past. Perhaps the people would have caught on in the end and gone along with the crown if the leaders of public opinion (that is, the 'Philosophes') had proved capable of enlightening them. But they, too, engaged themselves on the side of error, because of their ideas, because of their vanity and because of the stand that they had taken.[19]

Inspired by the great passion of their youth, deeply Prussophile and anti-Austrian, the Revolutionary leaders Brissot and Dumouriez reversed the monarchy's new policy at the first opportunity in 1792:

> In truth, the Revolution did not represent a continuation of the ancien régime in its European policy: it pretended to pursue the same policy, but with corrections. By the most curious of phenomena, the Revolution wished to return to the very purest traditions of French policy, which had been altered by the last two kings since the reversal of alliances. In this sense, the Revolution was reactionary.[20]

Thus, the secular policy of dividing Germany and keeping it in a mosaic anarchy was broken. Joined together by Napoleon, the Germanic peoples were never again to be controlled by the skilful counterbalancing of French diplomacy, which, contrary to its own interest, thereafter supported the growing nationalist movement. From Bismarck to Hitler, the unifying of Germany continued without surcease until the suppression of the last vestiges of federalism. So, Bainville ends on a note of paradox and foreboding, the history of the two peoples continues; but

> never have the French so little understood the Germans. Their reasoning and their sentiments escape us. Their intellectual and emotional

19. Bainville, *L'Histoire de deux peuples* pp. 119–20.
20. Bainville, *L'Histoire de deux peuples*, p. 137.

world is not ours. Never, perhaps, have they been so different from us. Even art is a breeding ground for misunderstanding. When we hear *Siegfried*, when the hero, crossing the circle of fire, awakens the sleeping Brunhilde, this theater is for us a puerile mythology, serving as a pretext for music. This music, for Wagner, was that 'of the future.' And the Walkyrie sings, 'Hail to thee, sun! Hail to thee, light! Bright day, hail! My sleep has been long. What hero awakened me?' Words from an opera libretto here. But there, a symbol of resurrection and metamorphosis. What destiny does this Germany, different and yet like unto herself, hold in store?[21]

Jacques Bainville's *L'Histoire de deux peuples* appeared in a revised and updated edition in 1933. It was in 1934, one year after the Nazi seizure of power, that Charles de Gaulle's book *Vers l'armée de métier* first appeared. The parallels are sufficiently striking to suggest at least a remarkably common outlook, if not a direct influence. Bainville's book opens on a note of warning:

As soon as the perseverance of several generations of Capetians had begun to give shape to France, the problem of the Eastern frontiers was raised. The kingdom, having expanded, found itself confronted suddenly by a hostile world. Germany stood guard before the Rhine, and it was towards the Rhine that France was destined to expand in order to satisfy reason. . . .[22]

De Gaulle's book picks up on the same warning note, and the same linking of geography and destiny: 'As looking at a portrait suggests the impression of the subject's destiny to the observer, so the map of France tells our own fortune.'[23] De Gaulle then describes France as a medieval fortress flanked by natural barriers on all sides, except for 'une brèche terrible' in the northeast:

This breach in the ramparts is the age-old weakness of the country. Through it, Roman Gaul saw the Barbarians hurl themselves upon her wealth. It was there that the Monarchy struggled to resist the pressure of the Holy Roman Empire. There Louis XIV defended his power against the combined forces of Europe. The Revolution nearly perished there. Napoleon succumbed there. In 1870, disaster and shame advanced along the same route. In this fatal boulevard we have just buried one-third of our youth. Quite apart from war crises, with what

21. Bainville, *L'Histoire de deux peuples*, pp. 251–2.
22. Bainville, *L'Histoire de deux peuples*, pp. 11–12.
23. De Gaulle, *The Army of the Future*, p. 11.

a heavy load has the anxiety of a poor frontier weighed upon France! How many projects have proved abortive, how many hopes have been shattered, how many enterprises brought to nothing, all for want of a good closure for the domain![24]

Like Bainville, de Gaulle also restates the theme of the incomplete hexagon. In a sweeping panorama of European topology, he explains how natural geography favours other countries, particularly Germany, and he laments the vulnerability of France. A traveller flying from Berlin to Paris, he suggests, will not fail to notice all that makes for the security of Germany and the weakness of France. For, while Germany is indeed a 'fortress',[25] barely does one cross the frontier into France when 'suddenly the land flattens out, grows gentler and more humane. No more mountains, gorges or precipices. *C'est la France*.'[26]

Gentle and humane in its geography, France is ever vulnerable to the nefarious designs of her well-protected neighbour. Moving nimbly through the pages of history, de Gaulle sketches in the heavy past conditioned by this natural fault in geography. Indeed, he begins his second chapter with a very appropriate quotation from Napoleon, to the effect that the policies of a state are dictated by geography; for what security is not provided by nature must find its compensation in diplomacy. He notes the secular struggles between the Germans and the French, and finds that they are therefore 'in the nature of things'.[27] And finally, picking up on the note where Bainville left off, he comes to what he calls 'l'opposition des tempéraments' which complements and animates the natural hostility between the two peoples. Incompatible qualities of national character contribute to the inevitable antagonism between the French and German nations.

De Gaulle's description of his countrymen is an impressionist portrait painted with delicacy and tenderness, embellished with a classical rhetoric and stylistic rigour:

This Frenchman, who has so much order in his mind and so little in his acts, this logician who doubts everything, this stay-at-home colonizer, this enthusiast for alexandrines, tailcoats and public gardens,

24. De Gaulle, *The Army of the Future*, pp. 12–13 (translation adapted).

25. The recurrent fortress image is suggestive of de Gaulle's mental vision of France and Germany as two warring feudal lords.

26. De Gaulle, *The Army of the Future*, p. 17 (translation adapted).

27. De Gaulle, *The Army of the Future*, p. 19.

who, nevertheless, sings comic songs, goes about in sloppy clothes and strews the grass with litter, this Colbert colleague of Louvois, this Jacobin shouting '*Vive l'Empereur!*' this politician who forms the *Union Sacrée*, this man defeated at Charleroi who attacks on the Marne, in short this fickle, uncertain, contradictory nation, how could the Teuton sympathize with it, understand it, or trust it?[28]

If de Gaulle relishes the paradoxical qualities of his own countrymen, when he turns to the Germans it is a different spirit that animates his description. He views the German people with mystery and bewilderment – a primitive, barbarous force at once fascinating and frightening:

And, conversely, we are preoccupied by Germany – a force of nature, to which she clings so closely; a bundle of powerful yet hazy instincts; born artists devoid of taste, technicians who remain feudal, bellicose fathers of families, with restaurants that are temples; factories in the midst of forests, gothic palaces for lavatories, oppressors who want to be loved, separatists who are slavishly obedient, chivalrous knights who get sick on too much beer; all that Siegfried the Limousin sees as epic in the morning, romantic towards midday, warlike in the evening; sublime and glaucous ocean from which the net draws forth a jumble of monsters and treasures; cathedral whose polychrome nave – assembled with noble arches – fills with harmonious tones and organizes in symphonic harmony for the senses, for the mind, for the soul, the emotion and light and religion of the world, but whose dark transept, echoing with barbarous noises, shocks one's eyes, mind and heart.[29]

'Monsters and treasures' – de Gaulle's fervent portrait of the Germans captures the *Sturm und Drang* romanticism that eludes his rational comprehension even as much as the intense contrasts between vulgarity and finesse shock his aesthetic and emotional sensibilities. Gone is the piquant taste for paradox which he reserves for his own countrymen: Germany evokes instead a tone of ominous contradiction, giving way to a romantic effusion in which are mixed equal ingredients of admiration and fear.[30]

How to deal with this burden of geography, history and incompatible national character? De Gaulle looks to the past, and like Bainville finds that traditional French policy succeeded

28. De Gaulle, *The Army of the Future*, p. 20.

29. De Gaulle, *The Army of the Future*, pp. 20–1 (translation adapted).

30. Yet, in the very midst of his lyrical effusion, de Gaulle evokes the image of Giraudoux's hero, Siegfried the Limousin – the German soldier suffering from amnesia, who discovers he is really French. Siegfried, that most German of heroes, is after all French. How much France and Germany share!

best in limiting the danger of the German colossus to the east by an astute game of diplomatic acrobatics – manœuvring, balancing, watching, threatening, buying-off, intriguing. Alas, the present situation no longer affords that opportunity:

> But this classic game of chess in which, by combining force with intrigue, we held the fury of the Teutons at bay, has been swept from the board. . . . German unity, favored by our illusions, cemented by our disasters, consolidated by our haste to limit the result of our recent victory of 1918, has put the colossus in a position to hurl itself upon the West in a single instantaneous bound.[31]

How can the valkyrian spirits be kept in check now? Delving deeper into the internal fabric of German life than Bainville, de Gaulle goes on to analyse the internal divisions which restrain German expansionism. He draws the commonplace distinction between the autonomous Bavarians and the Prussians, the Catholics of the Rhineland and the Protestant 'functionaries',[32] and points out that these internal divisions are both a hope and a threat. They are a hope in so far as they hinder internal cohesion and provide thereby a domestic constraint on national ambitions in the area of foreign policy; yet, they are still more a threat in that they encourage an activist foreign policy as a precondition for internal cohesion:

> It is just this threat of anarchy that eggs on the German Empire to undertake great enterprises. Its continued unity depends upon outside expansion and great designs, which alone in the eyes of the Germans justify the sacrifices they make for them. Bismarck understood this at first; when he seemed to forget it, a young emperor turned him out, with the approval of everyone. Today, the Reich follows along the same lines. Who can doubt that a fresh crisis will once more draw the Germans toward Paris?[33]

For Charles de Gaulle had no doubt that the Germans would march again toward Paris, and he even stated categorically the

31. De Gaulle, *The Army of the Future*, p. 21 (translation adapted).

32. It is worth noting that this division corresponds to the popular French distinction between a 'good' and 'bad' Germany. 'Good' Germany is the Catholic Rhineland, Bavaria, and the Romantic Route; 'bad' Germany is Prussia, the Protestant north, and ultimately any part other than the 'good' part. To appreciate the extent of this popular myth, see the ever-popular *Michelin Green Guide* for Germany, virtually *all* of which extols the wonders of the Rhineland, Bavaria and the 'Route Romantique'. The rest of Germany apparently goes unexplored by tourists following the *Guide Vert*.

33. De Gaulle, *The Army of the Future*, p. 22.

route they would take through Belgium. But French politicians of the day, confident that France's security was provided for in the Maginot Line and the series of international guarantees from Locarno to the Kellogg–Briand Pact, did not yet share his fears. In vain de Gaulle pleaded against the prevailing mentality of his time, warned against the passions stirring across the Rhine:

> At the very time when we declare that war should be outlawed and affect to efface the power of the sword from History and even its commemorative medals, in other places force is acclaimed, the nostalgia of danger is proclaimed as good and necessary, armaments are insisted upon and men are formed into militias, armies and storm troops. Where, then, will the torrent stop?[34]

34. De Gaulle, *The Army of the Future*, p. 26.

CHAPTER TWO

Security, Equality, Fraternity

I do not know what to do with de Gaulle. Possibly you would like to make him Governor of Madagascar.

Roosevelt to Churchill, 8 May 1943

Old France, weighed down with history, prostrated by wars and revolutions, endlessly vacillating from greatness to decline, but revived, century after century, by the genius of renewal!

De Gaulle, *War Memoirs*, Vol. III, p. 998

The torrent did not stop until 1945, when Europe lay in ruins, and Colonel Charles de Gaulle – now General de Gaulle – had become the hero of the Resistance epic. Relinquishing his lonely position of the 1930s, de Gaulle was now to hold the reins of government and to preside over the formation of the Fourth Republic. The new French Government was quite naturally to be preoccupied initially by the enormous task of postwar economic reconstruction and the delicate process of reorganizing internal political life in the wake of all the bitter divisions born of the Vichy experience. But Charles de Gaulle was above all interested in foreign policy.

As Alfred Grosser points out in his excellent analysis of de Gaulle's foreign policy,[1] for de Gaulle, foreign policy is the primary task of the state and its *raison d'être*. Internal organization ultimately serves to guarantee foreign policy. But for that reason, all the more, the state must be effectively organized internally. In the third volume of his war memoirs, de Gaulle declared:

I regard the state . . . not as it was yesterday and as the parties wished it to become once more, a juxtaposition of private interests which

1. Alfred Grosser, *La Politique extérieure de la Ve République*, Paris, Editions du Seuil, 1965; *French Foreign Policy under de Gaulle*, translated by Lois Pattison, Boston, Little, Brown, 1967.

could never produce anything but weak compromise, but instead as an instrument of decision, action and ambition, expressing and serving the national interest alone. In order to make decisions and determine measures, it must have a qualified arbitrator at its head.[2]

That 'arbitrator' was in the first instance to be Charles de Gaulle himself, who now presided over the translation into action of the ideas he had propounded in *Le Fil de l'épée* and *Vers l'armée de métier*. He did exactly that. Or at least, he tried to.

The main objectives of de Gaulle's foreign policy upon his triumphant return to Paris might be summarized as security, equality and fraternity. Together with his foreign minister, Georges Bidault, de Gaulle pressed obstinately for the realization of these objectives, whose details had, moreover, been well thought out in advance, and which are remarkably and precisely set forth in the third volume of his war memoirs.[3]

The claim to equality contained both immediate and long-range implications. Not surprisingly, the immediate objective of French foreign policy in 1944 was to obtain a voice for France in the European settlement, particularly in regard to the future of Germany. De Gaulle set forth that objective unambiguously as early as 12 September 1944, in an exposé of his policies at the Palais de Chaillot:

> We believe it is in the higher interests of mankind that the arrangements which will tomorrow settle Germany's fate should not be discussed and adopted without consulting France. . . . We believe any decision concerning Europe reached without consulting France to be a grave error.[4]

Of all the foreign policy issues facing the new French Government, the issue de Gaulle baptized 'le rang', or status, was indeed

2. As quoted in Alfred Grosser, *French Foreign Policy under de Gaulle*, p. 15.

3. For an excellent treatment of French foreign policy in the immediate postwar years, see A. W. De Porte, *De Gaulle's Foreign Policy: 1944–46*, Cambridge, Mass., Harvard University Press, 1968. See also, Alfred Grosser, *La IVe République et sa politique extérieure*, Paris, Armand Colin, 1961, 'Introduction' and pp. 193–231; F. Roy Willis, *France, Germany and the New Europe: 1945–1967*, Stanford, Calif., Stanford University Press, 1968, chapters I and II; and Adalbert Korff, 'Le revirement de la politique française à l'égard de l'Allemagne entre 1945 et 1950', *Documents*, XXI, no. 2 (mars–avril 1966), pp. 15–30.

4. *The Complete War Memoirs of Charles de Gaulle, Vol. III: Salvation 1944–46*, translated by Jonathan Griffin and Richard Howard, London, Weidenfeld, 1960; New York, Simon & Schuster, 1967, p. 675. All subsequent quotations are taken from this translation, hereafter referred to as *War Memoirs*.

the most crucial, for it entailed nothing less than the licence to have a foreign policy in the first place. The alternative was for France to acquiesce passively in whatever arrangements should be dealt out by England, the Soviet Union and the United States. De Gaulle chafed at his exclusion from Allied policy planning, remarking tersely, 'Everything occurred as if our Allies were intent on excluding France from the mere knowledge of their arrangements.'[5] However unpalatable this exclusion may have seemed to him personally, none the less, de Gaulle viewed France's options pragmatically.

> We could not bring this relegation to a halt immediately, but we could make it unendurable to those inflicting it upon us. For none of their decisions concerning Europe, particularly Germany, could be put into effect if France did not lend her voice. . . . Moreover, the war's end would leave us in force on the continent, while America would be back in her hemisphere and England on her island. Provided that we knew what we wanted, we would then have the means to break out of the circle of resigned acceptance and docile resignation inside of which our three partners intended to imprison us.[6]

'Resigned acceptance and docile renunciation' were neither an immediate nor a long-range alternative for a man of Charles de Gaulle's iron determination and stubborn resistance. His concept of 'status' was no ceremonial objective: he meant nothing less than to return France in the long run to her role as full equal in the councils of diplomacy:

> Thus I demonstrated that France was regaining the status she required to play her role again. This role was to be that of one of the greatest states.[7]

> Our remarks left . . . no doubt that the only situation we found acceptable was that of *full* associate.[8]

The means at de Gaulle's disposal in realizing this objective were certainly not impressive, but he pressed on, trading diplomatic skill for material advantage. His first goal was to obtain a seat for France at the forthcoming Allied summit meeting in February 1945, at Yalta. Hoping to strengthen his diplomatic

5. De Gaulle, *War Memoirs*, p. 722.
6. De Gaulle, *War Memoirs*, pp. 722–3.
7. De Gaulle, *War Memoirs*, p. 730.
8. De Gaulle, *War Memoirs*, p. 725. Emphasis added.

bargaining position and his bid for great power rank, de Gaulle made an eight-day trip to Moscow in December 1944.[9] At his first meeting with Stalin, de Gaulle came straight to the point. His plan was to obtain diplomatic leverage in dealing with the United States and England by establishing between Moscow and Paris a bilateral agreement on the future of Germany, with which they would subsequently confront the other Allies: 'I sketched the prospect of a direct entente between the Moscow and Paris governments in order to establish a settlement which they would propose in common to the other Allies. . . .'[10] Stalin rejected this proposal out of hand. De Gaulle obtained the Russian alliance he had counted on as a part of his security objectives, but he failed in his effort to win Stalin over to promoting France's great power aspirations. He later remarked icily in his memoirs that he supposed Stalin 'already had good reasons to anticipate Roosevelt's and Churchill's agreement with what he wanted'.[11]

On 15 January 1945, de Gaulle applied formally for an invitation to the forthcoming conference at Yalta. It was no secret to him that resistance would come from the direction of Washington. To make his refusal explicit, President Roosevelt dispatched Harry Hopkins to Paris at the end of January, in de Gaulle's words, 'to sugar-coat the pill'.[12] It was a bitter pill that de Gaulle would not forget. Yalta came to symbolize for him an ominous complicity, a deeply resented *Diktat* – the diplomatic poker game of the 'Big Three', with the world as the ante and France a powerless bystander.

It is worth dwelling a moment on de Gaulle's account of his conversation with Harry Hopkins and Ambassador Caffery prior to the Yalta Conference,[13] not merely as another episode in the long series of misadventures in Franco-American relations, but as a clearly delineated confrontation of opposed views on France's role. For de Gaulle does not make a straw man out of American policy – he presents it coolly and forthrightly. Hopkins's reply to de Gaulle's bid for equal status for France as a great power represents a recurrent theme in the American policy line.

Hopkins opened his discussion with de Gaulle on a by now

9. De Gaulle dwells at considerable length on this visit in his *War Memoirs*, pp. 735–57.

10. De Gaulle, *War Memoirs*, p. 738.

11. De Gaulle, *War Memoirs*, p. 738.

12. De Gaulle, *War Memoirs*, p. 760.

13. See de Gaulle, *War Memoirs*, pp. 759–63.

familiar theme: how could Franco-American relations be brought out of their present impasse? Shifting ground a bit, de Gaulle replied by asking Hopkins what, in American eyes, was the cause of the poor relations between the two countries? Hopkins lost no time in responding that the cause was above all America's shock and dismay at the news of France's collapse in 1940 and, added to that, the recurrent disappointments in French leaders that American diplomacy had relied on subsequently. Seeking to reassure de Gaulle, Hopkins added: 'Do not seek elsewhere for the true source of the attitude we have adopted toward your country. Judging that France was no longer what she had been, we could not trust her to play one of the leading roles.'[14] Of course, it was true that General de Gaulle had appeared on the scene, and that American policy had been mistaken in doubting that he could realize his political ambitions; nevertheless, this could not erase the bad experience American diplomats had had first-hand with French military and political leaders. And finally, 'knowing the political inconsistency that riddles your country, what reasons have we to suppose General de Gaulle will be in a position to lead her for long?'[15] This is the France-is-an-endemically-unstable-country line, combined with its variation by implication: *après de Gaulle le déluge*. In a more recent reincarnation, this same argument is advanced unaltered, though marinated in clichés, in George Ball's book, *The Discipline of Power*.[16]

For de Gaulle, there were two questions that dominated Franco-American relations both then and in the future: Did the United States believe that France was capable of becoming a great power again? Did the United States propose to help her? As for misgivings in regard to the past, France also had good enough cause to question America's record:

> In the mortal dangers we French have survived since the beginning of the century, the United States does not give us the impression that it regards its own destiny as linked with that of France, that it wishes

14. De Gaulle, *War Memoirs*, p. 760. Under the Fifth Republic, another theme is added: the United States cannot risk discriminating against West Germany by according France a privileged position, despite the preferential relationship with the British. French requests to be treated on a par with England were repeatedly dismissed as unreasonable, based on hubris, or both.

15. De Gaulle, *War Memoirs*, p. 762.

16. George Ball, *The Discipline of Power*, London, The Bodley Head, 1968; Boston, Little, Brown, 1968, p. 143.

France to be great and strong, that it is doing all it can to help her remain or become so again. Perhaps, in fact, we are not worth the trouble. In that case, you are right. But perhaps we shall rise again. Then you will have been wrong. In either case, your behavior tends to alienate us.[17]

When had America entered World War I? Only after three years, when France lay thoroughly exhausted; and then only because German submarines had disrupted American commerce. Had America supported France in its search for security in the twenties? No, and moreover, it had 'furnished Germany all the aid necessary for a return to power. "The result . . . was Hitler." '[18] Indeed, even when Nazi Germany unleashed its fury upon Europe, America clung to neutrality, and rejected Paul Reynaud's appeal for even secret aid – which would have sufficed to convince the French Government to continue the war. In fact, when had the United States entered the war in Europe? Only after the Japanese attack on Pearl Harbor, when coerced by Germany's declaration of war.

Hopkins acknowledged de Gaulle's 'incisive but accurate' explanation of the past, and shifted the discussion back to the future. How could Franco-American relations be improved so that the two countries could 'act in agreement and in full mutual confidence'? This time de Gaulle put his answer on the line:

> If this is really America's intention . . . I cannot understand how she can undertake to settle Europe's future in France's absence. Especially since after pretending to ignore her in the imminent 'Big Three' discussions, she must ask Paris to consent to whatever has been decided.[19]

There was apparently no direct comment on de Gaulle's query beyond the initial explanation Hopkins had offered. Concluding the meeting, de Gaulle summed up his position:

> The French have the impression that you no longer consider the greatness of France necessary to the world and to yourself. This is responsible for the coolness you feel in our country and even in this office. If you want relations between our countries to be established on a different footing, it is up to you to do what must be done. Until you reach a decision, I send President Roosevelt the salute of friendship on the eve of the conference that will bring him to Europe.[20]

17. De Gaulle, *War Memoirs*, p. 761.
18. De Gaulle, *War Memoirs*, p. 762.
19. De Gaulle, *War Memoirs*, p. 763.
20. De Gaulle, *War Memoirs*, p. 763.

De Gaulle subsequently announced publicly that France would be bound by absolutely nothing that she had not been invited to discuss and approve 'in the same capacity as the others'.[21]

This conversation between de Gaulle and Hopkins discloses the mainspring of the differences in outlook and attitude, in interpretation of the past and policies for the future that would lead directly to the sharp confrontations of the future. De Gaulle's concept of grandeur as the historical and natural right of France that must and shall be restored, Hopkins's contention that France was no longer what she had been and therefore not entitled to treatment as a great power: all the subsequent crises in American–French relations are revealed baldly in this confrontation. It was not so much that de Gaulle had carried with him grudges and bad humours from the past; it was rather that neither he nor American political leaders had fundamentally changed their minds.

In the final communiqué of the Yalta Conference, France was invited to join the Big Three in occupying a zone of German territory and to participate in the government of occupied Germany on an equal footing as the fourth occupying power. It was a partial satisfaction that was only diminished by France's exclusion once again from the final Big Three conference at Potsdam in the summer of 1945.[22] While de Gaulle constantly stressed the responsibility of the Americans in France's exclusion from Yalta and Potsdam, it should in fairness be emphasized that Stalin was still less a promoter of the French cause. In any case, the upshot of the Yalta and Potsdam conferences was that France was ostensibly to enjoy the rank of subordinate-on-equal-footing. Such was the Allied response to de Gaulle's bid for equality.

The objective of equality thus met with only a very limited success. France did not obtain a direct voice in the settlement agreed at Yalta and Potsdam, but was included in the occupation of Germany and in the institutions established to administer occupied Germany. These institutions therefore provided the forum through which France would seek to implement her own policies toward Germany, policies which, not surprisingly, often proved to be at variance with those of her allies during the subsequent months and years. The long-range objective of full

21. De Gaulle, *War Memoirs*, p. 764.

22. For an extended treatment of this episode, see De Porte, *De Gaulle's Foreign Policy: 1944–46*, pp. 153–82.

equality would reappear as a dominant theme with de Gaulle's return to power in 1958.

The second objective of French foreign policy in 1944 was security. Security meant first and foremost guarantees against Germany. Germany must be prevented at all costs from ever again posing a threat to the security of France and of Europe. It would perhaps be more correct to say that this was the primary objective of all French policy in 1944 – the objective of equality, in the short run, represented the means necessary to advance the French conception of a Europe safe from German designs. In concrete terms, de Gaulle's policy of security took two forms: (1) a traditional system of international guarantees, buttressed by bilateral alliances with England and Russia, to contain Germany; and (2) direct action on Germany itself.

The concept of international guarantees was, of course, not a French monopoly. Churchill also envisaged a tripartite alliance linking Britain, France and the Soviet Union, and telegraphed Stalin to that effect on the eve of de Gaulle's trip to Moscow in December 1944. De Gaulle, however, was opposed to a tripartite scheme and favoured a bilateral alliance system, mainly because a bilateral system would be less susceptible to immobilization in the event of one party's disagreement. His concept had at its core a personal theory of 'levels of involvement' in regard to the German danger, a view substantially formed by his earliest analysis of the interplay of history and geography. For de Gaulle, Russia and France were the states most immediately and directly threatened by Germany, and he was therefore unwilling to subject their action to the agreement of Britain, which he regarded as problematical in any event. Britain's concerns were, after all, not exclusively continental – she was also dependent on commonwealth relations: 'Must Paris and Moscow wait to act until London was ready to do so?'[23] That was to risk a repetition of the experience of the interwar years. De Gaulle therefore favoured a series of bilateral alliances, with Russia and Britain at the centre, in that order, and the United States as an ultimate recourse:

> As for alliances, we considered that they must be constructed in 'three stages': first a Franco-Russian treaty providing for initial security; the Anglo-Soviet pact and an agreement still to be made between France and Great Britain constituting a second degree; the

23. De Gaulle, *War Memoirs*, p. 745.

future United Nations pact, in which America would play a decisive role, crowning the entire edifice and serving as an ultimate recourse.[24]

De Gaulle obtained the bilateral Russian–French alliance against Germany at the end of a gruelling round of negotiations with Stalin in December 1944.[25] The Russian alliance was, of course, an old standby of French policy. 'In dealing with the German menace,' de Gaulle told Stalin, 'the mutual action of Russia and France was in the nature of things.'[26] France had sought vainly during the interwar years to replace *la belle et bonne alliance* by the Petite Entente, and, when that failed, turned again to Russia. But the 1935 Franco-Soviet Pact remained a paper treaty – it was the German–Soviet accord that prevailed at the crucial hour. To that extent, de Gaulle's priority to a Franco-Soviet pact in 1944 also represented a reassurance against the eventuality of future 'Rapallos'. The Anglo-French Treaty of Dunkirk was not signed until March 1947, long after de Gaulle had left office, at a time when it seemed already a sort of anachronism. It was in March 1947 that President Truman set forth the Truman doctrine in an address to the US Congress: the cold war and Britain's economic weakness were already in the process of transforming radically the status of occupied Germany.

The second aspect of France's security policy consisted of direct action on Germany in political, economic and military spheres, with the ostensible object of ensuring a permanent weakening of German power relative to French. The military defeat of Germany, of course, provided an unhoped-for opportunity to impose a political sentence entirely to France's advantage. There was no lack of schemes in the air for Germany's future during the last days of the war. De Gaulle's programme for Germany, which was continued long after he personally left office, was well defined in its specific demands even before his return to Paris in 1944, and to some extent represented an evolution in his thinking, as compared with his earlier writings. French policy on Germany consisted of four elements which were constantly reiterated in public speeches and declarations: (1) territorial dislocation, (2) political decentralization, (3) military occupation and (4) economic sanctions.

24. De Gaulle, *War Memoirs*, p. 745.
25. See de Gaulle, *War Memoirs*, pp. 745–57.
26. De Gaulle, *War Memoirs*, p. 739.

Territorial dislocation entailed the political detachment of the Saar and of Germany's eastern territories – yet France made no claim to annexation. The hexagon would remain incomplete: economic control of the Rhineland would substitute for political annexation. Political decentralization meant the end of a centralized Reich and the eventual establishment of a 'federal' regime within Germany – another theme from de Gaulle's earlier writings. Military occupation pertained to the interim policies pursued by the Allied governments within their respective zones. Finally, economic sanctions included material reparations, dismantling of factories, linking the economic potential of the Rhineland, Saar and Ruhr to the west through international control mechanisms in which France should enjoy a privileged position. The overall effect was to ensure a relatively weakened Germany as a future neighbour, and to institutionalize the relationship of political and economic inferiority on a permanent basis.

The first formal statement of the French position came in an interview with Foreign Minister Georges Bidault that appeared in the London *Sunday Times* of 12 November 1944:

> One thing, however, is certain: there must be a Germany, but one which will be unable to wage another war. This is in everybody's and particularly in France's interest, because she is her direct neighbour. Peace with Germany should not be one of vengeance; it must be just and humane. Germany will have to be controlled for years to come, but I am not calling for trying to make her harmless by dismembering her artificially. Germany in her death struggle against unconditional surrender may fall bit by bit, like the walls of a house, and thus find herself naturally and organically dismembered – but to force it would be ill-advised. On the other hand, the early establishment of a central authority in Germany may impede the natural desire to dissociate themselves from Prussian influence that may exist today in other parts of Germany.
>
> We do not want to incorporate any German territory. We do not want any Germany minority within our borders. Our greatest interest lies in the control of the Rhineland, because it represents our frontiers. International control has been suggested. We would not object to that, but there are different kinds of international control, and if such are set up, France, as a direct neighbour, perhaps ought to be given a privileged position in this control. British and Americans will one day want to go home. We will remain. We, therefore, must have a full

share in the control of Germany. I do not believe it would do good to convert her into an agricultural country, but her industries, and especially her laboratories, must remain indefinitely under Allied supervision. Germany has given us on our own soil a very good example of how to control industries efficiently without making the control too obvious to the public. This method deserves to be studied carefully.[27]

Striking by its absence in the French Government's programme was the note of revenge. Germany must be firmly controlled, but the settlement must be 'just and humane'. In keeping with de Gaulle's earlier writings, French policy placed primary emphasis on political decentralization, a theme which shines through Bidault's hope that other parts of Germany may want to dissociate themselves from 'Prussia'. Does this suggest that the Nazi adventure was considered another example of classic 'Prussian militarism'? French policy was opposed to the forced dismemberment of the Reich, preferring to encourage the latent centrifugal elements within Germany toward a 'federal' organization – 'federal' meaning the autonomy of the various regional units comprising Germany. Decentralization and firm economic control in the hands of the West – these were the two conditions that would guarantee that Germany would pose no future threat to France.

Yet already in the statements of 1944–5, there is also a faint promise of a future Franco-German reconciliation. That promise appears still more explicitly in the third volume of de Gaulle's memoirs, though it should not be forgotten that this volume first appeared in 1959:

The abolition of a centralized Reich! This, in my opinion, was the first condition necessary to prevent Germany from returning to its bad ways. Each time a dominating and ambitious state had seized the German polities, obliterating their diversity, imperialism had been the result. This had been only too evident under Wilhelm II and under Hitler. Conversely, if each of the states within the German federation could exist by itself, govern itself in its own way, handle its own interests, there would be every likelihood that the federation as a whole would not be led to subjugate its neighbors. This would be even more likely if the Ruhr, that arsenal of strategic matériel, were given a special status under international control. Further, the Rhineland would, of

27. *Keesing's Contemporary Archives*, 11–18 November 1944, pp. 6807–8, as quoted in A.W. De Porte, *De Gaulle's Foreign Policy, 1944–46*, pp. 160–1.

course, be occupied by French, British, Belgian and Dutch armies. But if its economy were moreover linked to a grouping of the Western powers – and with no opposition to other German units joining this alliance as well – and if the Rhine itself became an international freeway, then cooperation between complementary nations could be instituted forthwith. Lastly, there was every reason to suppose that the Saar, retaining its German character, would be transformed into a separate state and united to France by trade agreements which would settle the question of our reparations in terms of coal. Thus, the German federation, recovering its diversity and turning its eyes toward the west, would lose the means of war but not those of its own development. In addition, none of its fragments would be annexed by the French, thus leaving the door to reconciliation open.[28]

To remove from Germany the political motivation and the economic possibility of war: such was the twofold object of de Gaulle's programme. His conclusions on how to implement that goal were drawn from a schematic analysis of history: German imperialism arises whenever a centralizing force dominates the internal impulses toward diversity. Ignoring ideology and anti-Nazi passions, de Gaulle groups together Kaiser Wilhelm and Hitler as comparable examples of this phenomenon.

Following the German surrender, in May 1945, de Gaulle paid his first postwar visit to Germany. The account he gives of his reaction to the suffering of the German populations is revealing of the interplay of emotion and political reasoning so characteristic of de Gaulle. There is no note whatsoever of the triumphant general viewing his spoils – it is rather with compassion that de Gaulle looks upon the aftermath of war and the misery of fellow 'Europeans'. Indeed, his attitude toward Germany is altered by the first-hand sight of its ravaged countenance. He finds in the ashes of destruction and despair the promise of the future:

The countenance Germany showed us was certainly lamentable in any case. Observing the mountains of ruins to which the cities were reduced, passing through flattened villages, receiving the supplications of despairing burgomeisters, seeing populations from which male adults had almost entirely disappeared made me, as a European, gasp in horror. But I also observed that the cataclysm, having reached such a degree, would profoundly modify the psychology of the Germans.

It would be a long time before we would see again that victorious

28. De Gaulle, *War Memoirs*, pp. 720–1.

Reich which thrice during one man's lifetime had rushed to domination. For many years, the ambitions of the German nation and the aims of its policy would necessarily be reduced to the level of survival and reconstruction. Moreover, I scarcely suspected that it must remain severed and that Soviet Russia would insist on keeping at its disposal those very German territories which had nourished the impulses toward '*Lebensraum*'. Thus, amid the ruins, mourning and humiliation which had submerged Germany in her turn, I felt my sense of distrust and severity fade within me. I even glimpsed possibilities of understanding which the past had never offered; moreover, it seemed to me that the same sentiment was dawning among our soldiers. The thirst for vengeance which had spurred them on at first had abated as they advanced across this ravaged earth. Today I saw them merciful before the misery of the vanquished.[29]

Like Bidault, de Gaulle does not conceal his Prussophobe prejudices: his implication is that it was only those territories in the Soviet occupation zone (i.e. the old kingdom of Prussia) that had pressed for *Lebensraum*. There is little doubt that this same attitude contributed significantly to de Gaulle's subsequent intransigence toward the GDR.

But despite conciliatory musings, in the immediate postwar years it was the theme of firmness and not the theme of reconciliation that dominated French policy toward Germany. This policy undoubtedly enjoyed the support of the great majority of Frenchmen of all political tendencies. There were, to be sure, those who advocated a more draconian fate for Germany, often in the same spirit of racism as the Nazi policies they deplored. And there were also those prophets of a future day – many of whom had just returned from concentration camps where they had formed close friendships with German fellow-prisoners – who quietly but with determination set out to lay the foundations for Franco-German reconciliation. Then, Charles de Gaulle, too, had his dream of the far-off future.

The third theme in de Gaulle's postwar foreign policy was a long-range vision rather than a concrete objective. It is one which is too often overlooked. Yet, throughout the final volume of his war memoirs, the theme of European reconciliation – what I have labelled 'fraternity' in keeping with the French Republican credo – constantly counterbalances de Gaulle's

29. De Gaulle, *War Memoirs*, p. 903.

statements on Germany. Nor can this simply be written off as a '1959 prophecy' retroactively credited to de Gaulle's 1944 attitudes. In a magisterial study of de Gaulle's attitude toward the building of Europe,[30] Edmond Jouve has shown incisively the genesis and development of the European theme in the General's statements from the days of his London exile, his unbending effort to construct the future on the crest of his personal vision. Whatever the inspiration underlying de Gaulle's long-range vision of some form of pan-European co-operation, one thing is certain: by 1944–5 the theme of Europe appears solidly established as a principle in the General's political objectives. It appears perhaps as an embryonic concept whose form is not yet clearly defined in his mind. From time to time, he speaks with a certain ambiguity of a European 'federation', a word which most certainly does not merit dissecting for its legal refinements at this point. 'Federation' meant at least some form of established *association* – what form is by no means clear. 'Association' is, moreover, the word de Gaulle himself prefers to use in his memoirs:

This conception of tomorrow's Germany was closely related to my image of Europe. After the terrible lacerations she had undergone in the last thirty years, and the vast changes which had occurred the world over, Europe could find equilibrium and peace only by an association among Slavs, Germans, Gauls and Latins. Doubtless she must take into account what was momentarily tyrannical and aggrandizing in the Russian regime. Utilizing the procedures of totalitarian oppression and, on the other hand, invoking the solidarity of the Central and Eastern European peoples against the German peril, Communism was apparently trying to gain control of the Vistula, the Danube and the Balkans. But once Germany ceased to be a threat, this subjection, for lack of a raison d'être, would sooner or later appear unacceptable to the vassal states, while the Russians themselves would lose all desire to exceed their own boundaries. If the Kremlin persisted in its enterprise of domination, it would be against the will of the nations subject to its government. Yet in the long run there is no regime that can hold out against the will of nations. I believed, moreover, that timely action by the Western Allies with regard to the masters of the Kremlin, on condition that such action be concerted and categorical,

30. Edmond Jouve, *Le Général de Gaulle et la construction européenne 1940–1966*, 2 vols, Paris, Librairie Générale de Droit et de Jurisprudence, 1967. See especially vol. 1, p. 5 ff.

would safeguard the independence of the Poles, the Czechs, the Hungarians and the Balkan peoples. After which the unity of Europe could be established in the form of an association including its peoples from Iceland to Istanbul, from Gibraltar to the Urals.[31]

The future European 'association' was thus in de Gaulle's mind bound up with the 'equilibrium', or balance of power, on the continent, and it was a counterpart for his vision of the future of Germany.[32] Conspicuous by their absence from the list of peoples included in de Gaulle's 'association' of Slavs, Germans, Gauls and Latins are the Anglo-Saxons, though he closes on a wider geographic sweep from Iceland to Istanbul, and from Gibraltar to the Urals. In 1944–5, de Gaulle did not place the English outside his vision of Europe. At the very least, it must be said that de Gaulle's vision of Europe was never that of a Little Europe, a Carolingian Europe, a *Christliches Abendland*: his concept was more political than cultural, more predicated on balance of power than utopian or economic aspirations. The European association was above all to solve the problem of Germany on a continental basis. This can be seen clearly in his analysis of the motives behind Soviet imperialism in Central Europe. Its motor force and cement was fear of Germany. Once Germany had ceased to be a threat, he reasoned, the bloc would fall apart, and furthermore the Soviet Union would lose its taste for domination. Then, Europe could be unified in an organization that would preserve its peace, and ultimately its cultural values as well.

De Gaulle went to considerable pains to promote his scheme in the last days of the war. In November 1944, he attempted to win Churchill over to his concept of an Anglo-French foundation for the new order he foresaw, but Churchill was naturally more concerned at the time with his relations with Stalin and Roosevelt than with promoting Gaullist visions. Still, de Gaulle's comments on his proposal to Churchill are interesting; for they display his abiding concern with the effects of technical civilization on man, a humanistic concern that echoes the themes of *Le Fil de l'épée* and *Vers l'armée de métier*:

The equilibrium of Europe, . . . the guarantee of peace along the Rhine, the independence of the Vistula, Danube and Balkan states, the creation of some form of association with the peoples all over the

31. De Gaulle, *War Memoirs*, p. 721.

32. See below, pp. 38–41.

world to whom we have opened the doors of Western civilization, an organization of nations which will be something more than an arena for disputes between America and Russia, and lastly the *primacy accorded in world politics to a certain conception of man despite the progressive mechanization of society* – these, surely, are our great interests in tomorrow's world. Let us come to an agreement in order to uphold these interests together.[33]

De Gaulle spoke of Europe again, on 22 November 1944, in his major address on foreign affairs before the Consultative Assembly. This time, it came at the end of the section dealing with the future of the 'German peoples'. Stressing the importance of providing for French security in a future settlement, de Gaulle then concluded:

But I declared that by imposing upon Germany a fate that was obligatorily pacific, France intended to lay the foundations for that valuable edifice which would be the unity of Europe. 'We believed in this unity!' I proclaimed, 'and we hope that it will be translated, to begin with, into specific acts binding its three poles, Moscow, London and Paris.'[34]

In the two years that followed the liberation of France, the realities that were to dominate the postwar world had already taken form. The cold war began to divide Europe and the world into two opposing blocs dominated by Moscow and Washington, with Germany as the major stake in Europe. De Gaulle resigned his office in January 1946, and withdrew to twelve years of contentious semi-retirement. From his retreat at Colombey-les-deux-Eglises, he continued to issue Cassandra-like statements and to deliver occasional speeches on the topics of the day as leader of the Gaullist Party, Le Rassemblement du Peuple Français (RPF).

At the end of July 1946, at Bar-le-Duc, de Gaulle spoke again of his concept of an association of European states to protect the balance of power. By 1946, however, one is struck by the restructuring of his earlier ideas under the impact of the American–Soviet competition. In the Bar-le-Duc speech, one sees clearly delineated the theme of Europe as a sort of 'third force' between the United States and the Soviet Union. It is not, however, that

33. De Gaulle, *War Memoirs*, p. 727. Emphasis added.
34. De Gaulle, *War Memoirs*, p. 731.

this theme entirely replaces the older and more extensive Europe 'from Gibraltar to the Urals' in de Gaulle's mind – it becomes rather superimposed upon it in the manner of a reluctant concession to dreaded new realities. For the cold war must at all costs be attenuated in Europe, not least because France's internal politics paralleled most closely the division of the international scene, with a quarter of its voters pledged to support of the Communist Party. Against this shift in the international situation, de Gaulle set forth a new role for a more circumscribed Europe: that of buffer and broker between the two superpowers. A united Europe should transform the rigid bipolar balance by adding an additional factor to the equilibrium:

> The war which has just ended has put into immediate contact the forces and the influences of the two principal partners. No one can henceforth escape the heavy worries imposed upon the destiny of each country and each individual by the future of the relations between America and Russia.
>
> What then can reestablish the equilibrium, if not the Old World between the two new ones? Old Europe, which for so many centuries has been the guide of the universe, is capable of constituting in the heart of a world tending to cut itself in two, the necessary element of compensation and understanding. The nations of the ancient Occident, whose vital arteries are the North Sea, the Mediterranean, the Rhine, geographically located between the two new masses, resolved to conserve an independence which would be gravely threatened in the event of a conflagration, physically and morally identified with the agglomerate effort of the Russians as well as the liberal rise of the Americans, globally powerful by their own resources and by those of vast territories linked to their destiny, projecting far their influence and their activities – what a weight they could bring to bear if they arrived at conjugating their policies, despite their grievances exchanged from age to age![35]

The theme of fraternity, or European reconciliation, as an objective of postwar Gaullist policy was to remain, however, largely in the realm of rhetoric. As cold war priorities began to alter Anglo-American policies in Germany, French policy remained long after de Gaulle's retreat stubbornly attached to its initial strategies of constraint. Continuity in foreign policy was in part assured by the long tenure in office of two foreign ministers,

35. De Gaulle, *Discours et messages*: *dans l'attente* (*février 1946–avril 1958*), Paris, Librairie Plon, 1970, pp. 15–16.

Georges Bidault and Robert Schuman, despite the game of political musical chairs in other cabinet posts. Control over Germany remained the primordial issue in French policy: French diplomacy retreated from its positions with extreme reluctance, most often under combined pressure from the United States and Britain and constraining economic circumstances.[36]

The Schuman proposal of 1950 represented the first significant effort on the part of the French Government to transform the new Western policy toward Germany, which it had sought to prevent and agreed to only under duress, into a progressive French initiative. It is true that the divided Germany of 1950[37] was less threatening than a united Germany. It is also true that Schuman's proposal of a supranational coal and steel community provided France with control of the key strategic sector of the West German economy. Yet, there is little doubt that in choosing deliberately the path of reconciliation within the framework of supranational European institutions as the future direction of French policy toward Germany, Schuman acted courageously, committing himself to a course that by no means yet enjoyed the support of public opinion of the day. In fact, the Schuman Plan was sold to the French Parliament more in its capacity as a continuation of the old policy of control over Germany than as a gesture of reconciliation and faith in the European movement. The latter appears largely as the then available means to achieve the former. M. Alfred Coste-Floret, *rapporteur* for the ECSC proposal, illustrates this aptly in his report to the French National Assembly:

> Germany is growing steadily, but this growth has never ceased; and precisely in a moment when we might entertain anxieties over its eventual outcome, the Schuman Plan intercedes opportunely to stabilize the situation and to remove from the German national State, as it does likewise from the French national State, the availability of its heavy industry for purpose of war.[38]

36. See Korff, 'Le revirement de la politique française à l'égard de l'Allemagne entre 1945 et 1950'.

37. Germany was divided *de facto* in 1949 with the establishment of the Federal Republic in the West and, shortly thereafter, the German Democratic Republic in the East.

38. Quoted in Alfred Grosser, 'A la recherche d'une politique franco-allemande', in Raymond Aron and Daniel Lerner (eds), *La Querelle de la CED*, Paris, Colin, 1956, pp. 102–3.

Conceived in response to the international politics of the cold war, once begun, the process of Franco-German rapprochement continued. Slowly and not without obstacles (the EDC affair, in particular), during the course of the Fourth Republic Frenchmen were won over to the cause of Franco-German reconciliation within the framework of Western European union. This was certainly one of its most creative achievements in foreign policy. The Coal and Steel Community was eventually followed in 1957 by Euratom and the Common Market, after a period of relative stagnation resulting from the abortive EDC episode. When the Fourth Republic fell in 1958, only two major political groups had public records of opposition to this policy: the Communists on the Left, and the Gaullists on the Right.

CHAPTER THREE

Nato: Directorate *Oui*, Protectorate *Non!*

Gaullist foreign policy is not based on any principles: it merely consists of a series of contradictory policies originally motivated by illusions and later by grudges.

Paul Reynaud, *The Foreign Policy of Charles de Gaulle*, translated by M. Saville, New York, Odyssey Press, 1964, p. 150

France obviously cannot leave her own destiny and even her own life to the discretion of others.

De Gaulle, Press Conference, September 1960

By the late 1950s, the Fourth Republic was widely considered the best available candidate for the role of 'sick man of Europe'. Yet when Charles de Gaulle returned to power in 1958 to preside over its interment, there was little rejoicing outside of France. Internally, France stood on the verge of a civil war precipitated by the Algerian rebellion. Externally, a tri-coloured question mark now loomed over the major foreign policy choices of the Fourth Republic concerning Europe and the Western Alliance. Choices made with no little deliberation, and conscientiously (often grudgingly) embarked upon were called into question because of the notorious opposition of the Gaullists, who now held the reins of power. On two decisive points, de Gaulle had time and again made his position clear: on the one hand, he had inveighed sharply and sardonically at every opportunity against the supranational concept of European integration, premised on the progressive surrender of national sovereignty to common federal institutions; and on the other, he had roundly condemned the system of military integration in Nato, which he denounced as the subordination of European forces to a system entirely at the disposal of United States policies. In simplest terms, both attitudes represented de Gaulle's stubborn commitment to French national autonomy, to France as master of her own destiny. To remove French policy from subordination to the Anglo-American lead had been a central objective of de Gaulle's policy in the immediate postwar period. By 1958, the international context had been transformed under the pressures of the cold war. The search for release from the frustrations of the continued subordination of French policy fostered by the cold war took the form of an active reassertion of French autonomy. The Fifth Republic's noisy clamouring after grandeur and independence represented a variation on and development of the earlier theme of equality in a changed context.[1]

De Gaulle's attachment to independence as a foreign policy objective can be understood as a lesson drawn from the traumas of the 1930s, a formative period in his generation's political experience. Throughout the 1930s, France's political system was plagued to the point of paralysis by the interpenetration of foreign policy and domestic issues, with the result that French foreign policy suffered both from the absence of national unity internally, and from its obsession with dependence on the policies of other countries – principally, Great Britain and the United States. Rightly or wrongly, French policy was immobilized by the assumption that France could not act unilaterally to check German moves; that France could only act if supported by England, which was swept in a wave of pacifism. This frustration of impotence was the mainspring both of de Gaulle's determination to forge national unity and strength out of the debris of the Liberation, and also of his unflagging efforts to eliminate all fetters of external dependence. The cold war, however, had the unfortunate effect of prolonging both the internal divisions and the malaise of dependency.

There was a certain historical irony attending de Gaulle's return to power in 1958. The stage of international relations was again for a brief time to be occupied by the same actors as in Algiers in 1943: Harold Macmillan, then British Secretary of State in Algiers, working hand in hand with Roosevelt's representative, Robert Murphy, was now Prime Minister of England.

1. Critics of de Gaulle's foreign policy, such as Raymond Aron, have at various times suggested that his fetish for national autonomy represented an end in itself rather than a means at the service of a wider, more imaginative policy. This is a question that we shall have occasion to return to. 'Quel est le Grand Dessein?' *Le Figaro*, 4 février 1966.

And Dwight Eisenhower – 'this great soldier, this generous-hearted man'[2] – who had also played his role in the test of will between Giraud and de Gaulle in Algiers, was now President of the United States. Robert Murphy was also briefly to reappear on stage later in 1958.

Whatever difficulties attended their wartime relations, de Gaulle writes unabashedly in his memoirs of his personal respect and admiration for Dwight Eisenhower. Eisenhower's image is that of the good soldier, military strategist and chief, uninterested in the 'political' intrigues of the Allies in Algiers. Problems in de Gaulle's relations with Eisenhower were not therefore personal, but rather attributable to regrettable American policy: 'The United States was less affected by our distress than by the appeal of domination',[3] a fact independent of Eisenhower's impartial military leadership. Eisenhower was, in any case, perforce to benefit from de Gaulle's admiration for the soldier-statesman and his distaste for 'politicians'.

Macmillan's role in de Gaulle's eyes was somewhat more ambiguous. Macmillan was, in the first place, above all a 'politician'. The only quotation directly ascribed to Macmillan in his memoirs is doubtless a bitter-sweet in de Gaulle's personal archives:

> The British Secretary of State gave vent to a violent outburst of irritation. 'If General de Gaulle refuses the hand held out to him today,' he exclaimed, 'be assured that America and Great Britain will abandon him altogether, and then he will be nothing.'[4]

But in his role as villain, Macmillan always performs in a kind of tandem act with Robert Murphy. 'Macmillan and Murphy' appear inseparable in the wings of the political manœuvring in Algiers. De Gaulle recounts that relations between him and Macmillan were at first strained but evolved with time. However strained they had been, by the time Macmillan was transferred to Italy in December 1943, he had won de Gaulle's esteem as a fruit of Macmillan's own apparent disenchantment with American policy:

> Originally directed by Churchill to associate himself, although with some reservations, with the political actions of the Americans in North

2. De Gaulle, *War Memoirs*, pp. 436–7.
3. De Gaulle, *War Memoirs*, pp. 435–7.
4. De Gaulle, *War Memoirs*, p. 409.

Africa, Macmillan had gradually come to understand that he had better things to do. His independent spirit and lucid intelligence had found themselves in sympathy with the French group that desired a France without fetters. As our relations developed I sensed that the prejudices he had nursed toward us were dissolving. In return, he had all my esteem.[5]

Robert Murphy, however, did not fare so well in de Gaulle's estimation. Considered something of a political schemer, with whom he did not get on at all well, from the first to last, Robert Murphy comes in for stinging treatment at de Gaulle's hand: 'Mr Murphy, skillful and determined, long familiar with the best society and apparently rather inclined to believe that France consisted of the people he had dined with in town. . . .' As American consul general in Algiers, Murphy was held personally responsible for the Giraud episode and for all the indignities that de Gaulle had had to suffer at the hands of the Americans. When finally Murphy was also transferred to Italy, de Gaulle was delighted:

> Mr Murphy's departure and his successor's attitude produced an agreeable relaxation in our relations with the American Embassy. For if the first incumbent scarcely appreciated the 'Gaullist's' success, the second, on the other hand, appeared to be greatly pleased by it. Mr Wilson's visits were as agreeable and numerous as my interviews with Mr Murphy had been infrequent and uncomfortable.[7]

If the actors on stage in 1958 were the same as those in Algiers in 1943, the stage itself had changed and so had their respective roles. Thirteen years after the German surrender, Western Europe had erased all signs of the physical destruction of the war, and had embarked on a period of internal peace and prosperity, stimulated by the combined effects of the Marshall Plan and the North Atlantic Treaty. Under the pressure of the Russian threat, US policy had fostered a rapprochement between victors and vanquished in Europe. Traditional hostilities dwindled before the need for a common defence. The Atlantic Alliance had successfully provided for security and stability. The Fourth Republic had turned necessity into virtue by transforming the inevitable Franco-German rapprochement into the occasion for

5. De Gaulle, *War Memoirs*, p. 541.
6. De Gaulle, *War Memoirs*, p. 314.
7. De Gaulle, *War Memoirs*, p. 540.

embarking on a bold new initiative to build Europe. The European Communities were the product of that effort. But the consequences of Yalta and Potsdam remained in the form of the physical division of Germany, which was but the outward and visible sign of the deeper divisions of the European continent: American and Soviet bayonets continued to face each other across the Elbe.

Politically speaking, the strategic predominance and rivalry of the United States and the Soviet Union over Europe were translated into the two alliance systems of Nato and the Warsaw Pact, dominated politically by the two superpowers, and dedicated to the rigid defence of the *status quo*. The integrated Command structure of Nato, under American leadership, had made it possible, since 1954, to reconcile the existence of German military contingents with the absence of a German General Staff; it also made possible the co-ordination of European conventional forces with the nuclear deterrent, which remained under exclusive United States control. So long as the political interests of the European states and the United States were perceived as identical, this organization of the Alliance would go unchallenged. The political challenge, bolstered by a shifting strategic balance,[8] was to come from Charles de Gaulle immediately upon his return to power in 1958.

Throughout the Fourth Republic, de Gaulle had denounced policies aimed at subordinating or lessening the morale of the French Army. The European Defence Community, a French initiative intended to forge a European army, was later defeated by a French parliament in which a combination of Gaullist concern for the army, and Leftist opposition to Atlantic policy and anti-German sentiment, joined to defeat the proposal. Gaullist concern for army morale was not merely a nationalist reflex. France emerged from the war more vanquished than victor, with an army stung by the memory of defeat. That same

8. By 1958, the non-vulnerability of the United States to a potential Soviet attack had ended, with the development of an operational Soviet ICBM system. The relative numerical inferiority of European conventional forces on the continent and the vulnerability of Western Europe to Soviet intermediate range missiles had led to the installation of American IRBMS on European territory. The strategic theory of massive retaliation, which had been adopted during the period of US atomic monopoly as a guarantee of an automatic US nuclear response to attack on Europe and which remained the official strategy of Nato, was consequently in a period of official revision in American defence circles.

army had suffered eighteen years of colonial warfare, as France retreated from the tarnished glory of Empire reluctantly, step by step, into defeat and withdrawal. Finally, an army revolt had brought de Gaulle back to power in 1958, as France hung on the verge of civil war. The French army had more than one reason to feel betrayed by its Nato ally, as US policy was resolutely anti-colonial, and persisted in viewing the Algerian tragedy as another episode in decolonization.

De Gaulle, therefore, could unite domestic support behind his indignation at the political and military implications of Nato. The French Left – especially the Communists – viewing Nato as a cold war instrument of American policy, would be solidly behind a challenge to Nato, while the army and the Right could be bolstered in morale by affirmations of independence and appeals to France's historic destiny, pending the difficult search for a political solution in Algeria. De Gaulle's resistance to Nato, thus, served as an important outlet for national frustration, and a salve for the chaotic domestic political context de Gaulle had to master in order to survive. De Gaulle's Nato policy was, therefore, both a restatement of his old positions and an opportune political lever, given his fragile domestic context and his global ambitions for France. In addition, his effort to extend the geographic scope of the Alliance was, without doubt, an oblique bid for US support for French policy in Algeria. The latter was certainly never forthcoming. On the contrary.

De Gaulle's political challenge to Nato came from two directions: first, he attacked the concept of military integration as such, labelling the Alliance an American protectorate incompatible with the independence of France; and second, he attacked the concept of the identity of US political objectives and European ones, questioning alternatively whether European nations were prepared to be dragged into a nuclear confrontation that did not concern them because of their dependence on American policies, and whether the US 'automatic' commitment to the defence of Europe could really be considered credible in all cases – particularly in the event of a relatively minor incident in Europe that would run the risk of the destruction of Detroit, Omaha or Washington. Not only was Nato a protectorate, but it was doubtful whether the protectorate afforded much protection: such was the gist of the Gaullist psychological siege on Nato.

But this was not new in 1958: already, in his statement on the European Defence Community on 26 August 1954, de Gaulle had made his position regarding the Alliance clear: 'Faire prendre au Pacte Atlantique le caractère d'une bonne alliance, non d'un mauvais protectorat, voilà la grande entreprise que le destin offre à la France.'[9] Now that he was once again in control of foreign policy de Gaulle addressed himself immediately to transforming Nato from bad protectorate into good alliance.

De Gaulle held his trial run in meetings with Belgian Premier Paul-Henri Spaak and Prime Minister Harold Macmillan during the course of June 1958; but, of course, the most important confrontation would be with American diplomacy, since Washington held the effective reins of Nato. John Foster Dulles's trip to Paris on 5 July would provide that opportunity. The full details of the de Gaulle–Dulles meeting, long a carefully guarded secret, were given to the American journalist, David Schoenbrun, in an off-the-record interview with Dulles, and were first reported in his book, *The Three Lives of Charles de Gaulle*.[10] The encounter was a striking re-run of the de Gaulle–Hopkins meeting on the eve of Yalta: even the rhetoric had not changed substantially. De Gaulle explained France's need for grandeur – in practical terms meaning status as a major power – not only as her historical right, but also as imperative to strengthening the flagging French morale without which France might disintegrate under the strain of decolonization. He told Dulles that ' "grandeur" is not a romantic notion; it is a reality, a tangible factor in a nation's efforts. The French "have the need to believe in themselves and the right to believe in themselves" '.[11] In de Gaulle's view, the attribute of grandeur was therefore an immediate psychological necessity as well as a French historical tradition. It meant a role of major international responsibility based on national self-esteem. It was above all the cement necessary to hold the nation together in the face of the divisive strain of Vichy and a decade of defeat in French colonial policy. Dulles replied in an avuncular manner that the spirit of France must certainly be kept strong, and that the

9. Quoted in Guy de Carmoy, *Les Politiques extérieures de la France: 1944–1946*, Paris, La Table Ronde, 1967, p. 329.

10. David Schoenbrun, *The Three Lives of Charles de Gaulle*, New York, Athenaeum, 1968, chapter 10.

11. Schoenbrun, *The Three Lives of Charles de Gaulle*, p. 300.

French must continue to think of their nation as 'the spirit of Western civilization', but he warned that

> there might be a clash of wills if France, striving to maintain the status of a great power, were to appear to be setting herself up separately and above Germany and Italy. The Secretary pointed out that the Germans and Italians had their serious emotional and political problems; that they might misunderstand French motives and become mistrustful, and thereby severely strain the entire Atlantic Alliance.[12]

De Gaulle's rejoinder was that he appreciated the problems of his neighbours very well, but that Germany and Italy had historically been continental powers, while France had, like Great Britain, always been a world power; and that he could see no reason why Germany or Italy would mistrust French aspirations any more than Britain's. He further indicated France's intention to become a nuclear power and to subject the location of nuclear weapons on French territory to French control and dispositions. De Gaulle closed their meeting by pointing to his view of France's interests and responsibilities, concluding, 'France, Sir, has a world vocation.'[13] This vocation he saw as France's historical legacy, her right, and her imperious need in the midst of present trials. The United States was apparently prepared to concede a major role for Great Britain, but it placed France on a footing with defeated Germany and Italy as continental powers. Finally, de Gaulle's view of relations between allies as based on consultation and co-operation among independent states collided headlong with the American thesis of integration under US leadership. US and French interests were in fundamental conflict over Algeria. Little wonder that the strain appeared in the form of resistance to the domination by the US of the Alliance.

All the basic characteristics of the on-going French–American controversies can be found in this encounter between Dulles and de Gaulle, as they could also in the meeting between Hopkins and de Gaulle thirteen years earlier. As in the meeting with Hopkins, de Gaulle's primary objective continued to be full recognition of France's status as a great power with a role of world-wide

12. Schoenbrun, *The Three Lives of Charles de Gaulle*, p. 300.

13. Schoenbrun, *The Three Lives of Charles de Gaulle*, p. 307. See also the excellent discussion of this episode in John Newhouse, *De Gaulle and the Anglo-Saxons*, New York, Viking Press, 1970, pp. 56 ff.

diplomatic responsibility. The bipolar international system resulting from the war he looked upon with opprobrium, declaring his determination to reverse its effect through the currency of nuclear power and diplomatic skill.

De Gaulle continued his diplomatic manœuvring two months later in a secret letter to President Eisenhower – actually, the first in a series of secret letters. This did not in the least prevent their contents from being discussed widely, however, and the shroud of secrecy probably served more in the end to dramatize and confuse the issues raised than to facilitate diplomacy. The content was, to say the least, an open secret. Before addressing Eisenhower, however, de Gaulle took care of another detail. Since Dulles had made plain that the main thrust of American opposition to his bid for French status would lie in an appeal to Italian and German mistrust, de Gaulle quietly and effectively set out to neutralize that objection. He lost no time in dispatching Foreign Minister Couve de Murville to Rome and to Bonn, crowning this diplomatic initiative with an invitation to Chancellor Konrad Adenauer to meet at his private retreat in Colombey-les-deux-Eglises on 14 September.

To Konrad Adenauer, who had from the beginning made of reconciliation with France the cornerstone of his European policy, the meeting with de Gaulle on French soil symbolized both a political victory and a deep personal tribute. As it turned out, it was still more of a success for de Gaulle; for Adenauer, completely enchanted by de Gaulle's courtly charm and political astuteness, gave de Gaulle exactly the cards he needed to play his next round against the Americans. The final communiqué of their conversations stated that 'Franco–German co-operation is the foundation of the European construction', and further that it would 'reinforce the Atlantic Alliance and serve the causes of all peoples in the domain of the great problems of the world'.[14] Adenauer glowed still more effusively in his personal comments to the press following the meeting. Clearly, the meeting had been a great triumph for de Gaulle. It would be wrong, none the less to infer that de Gaulle's rallying to Franco–German reconciliation was a purely tactical move geared to reinforce his bargaining position. First of all, de Gaulle's moves were seldom 'purely' anything. They tended to create and multiply options. Second, reconcilia-

14. *Le Monde*, 16 septembre 1958.

tion with Germany had always been implicit in de Gaulle's long-range objectives. What was clear, however, was that he would now appropriate the Fourth Republic policy for his own purposes. It was the timing of his courtship of Adenauer that was particularly adept. In adopting the policy of Franco–German rapprochement, he had deftly silenced his puzzled internal critics and stolen the thunder from the American objections to France's bid for great power status. The time was now ripe to make the big move.

In his secret letter to Eisenhower, dated 17 September 1958, de Gaulle took dead aim at the internal contradictions of the American 'protectorate' over Nato.[15] De Gaulle had no problem, of course, in appreciating the possible divergence of American and European political interests and policies. If his experience of the past were not sufficient, the humiliating episode of Suez was not that far behind, and indeed the Algerian war provided a daily example of the non-identity of views. But in his letter to Eisenhower, de Gaulle chose instead to focus on the dramatic Middle East crisis, including the landings in Lebanon over the summer of 1958. He pointed out that there was indeed a danger of such a crisis deteriorating into a general war – a situation demonstrating clearly the risks that France ran as a Nato ally of the United States who would perforce share its fate. Yet France, a power with world-wide interests, was not consulted concerning American decisions potentially affecting her fate. Having recovered fully from the setbacks of the war, France in 1958 was ready to assume its 'historical role in world affairs'. He could therefore no longer see any justification for delegating to the United States exclusive responsibility for vital decisions concerning common defence.

This argument served as a springboard for the real message:

> The French Government does not consider that the security of the free world, or indeed France itself, can be guaranteed by the North Atlantic Treaty Organization in its present form. In its view, political and strategic questions of world, as opposed to regional, importance should be entrusted to a new body consisting of the United States, Great Britain, and France. This body should have all the responsibility of taking joint decisions on all political matters affecting world security,

15. See the excellent discussion of this episode in Schoenbrun, *The Three Lives of Charles de Gaulle*, p. 305 ff. Schoenbrun had access to the original letter. See also, 'De Gaulle's 1958 Tripartite Proposal and U.S. Response', *Atlantic Community Quarterly*, IV, no. 3 (Fall 1966), pp. 455–8.

and of drawing up and, if necessary, putting into action strategic plans, especially those involving the use of nuclear weapons. . . .[16]

The wording of the French proposal was such that the thorny issue of nuclear control appeared to have been tucked in almost as an afterthought. The memo referred to 'drawing up and, if necessary, putting into action strategic plans . . . involving the use of nuclear weapons'. What de Gaulle was calling for amounted to nothing less than a full formal reform of the Atlantic Alliance, including a veto over the use of nuclear weapons. Not even Britain enjoyed such broad control over nuclear weapons, its veto being restricted to weapons actually located on British territory. Most crucially, de Gaulle was not prepared to settle for some nebulous 'participation' in alliance 'planning': he wanted the scheme to be formally recognized and institutionalized at the highest level. Participation meant power to exert effective influence, not talkathons among subordinates. In his concluding paragraph, de Gaulle declared that henceforth France would subordinate French participation in Nato to equal participation by France in global strategy: 'The French Government regards such an organization for security as indispensable. Henceforth, the whole development of its present participation to Nato is predicated on this.'[17]

Schoenbrun and Newhouse both question whether de Gaulle could realistically have expected the 'Anglo-Saxons' to agree to these proposals when one considers their implications. Raymond Aron answers this question in the negative, contending that the whole scheme amounted to nothing more than a tactical diplomatic manœuvre, deliberately designed to provoke a refusal, thereby setting the stage for an alternative course.[18] He points in support of that conclusion to two proofs: the first being that the French Government 'never revealed its proposal in detail or with precision'; and the second being de Gaulle's congenital allergy for the kind of deliberations among equal partners, with the implication of give-and-take and the concessions, that would be involved in such a scheme. The latter argument can be dismissed by pointing to two other Gaullist proposals which were, to say the very least, serious: the Fouchet Plan and the Franco-German

16. Quoted in Newhouse, *De Gaulle and the Anglo-Saxons*, p. 70.
17. Newhouse, *De Gaulle and the Anglo-Saxons*, p. 70.
18. 'Quel est le Grand Dessein?' *Le Figaro*, 4 février 1966.

Treaty – both of which likewise would have required a different style of diplomacy. The inability to adapt one's style of diplomacy to the necessities of a new situation may be an operational flaw in the scheme, but it should not perforce cast doubt on the seriousness of the original intention. As for the former argument, it appears at the very least implausible that de Gaulle would have gone to such pains to set the stage for his letter to Eisenhower, if it were merely designed to provoke a refusal – or indeed that he would have followed up his original letter with additional ones.[19] That the French Government never made its proposals public is at least susceptible of another interpretation and an objection: (1) that when it *subsequently* became apparent that the proposal would not be accepted, it was then discarded; (2) even granting Aron's conclusion that the whole proposal was from the outset a tactical manœuvre, would it not have served the French Government's propaganda purpose, in that case, far more to have made the whole transaction public, not the contrary?

Given his fundamental objections to the Nato *status quo*, de Gaulle had two options: to revamp the present system, or to substitute an alternative policy. De Gaulle surely entertained no illusions about the success of his Directorate scheme, but the proposal was indeed a serious one and not a mere contrivance.[20] The events of September to December 1958 tend to support this interpretation as the more probable one.

President Eisenhower responded to de Gaulle's letter on 20 October.[21] Eisenhower's letter was brief, breezy and blunt. He did not discuss de Gaulle's proposals more than superficially, and then in order to make the somewhat patronizing point that American policy had already considered them. Agreeing with de Gaulle that the threat to the free world was global, Eisenhower's anodyne answer was that American policies already took that into

19. This conclusion is supported by Kulski's claim that de Gaulle resubmitted the memorandum in a personal letter to Kennedy in January 1962. W.W. Kulski, *De Gaulle and the World*, Syracuse, NY, Syracuse University Press, 1966, p. 166.

20. See De Gaulle, *Mémoires d'espoir: le renouveau, 1958–1962*, Paris, Librairie Plon, 1970, p. 211 ff., translated as *Memoirs of Hope: Renewal and Endeavour*, London, Weidenfeld & Nicolson Ltd; New York, Simon & Schuster, 1971. See also Maurice Couve de Murville, *Une Politique étrangère: 1958–1962*, Paris, Librairie Plon, 1971, pp. 33 ff. and 53 ff.

21. Letter from President Eisenhower to General de Gaulle dated 20 October 1958, *Atlantic Community Quarterly*, no. 3 (Fall 1966), pp. 457–8. See text of letter in Appendix 1.

account through regional alliance systems and world-wide economic aid and technical assistance programmes. This was a clear case of side-stepping, in favour of the *status quo*, de Gaulle's demand for a tripartite global strategy. The message is plain: rely-on-Uncle-Sam-and-don't-rock-the-boat. In regard to Nato, Eisenhower pointed to the extension of 'the habit of consultation' in the Nato Council and 'developing intimacy among all the members' as positive signs of evolution, eschewing consideration of whether the US 'informing' its Nato allies of policy decisions constituted any form of bona fide participation on their part in the actual framing of the policies. Finally, the crux of the matter is contained in the next to last paragraph, which is a sort of monument of irony: 'We cannot afford to adopt any system which would give to our other Allies, or other Free World countries, the impression that basic decisions affecting their own vital interests are being made without their participation.'[22] But that was precisely de Gaulle's point.

In an effort to accommodate de Gaulle's proposal of joint planning at least to some extent, President Eisenhower instructed the Secretary of State in November to set up a 'tripartite committee' beneath cabinet level. But Dulles made two fatal errors along the way – errors which amounted to an incomprehensible diplomatic gaffe. In the first place, he appointed as the American member of the committee the one American diplomat guaranteed to offend de Gaulle, Robert Murphy. In the second place, he reassured German and Italian diplomats that the committee would merely provide a forum for de Gaulle's proposals – nothing more – news which promptly made it back via the diplomatic grapevine to de Gaulle.[23] Such unseemly *maladresse* in diplomacy is difficult to account for in one ordinarily so circumspect as John Foster Dulles.

The final encounter in the first round of the French bid for a

22. Eisenhower, *Atlantic Community Quarterly*, no. 3 (Fall 1966), p. 458. Compare with Couve de Murville's analysis: 'Either France would be closely associated with the United States . . . in security matters – beginning with the deployment of atomic weapons – or else she would be obliged to reconsider her policy, and notably her membership in NATO which bound her in practice to follow Washington, *without being either truly consulted or even perhaps in agreement*. This was the point of the memorandum which de Gaulle addressed to President Eisenhower and Prime Minister Macmillan on September 17th. . . .' Couve de Murville, *Une Politique éhtrangère*, p. 33. Emphasis added.

23. Schoenbrun, *The Three Lives of Charles de Gaulle*, p. 310.

tripartite reorganization of Nato policy and strategy took place on 15 December at an icy meeting between Dulles and de Gaulle in Paris. In an effort to placate de Gaulle, if not to respond directly to the issues he raised, Dulles proposed creating a tripartite planning committee on policy toward Africa. Under no illusion regarding the importance of a 'committee', de Gaulle nevertheless acknowledged Dulles's suggestion coolly, making plain that his idea of a concerted policy toward North Africa entailed purely and simply an endorsement by the US and Britain of French policy there, since North Africa was primarily an area of French influence. Dulles returned to Washington with a nominal agreement, but in fact empty-handed, while de Gaulle prepared to draw the necessary conclusions from the diplomatic impasse. He, in any case, never appointed a French delegate to Dulles's proposed 'committee'.

> As I expected, the two recipients of my memorandum replied evasively. So there was nothing to prevent us from taking action. But circumstances decreed that we should act with circumspection.... We, therefore, proposed to take appropriate steps in the direction of Atlantic disengagement while at the same time maintaining our direct cooperation with the United States and Britain.[24]

De Gaulle had had ample practice in the art of the contentious *grand geste*. He now stage-managed his scenario masterfully, punctuating his gestures with dramatic public rhetoric. Round two of *le défi gaulliste* began.

In early March 1959, France abruptly informed the Nato Command of her intention to withdraw her Mediterranean fleet, which was supposed to be committed to Nato Command in time of war. A move of virtually no strategic significance, it was clearly aimed at prodding Washington to take the French proposals seriously by stirring up some commotion. At the first of his spectacular presidential press conferences, on 25 March 1959, de Gaulle defended the political logic behind the French move:

> The zone of possible NATO action does not extend south of the Mediterranean. The Middle East, North Africa, the Red Sea, etc. are not part of it. Who can deny that France may possibly find herself obliged to act in these different areas? She would therefore have to act

24. De Gaulle, *Mémoires d'espoir*, p. 203.

independently of NATO. But how could she do so if her fleet were not available?[25]

De Gaulle further explained that since neither the United States nor Great Britain had committed the greater part of their naval forces to Nato, he therefore found it natural for France, too, to resume the power to dispose of her fleet. The message was clear: if Eisenhower were unwilling to accept his scheme for a tripartite global Directorate for Nato, de Gaulle would reclaim French freedom of action in the name of France's world-wide responsibilities. Withdrawal of the fleet was a stinging political gesture, of more nuisance value than military significance. It was a firecracker. Yet, while stage-managing his uncivil public image, on the back stages of diplomacy de Gaulle was penning still another secret letter to Eisenhower, promoting his plan for global strategic co-operation. He had by no means given up. The well-staged public show cum more courteous secret approaches marked the Gaullist style of political warfare.

The year 1959 provided two more such spectacular gestures in the name of French autonomy and grandeur. De Gaulle summarily ordered the nine US squadrons of F-100s equipped with nuclear warheads off French soil, and on 2 November he announced publicly in an address at the Ecole Militaire that France would build an independent nuclear force, the much celebrated *force de frappe*. The development of a French atomic bomb together with the construction of the nuclear installations at Pierrelatte were, in fact, a legacy of the Fourth Republic. But the timing of the announcement, coming as it did shortly on the heels of the September speech proclaiming the possibility of self-determination for Algeria, was certainly calculated to temper by gestures of self-assertive confidence the internal disarray over Algeria – above all, the demoralization of the French army. The assertive stance in regard to Nato provided a tactical counterpoint to the on-going ordeal in Algeria. None the less, the message was plain: the system of military integration under the American protectorate must end.

France exploded her first atomic bomb in the Sahara in 1960, shortly after the Generals' revolt in Algiers in response to the

25. French Embassy, Press and Information Division, New York, NY, *Major Addresses, Statements and Press Conferences of General Charles de Gaulle, May 19, 1958–January 31, 1964*, p. 49. Hereafter referred to as *Major Addresses*.

Government's announced policy of independence for Algeria, and on the eve of the Big Four summit conference in Paris. Were it not for the threat of civil war that hung over France during the next two years, it is altogether probable that the pace of de Gaulle's anti-Nato measures would have been maintained. As it turned out, the first half of 1960 was taken up with the aftermath of the Generals' revolt and with preparations for the ill-fated Big Four summit conference in Paris. But even this did not prevent de Gaulle from continuing behind the scenes to press for his version of Nato reorganization during visits with Macmillan and Eisenhower in April, and from following up his personal conversations with still another spate of secret correspondence urging an organization for three-power global strategic co-operation, including French participation in joint nuclear decision-making.[26]

The de Gaulle–Eisenhower correspondence ended in an impasse, over de Gaulle's insistence on a formal Big Three summit conference to map out global strategy and to reorganize Nato, countered by the continued American insistence on a more discreet, lower-level approach that would not risk offending other continental Allies. De Gaulle's objective was to reassert unequivocally France's autonomy and resumption of responsibility for her own security.[27]

The chapter of secret diplomacy was sealed at de Gaulle's press conference on 5 September 1960, in a broadside public attack on Nato. Having failed in his effort to win over Eisenhower to the idea of a summit, he now would make one by public proclamation.

De Gaulle's attack on Nato was the more stinging for its tone of common-sensical simplicity. The planted question invited him to 'throw some light' on his 'concept of co-operation with Nato', which he had 'asked to have reformed'. Beginning on a note of times-have-changed, de Gaulle sketched in the circumstances under which the present Nato structures had been set up ten years earlier. The states of Europe in collapse, weak, incapable of defending themselves:

> So the Alliance was set up on the basis of integration, that is to say, of a system whereby the defense of each of the countries of Continental Europe, of Western Europe – not counting England – does not have a

26. Schoenbrun, *The Three Lives of Charles de Gaulle*, p. 316.
27. See Couve de Murville, *Une Politique étrangère*, p. 58.

national character, a system in which, in fact, *everything is under the command of the Americans*, and in which the Americans decide on the use of the principal weapons, in other words, the atomic weapons.[28]

Two important changes had occurred since then. First of all, Nato was restricted in scope by its charter to Europe, while the areas of conflict were spreading all over the world – revealing profound political differences among the Nato allies. And second, as the countries of continental Europe – France, in particular – regained their strength, they naturally desired to resume their own responsibilities in regard to defence.

Brushing off parenthetically the American argument that the situation of other Nato allies must be kept in consideration (Dulles was thinking primarily of Germany), de Gaulle proposed to speak only of France's interest. 'As for other countries . . . they will speak for themselves.'[29]

It was therefore high time to reform Nato, both in regard to 'the limitation of the Alliance to the single area of Europe', and in regard to the concept of military integration. National defence must have a 'national character' in order that countries should assume political responsibility for their own defence. Reliance on American protection is no defence policy. 'France obviously cannot leave her own destiny and even her own life to the discretion of others.'[30] De Gaulle emphasized this point time and again, both in principle and in concrete example. In September 1959 he told Eisenhower:

In the course of the two world wars, America was France's ally, and France has not forgotten what she owes to American help. But neither has she forgotten that during the First World War, that help came only after three long years of struggle which nearly proved mortal for her, and that during the Second she had already been crushed before you intervened. In saying this, I intend not the slightest reproach, for I know, as you yourself know, what a nation is, with its geography, its interests, its political system, its public opinion, its passions, its fears, its errors. *It can help another but it cannot identify itself with another.* That is why, although remaining faithful to our alliance, I cannot accept France's integration into NATO.[31]

28. *Major Addresses*, p. 95. Emphasis added.
29. *Major Addresses*, p. 96.
30. *Major Addresses*, p. 96.
31. De Gaulle, *War Memoirs*, p. 214. Emphasis added.

Secret diplomacy having failed, war-by-press-conference had begun. De Gaulle knew the power of the public media well, having made his political career through his ability to mobilize opinion, and he marshalled his forces with the skill of a craftsman. Positions had hardened since 1958, but there was little change in the arguments. It remained to be seen whether the next administration in Washington would be more receptive to de Gaulle's bid for a voice in world policy-making than the previous one.

With his government's policy toward Nato now on public record, de Gaulle turned to another forum. At the same press conference at which he buried Nato, de Gaulle slipped in another of his planted 'spontaneous' questions, concerning the future of European co-operation. For a brief time, France would again resume her role of leadership of the movement toward European political unity – but, of course, the Gaullist vision of Europe was not the tidy institutional framework of Robert Schuman and Jean Monnet. *Le défi gaulliste* took aim at another old foe – European integration.

CHAPTER FOUR

Europe for What? 'Integrated *Volapük*' and the Fouchet Fiasco

By defending our own independence, we are defending that of the Europe to which we belong, and we are the real Europeans.

Premier Georges Pompidou, speech to French National Assembly, 17 June 1965

To build Europe, that is to say, to unite it, is evidently something essential. . . . All that is necessary, in such a domain, is to proceed, not by following our dreams, but according to realities.

To imagine that something can be built that would be effective for action and that would be approved by the peoples outside and above the States – this is a dream.[1]

Whatever dreams of the future of Europe de Gaulle had nurtured in 1945 and during the years immediately following the war,[2] by 1960 there was at least one additional 'reality' in the continental landscape, namely, the three European communities established between 1950 and 1957 prior to his return to power. Two other projected communities had been relegated in the same period to the cemetery of dashed dreams of European unity. The Coal and Steel Community, established in 1950, now stood alongside Euratom and the Common Market, established in 1957 and scheduled to begin operation in January 1959. The European Defence Community, proposed by the French in 1950, went down in defeat four years later in a bitterly divided French parliament,

1. *Major Addresses*, press conference of 5 September 1960, pp. 92–3.

2. See chapter II. It should again be pointed out that Vol. III of de Gaulle's *War Memoirs*, covering the early postwar period, did not appear until 1959. It is therefore probable that much of de Gaulle's reflection on Europe bears the stamp of later developments, at least in emphasis.

and along with it a proposed European political community, which represented the dream-come-true of the most ardent European federalists. During this whole period of European construction, the attitude of the Gaullists had been one of unwavering and noisy opposition at every turn to projects that would subordinate French policy to the decisions of others. It was not so much the *goal* of European unity they objected to, as the form it was being given in the various institutions of 'supranational' authority, as a foundation for federation.

When de Gaulle returned to power in 1958, therefore, the reaction in 'European' circles was one of understandable dismay. What would be de Gaulle's attitude toward the treaty establishing the Common Market, which had been signed but remained to be implemented? From his return to power in May 1958 until his news conference of September 1960, de Gaulle made no major public statements concerning Europe. But to the astonishment of his European critics, he had indeed initiated the internal reforms necessary to the entry into force of the Treaty of Rome on schedule in January 1959. The Common Market Treaty was unworkable without the financial decisions of 28 December 1958.[3] De Gaulle proceeded to delight and silence his European critics further by adopting the stance of staunch defender of the treaty's provisions in the domain of agriculture. Where de Gaulle and the Europeans parted ways was in regard to the political future of Europe: What Europe? and, For what?

Political unity remains the ultimate goal of all advocates of European unity, but they differ on the ways and means of attaining that objective, on *how* to establish a common foreign policy and defence. One method, which had been rejected in 1954 with the package defeat of the proposed European Defence Community and its bedfellow, the Draft Treaty for a European Political Community, was purely and simply to write a treaty creating a new federal political institution. Another route, explored in the unsuccessful Dehousse Plan of 1960,[4] lay in enlarging the supranational powers of the existing Community institutions – in particular, the European Parliament. That route

3. See Grosser, *French Foreign Policy under de Gaulle*, p. 82. They included, among other things, a restoration of the external convertibility of the franc. De Gaulle's objectives are discussed below, p. 62.

4. See Pierre Gerbet, *La Politique d'unification européenne*, Amicale des Elèves de l'Institut d'Etudes Politiques de Paris, 1964–5, pp. 550 ff.

had been rejected by France, and met with little enthusiasm in Italy and Germany as well. Theories on political integration abounded. Verbal formulas likewise abounded: mechanisms of rapprochement, spill-over effects, upgrading the common interest . . . But the fact of the matter was that an institutional framework for political unity continued to remain a distant dream. Hence, despite his ostensibly cynical rhetoric, in taking up the challenge to forge political unity at his September 1960 press conference, de Gaulle was dealing in the dream market. In the process, he was gradually to reveal the kind of Europe he had in mind as well.

De Gaulle's vision of Europe had, of course, changed in focus somewhat since 1945. For one thing, the situation of Europe had changed dramatically. Divided and politically weakened, Germany had ceased to pose a challenge to French security. Driven together by the common threat of the cold war, France and West Germany had embarked on a policy of rapprochement whose concrete manifestation was the institutions of the European communities. Europe in 1960 had no longer to be kept safe from German designs, but set free from the paralysing threat and counterthreat of Soviet and American hegemony locked in immovable conflict symbolized by the on-going confrontations over Berlin. The objective of de Gaulle's 1960 initiative was, therefore, the creation of that 'third force' Europe already alluded to in the Bar-le-Duc speech of 1946[5] – a Europe in charge of its own destiny and no longer a mere pawn in the contest between the two superpowers. In promoting political unity under French leadership, de Gaulle saw France's role as *l'élément moteur*[6] of a new Europe, which would, in turn, guarantee a more assertive and independent European voice in the world. Europe was, therefore, in de Gaulle's scheme of things, both a means and an end in itself.

The timing of the French European initiative demonstrates de Gaulle's skill as a political strategist, choosing the ground for his foreign policy initiatives so as to enhance his position in the difficult domestic political arena. Assuming a stance of leadership and strength in foreign policy helped no little to consolidate his government's shaky position internally during the long, drawn-out period of the Algerian negotiations, from 1958 to 1962. De

5. See above, chapter II, pp. 38–9. His advocacy of a more autonomous role for Europe should not be confused with an *a priori* commitment to neutralism.

6. Couve de Murville, *Une Politique étrangère*, p. 303.

Gaulle had been brought to power by an army revolt, and had continuously to contend with the threat of further attempted *coups* on the part of the army, supported by the violent street tactics of the OAS. With bombs exploding in public buildings in Paris, and multiple attempts at assassination, the government maintained at best a precarious hold over public order, as it stepped up the process of disengagement. Riveting attention on foreign policy, therefore, served a vital function in focusing the attention of public opinion off Algeria intermittently, toward other arenas where France could perform masterfully rather than suffer humiliating defeat. By 1960, the Nato card had been played. Another effort to reap the rewards of leadership was the Big Four summit conference in Paris, in June 1960, where de Gaulle had doubtless hoped to score some diplomatic points. Khrushchev's intransigent torpedoing of the conference sealed that opportunity. De Gaulle's European initiative at Rambouillet came right on the heels of the failed summit in Paris. Given the popularity of the goal of European unity in public opinion,[7] it was an adroit card to play, tactically. It was also in substantial continuity with his long-standing policy objectives.

Following the failure of his bid through a Nato Directorate to obtain a voice in world diplomacy, the European substitute provided an alternative vehicle, an enhanced power base, for France's claim to pursue policies independent of the US lead. But the European option was, indeed, far more than a contrivance designed to accomplish for French nationalist ambitions what France's own relative weakness could not obtain. De Gaulle's European policy stemmed from a pragmatic assessment of France's fate as inextricably bound to the future of her European neighbours, and represented a conscientious decision to move in consequence toward an institutional framework for political co-operation, beyond the economic mechanisms that had already been set up.

> The point was to decide and to act. At least, this was how France conceived of a European political union. For France, the main concern was for a Europe capable and eager to assert itself, to determine its own international policy and to stick to the positions thus arrived at – in other words, an independent Europe.[8]

7. See Raymond Aron, 'Old Nations, New Europe', in Stephen R. Graubard (ed.)' *A New Europe?*, Boston, Beacon Press, 1964, pp. 42 ff.
8. Couve de Murville, *Une Politique étrangère*, p. 348.

> In this way, a solid entity could be built in the West of the continent, representing at least a relative counterweight to the East and enabling us then to embark under more favorable conditions on that *politique d'ouverture*, opening the continent to itself, failing which, neither the eventual solution of European problems – that is, the German problem – would be conceivable, nor true peace for our nations.[9]

De Gaulle's initiative on European political union was a cornerstone of his foreign policy.[10] While he entertained few illusions regarding the chances for success of his Nato proposals, he regarded no policy as so urgent and paramount as the realization of European political union. He sought, therefore, to build on the 'diffused sentiment' in favour of political unity[11] by giving it a precise form, supported by a sustained political will.

The problem of institutional form is inextricably bound to that of policy outcomes. As Pierre Gerbet put it, 'An institution is acceptable only providing there is the assurance that one will not be dragged into a policy that is unacceptable.'[12] The French proposals of 1960 represented a conceptual framework for institutions which would assure that French priorities would be respected. There remained the problem of winning over France's European partners to the French plan.

Three years after the signing of the Treaty of Rome, during the summer of 1960, de Gaulle launched his trial balloon on political union at a meeting with Konrad Adenauer at Rambouillet. Relations between de Gaulle and the German Chancellor had had their ups and downs since 1958, but they had recently been extremely cordial. And, of course, no proposal for European co-operation stood any chance of success without the support of both France and Germany, whence de Gaulle's concern to enlist West German support for his plan before proceeding further.

The plan de Gaulle disclosed at Rambouillet called for setting up a mechanism for intergovernmental co-operation, providing for periodical meetings of the heads of state or government of the Six, and a series of subordinate permanent intergovernmental commissions charged with political, cultural, economic and mili-

9. Couve de Murville, *Une Politique étrangère*, p. 348.

10. 'Pour de Gaulle, il s'agissait d'une affaire capitale . . .', Couve de Murville, *Une Politique étrangère*, p. 362.

11. Courve de Murville, *Une Politique étrangere*, p. 384.

12. Gerbet, *La Politique d'unification européenne*, p. 554.

tary affairs. A permanent secretariat would make preparations for the various consultations and supervise the implementation of decisions. Subsequently, at his press conference of 5 September 1960, he added to his proposal an assembly of delegates appointed by the various national parliaments and 'a formal European referendum' to give the sanction of effective popular support to this 'launching of Europe'.[13]

Political consultations at the level of foreign ministers had already become a regular practice among the Six, following de Gaulle's meeting with the Italian Government in Rome in June 1959. They represented a kind of empirical approach to co-operation, but their end result had been disappointing. At most, they had permitted a certain airing of differences.[14] A permanent secretariat had been proposed at the same time, but it was eventually abandoned. In other words, aside from the fanfare, what de Gaulle's 'départ de l'Europe' involved was essentially an expansion and institutionalization of the process of consultation, a proposal toward which France's partners had already displayed a certain reticence a year earlier.[15]

There was a spate of diplomatic activity in Europe during the late summer, even before de Gaulle's press conference, to sort out the significance of the Rambouillet proposals. What Adenauer actually agreed to at Rambouillet subsequently proved unclear, and this confusion proved all the more difficult to clarify in the wake of the openly negative domestic reactions to de Gaulle's proposals in West Germany. In any event, Adenauer could not possibly have agreed to a referendum, since referendums are specifically prohibited by the West German constitution. Whether the Chancellor did or did not in fact express objections regarding Nato and the existing European Communities,[16] de Gaulle came away convinced that he had Adenauer's support. What he did not

13. *Major Addresses*, p. 93. The parallels between these proposals and the political techniques of the Fifth Republic internally are, of course, not coincidental – especially the concept of a limited parliament and the referendum.

14. Gerbet, *La Politique d'unification européenne*, pp. 554 ff. See also, *Le Dossier de l'Europe politique*, documents published by the Political Committee of the European Parliament, Luxembourg, January 1964.

15. For an excellent analysis of the earlier discussions, see Couve de Murville, *Une Politique étrangère*, pp. 356–8.

16. See Alessandro Silj, *Europe's Political Puzzle: a Study of the Fouchet Negotiations and the 1963 Veto*, Cambridge, Mass., Harvard University Center for International Affairs, Occasional Paper no. 17, December 1967, note at bottom of p. 5.

suspect was that the aging Chancellor had already begun to lose domestic support within both his government and the governing CDU party.

It would have been easier to cope with de Gaulle's proposals on European unity had they not been served in such an unappealing package. For while de Gaulle was urging European unity, he was also laterally attacking the existing institutions of the European Communities. Why had it proved so difficult to unite Europe? de Gaulle patronizingly inquired. Because the process had been based on 'dreams' rather than on 'realities': 'Now, what are the realities of Europe? What are the pillars on which it can be built? . . . States are the only entities that have the right to command and the authority to act.'[17] What, then, of the three existing Communities? They, of course, had their 'technical value', but no ultimate political authority. They were merely partial arrangements pending a real organization of Europe:

> Of course, it is true that, while waiting to come to grips with Europe's problem and tackle it as a whole, it has been possible to institute certain organs that are more or less extranational. These organs have their technical value, but they do not have, they cannot have, authority, and consequently, political effectiveness. As long as nothing serious happens, they function without much difficulty, but as soon as a tragic situation appears, a major problem to be solved, it can then be seen that one 'High Authority' or another has no authority over the various national categories and that only the States have it. . . .
>
> To ensure regular cooperation between the States of Western Europe is what France considers as desirable, possible, and practical in the political, economic, and cultural domains and in that of defense.[18]

The press conference raised a predictable storm of protest in 'European' circles, both inside France and abroad. The principal objection was that the loose confederal intergovernmental commissions proposed by de Gaulle would have the effect of weakening the federal character of the existing European Communities, on the one hand,[19] and Nato, on the other. This was all the more apparent in the light of the explicit attacks de Gaulle had un-

17. *Major Addresses*, p. 92.

18. *Major Addresses*, p. 93.

19. This objection was to some extent tempered by the timely appearance in the newspaper *Le Monde* of a series of articles on the future of Europe by the influential Gaullist Deputy, Alain Peyrefitte, emphasizing the fact that historically 'les confédérations ont tendance à devenir des fédérations', and suggesting that the proposed system could evolve toward an organization operating by majority rule. *Le Monde*, 14–17 septembre 1960.

leashed against both organizations at the press conference. Implicit in de Gaulle's policy of movement was a rejection of the *status quo*. The Benelux countries also feared reinforcing the division of Western Europe if England were not immediately invited to participate in the discussions – a concern which actually masked a more profound mistrust of a European order based on potential French hegemony in a kind of *directoire à trois* of France, Germany and Italy.

The French made some concessions – or what then appeared to be concessions – in Bonn, on 7 and 8 October, when Premier Michel Debré and Foreign Minister Maurice Couve de Murville met Adenauer. In return for formal assurances on the part of the French in regard to Nato, Adenauer agreed to sponsor the French plan.[20] German objections were apparently also tempered by the decision of Jean Monnet's Action Committee for Europe to endorse the French proposal as a first step toward a European federation.

At the first European summit conference held in Paris on 10 February 1961, in response to the French initiative, Christian Fouchet, the French Ambassador to Denmark, was named chairman of a commission instructed to submit 'concrete proposals concerning meetings of the Heads of State or Government and the Ministers of Foreign Affairs as well as all other meetings that might appear desirable', in keeping with the French plan.[21] But the Dutch had already made plain their intention to hold out for British participation in the discussion prior to any decision. The dynamics of the future negotiations were already clear: the French pushing for their plan, the Dutch dragging their heels and leading the opposition, with the others arrayed in between – Italy mediating, and Germany openly supporting the French formula. The Fouchet Commission was, therefore, at the outset, a cover-up for basic disagreement. In essence, in the absence of consensus, a committee was named 'to study the matter'.[22]

20. What the French actually agreed to was that 'the closest possible cooperation between the European members and the North American members of the Atlantic Alliance is vital to the defense of the free world'. The Germans of course meant the entire Nato organization; what the French meant appears more ambiguous in the light of their subsequent withdrawal from the Nato 'organization', while protesting loyalty to the 'alliance'. See Silj, *Europe's Political Puzzle*, p. 8.

21. Quoted in Silj, *Europe's Political Puzzle*, p. 9.

22. See Couve de Murville, *Une Politique étrangère*, pp. 361–2.

At a second conference held in Bonn, on 18 July 1961, the heads of state of the Six further instructed the Fouchet Commission to generate proposals by which a 'statutory form [could] be given as soon as possible to the union of their peoples'.[23] This was agreed to after an important series of concessions on the part of the French, concerning Nato, the existing Communities, and the exclusion of defence and economic questions from the work of the intergovernmental commissions. The final communiqué stated:

The Heads of State or Government . . .

- convinced that only a united Europe, allied to the United States of America and to other free peoples, is in a position to face the dangers that menace the existence of Europe; . . . resolved to develop their political cooperation with a view to the union of Europe and to continue at the same time the work already undertaken in the European Communities;
- desiring the adhesion to the European Communities of other European states . . . have decided: . . .
- To hold, at regular intervals, meetings whose aim will be to compare their views, to concert their policies, and to reach common positions in order to further the political union of Europe, thereby strengthening the Atlantic Alliance.[24]

Shortly thereafter, on 31 July 1961, the British formally applied for membership in the EEC.

During the autumn of 1961, the governments of the Six duly submitted various position papers to the Fouchet Commission, but only the French Government presented a formal draft *Traité d'union d'Etats*, more commonly referred to as the Fouchet Plan.[25]

The proposed Fouchet Plan faithfully translated the political ideas of de Gaulle. The Plan provided for a Council of Heads of State and Government, with competence in the fields of defence, foreign policy, and scientific and cultural affairs. A European Parliamentary Assembly, as a deliberative body, would make recommendations to the Council, but could not censure the Council. And finally, a European Political Commission, composed of top civil servants appointed by the member states, and there-

23. Quoted in Silj, *Europe's Political Puzzle*, p. 11.

24. For the full English text of the communiqué, see Silj, *Europe's Political Puzzle*, Appendix 1, pp. 133–5.

25. See Appendix 2. It is noteworthy that the text of the Fouchet Plan never appeared in the semi-official French reference book, *l'Année politique*.

fore acting as an intergovernmental commission rather than a 'community' one, would 'prepare' the work of the Council. The Council would function by the unanimity rule for three years, at the end of which Article 16 provided loosely for a 'general revision' of the treaty with a view toward strengthening it. Thus, there was no explicit commitment to pass from unanimity to majority rule, as in the Common Market Treaty, but the door to hope was left ajar for the more ardent partisans of federation. The wording of Article 16, indeed, remained ambiguous. It stipulated as the main objectives of a general revision 'the introduction of a unified foreign policy and the gradual establishment of an organization centralizing, within the Union, the European Communities. . . . ' Did this mean in practice a subordination of the Communities, or a supranational reform?

The Council of Heads of State and Government, which was to meet every four months, was thus the political executive of the proposed Union, and, in keeping with the French concessions made at the Bonn conference, it had no competence in economic affairs at all. Defence had, on the other hand, been slipped back in. Most critics of the proposal could echo the summary judgment of Pierre Gerbet: 'Basically, it hardly did more than to confer formal blessing on the practice of consultations among the Foreign Ministers.'[26]

But the Dutch stood firm in their opposition to the project, and their position of isolation in the negotiations did not in the least deter them from sharpening their protests. They immediately objected to the inclusion of defence policy, without reference to Nato, among the powers of the Council. They preferred the existing European institutions, in which their voice carried more formal weight, to 'organized co-operation'; and, at the very least, if the existing supranational institutions were to be compromised, they then insisted all the more vehemently on the prior inclusion of the British, to offset the prospect of a Paris–Bonn axis, which they feared.[27]

The French, equally dedicated to reaching agreement on a political union *à la française*, presumably before admitting the British, were again prepared to make a few concessions. It was under these circumstances that Christian Fouchet apparently

26. Gerbet, *La Politique d'unification européenne*, p. 559.
27. See Jean Monnet, *Mémoires*, Paris, Arthème Fayard, 1976, p. 513.

circulated another, non-official, version of the Plan, a draft never published.[28] The revised draft was clearly intended to mollify the Dutch opposition. Article 16 was notably modified so as to provide some guarantees for the existing Community institutions. They further conceded at the December meeting of the foreign ministers that membership in the EEC would *automatically* confer membership in the political union. But while the press emphasized the French concessions, and concluded by implication that final agreement was imminent, the Dutch remained obdurately attached to their initial objections. The controversy over British participation in the negotiations and the question of supranationality stood in the end as insuperable obstacles to agreement. The Dutch intransigence finally prompted a harsh, dramatic and ultimately counterproductive French response:

> At the very least we would serve notice that we were not the dupes of exasperating delaying tactics and that after all, if – as our October draft showed – we were prepared for reasonable compromise, since others remained immobile, we were also entitled to mark our preferences.[29]

The surprise presentation of a second official version of the Fouchet Plan by the French Government on 18 January 1962 proved a brusque turn of events.

In presenting the new draft to the committee, the French representative contended that it contained merely 'quelques améliorations de style' in comparison with the earlier draft; but France's partners were undeterred in their common judgment that the new French draft constituted a giant step backwards.[30] The Amsterdam newspaper, *Algemeen Handelsblad*, branded the new French ploy a complete reversion to de Gaulle's original concept of *l'Europe des patries*, a confirmation of their worst suspicions, leaving no hope whatsoever to integrationists. Indeed, the second Fouchet Plan reasserted as unqualified goals of the Union both defence and economic policy, undermining *de facto* thereby the status both of Nato and of the existing European Communities. The controversial Article 16 was reworded so as to eliminate

28. See Irving Destler, *Political Union in Europe 1960–1962*, Washington, DC, Woodrow Wilson School of Public Affairs, 28 September 1964.

29. Couve de Murville, *Une Politique étrangère*, p. 371.

30. *L'Année politique 1962*, Paris, Presses Universitaires de France, 1963, p. 388. It is worth noting the timing of the French move, which came four days after an agreement on agricultural policy had been reached.

specific reference to the existing Communities altogether, and to remove the ambiguity allowing for the interpretation of an eventual evolution toward majority rule.[31] Instead, it suggested implicitly that the unmentioned Communities were to be 'rationalized'. And finally, the new draft did not provide that new members of the EEC should automatically become members of the Union, but rather that they should be subject to the unanimous vote of the Council. This meant, concretely, that the British might become members of the economic community, but not automatically of the political union. Whatever de Gaulle's objectives actually were, the result of his Jupiterian diplomacy was to end the isolation of the Dutch and to convince France's other partners that perhaps the Dutch had been correct in their misgivings all along.

De Gaulle's *coup de théâtre* was obviously a calculated risk. He acted boldly, weighing the possibility of failure against the prospect, presumably, of jolting both the project's opponents and supporters into serious negotiations by shifting to a hard line. But the atmosphere surrounding the negotiations continued, unfortunately, to deteriorate.

Though lines had indeed hardened irrevocably, the discussions on the Fouchet Plan did not terminate just yet. They dragged on until April, with intermittent initiatives that never got off the ground. De Gaulle attempted to shore up his position somewhat, even in the midst of a particularly difficult phase of the Algerian

31. A comparison of Article 16 in the two versions of the Fouchet Plan is revealing. In the first version, Article 16 read:

> Three years after this Treaty comes into force, it shall be subjected to a general review with a view to considering suitable measures for strengthening the Union in the light of the progress already made.
>
> The main objects of such a review shall be the introduction of a unified foreign policy and the gradual establishment of an organization centralizing, within the Union, the European Communities referred to in the Preamble to the present Treaty.
>
> The amendments arising from this review shall be adopted in accordance with the procedure outlined in Article 15 above.

(Article 15 provided for the unanimous agreement of the members.) By contrast, the the 1962 version of Article 16 was far briefer:

> Three years after this Treaty comes into force, it shall be subjected to a review in order to consider suitable measures for strengthening the Union in general in the light of progress already made or, in particular, for simplifying, rationalizing and co-ordinating the ways in which Member States co-operate.

For the full texts of the two French proposals, see Appendices 2 and 3.

peace negotiations, by paying visits to Adenauer in February and to Italian President Segni and Foreign Minister Fanfani in early April, but the result was mainly to increase the mistrust of the other partners *vis-à-vis* the spectre of a Directorate of the *Trois Grands*. The German Government, none the less, consented to continue supporting the revised Fouchet Plan in return for two concessions. At Adenauer's insistence, de Gaulle agreed that the preamble should contain a reference to Nato, and that the article describing the powers of the Council should make specific that discussions of economic affairs would take place in the context of 'respect for existing institutions'.[32] The Italians, while less enthusiastic than the Germans, likewise continued to support the revised French plan and attempted to continue in the role of mediator. But in the end, the Fouchet Commission was never able to bridge the differences over the timing of British membership. At the crucial meeting of the foreign ministers in Paris, on 17 April 1962, the Belgian Minister, Paul-Henri Spaak, rallied to the Dutch position, declaring that he was not prepared to sign any proposed treaty until after the British had been admitted to membership in the EEC. Couve de Murville, who was presiding, summarily closed the meeting. Negotiations were thus formally 'suspended', and the Fouchet Plan went quietly and unceremoniously to the file drawers.

In the end, the negotiations had failed not over the issue of more or less integration, supranationality, or the role of Nato, but over the issue of the timing of the British entry. Spaak's motives for rallying to the Dutch opposition are at least as unclear as the true nature of the Dutch objections themselves. Perhaps he thought, as a loyal 'European', that by delaying, he could wrest more concessions from the French, albeit to force de Gaulle's hand on the British question.

The Dutch position, in retrospect, appears more discreet and unyielding. Their objections in the name of political 'integration' appear at best tactical and sporadic, while their defence of the existing community structures, their constant concern for the role of Great Britain, and their unflagging attachment to Nato carry throughout the negotiations. Even without Spaak's eleventh-hour support, it remains dubious whether or not they could have been pressured into signing the Treaty – no matter

32. See Roger Massip, *De Gaulle et l'Europe*, Paris, Flammarion, 1963, p. 78.

what compromises the French were prepared to offer. From the outset, they appeared less interested in a political organization of Europe than in maintaining Atlantic ties. It has been suggested that they were in fact basically opposed to *any* European political organization, and did everything in their power to impede its realization.[33] Their trump card, if forced to a showdown, was to exchange agreement on some minimal political scheme for the certainty of British entry into the EEC, which would in turn have guaranteed, given the orientation of British policy, that a future organization would not be supranational in character and that it would not be dominated by French policy – in other words, that it would remain 'Atlantic' in orientation.

When Couve de Murville closed the foreign ministers' meeting on 17 April, few people actually thought that the Fouchet Plan would suffer the fate of a political Humpty-Dumpty. There had, after all, been sharp disagreements and temporary setbacks all along the route of European construction – times when the public forum took over until the diplomats returned to the bargaining table. Was it just a question of time? Perhaps, once the British entry had been settled, there would no longer be any obstacle. . . . Hopes for resuming the negotiations on political unity, therefore, lingered on over the summer of 1962, despite a convincing series of indications to the contrary. The first was another of de Gaulle's ceremonious press conferences, held on 15 May.

The scenario was as per usual. After soliciting the standard handful of planted questions, de Gaulle turned immediately to the question of Europe. Rehearsing the reasons that had originally inspired the French initiative, de Gaulle reaffirmed once more France's attachment to the political union of Western Europe. Economic construction is 'a great deal', he acknowledged, but it is not everything:

> Europe must have institutions that will lead it to form a political union, just as it is already a union in the economic sphere.
>
> What is it that France is proposing to her five partners? I shall repeat it once again: to organize ourselves politically, let us begin at the beginning. Let us organize our cooperation. . . .[34]

33. For an excellent discussion of the Dutch attitude toward both European and Atlantic policy, and the Dutch role in the Fouchet negotiations, see Silj, *Europe's Political Puzzle*, chapter 3, pp. 40–64.

34. *Major Addresses*, press conference of 15 May 1962, p. 174.

De Gaulle then took pains to defend and explain in the simplest terms the institutions of the Fouchet Plan.

> After we have tried it, we shall see, in three years' time, what we can do to strengthen our ties; but at least we shall have begun to acquire the habit of living and acting together. This is what France has proposed. She believes that this is the most practical thing that can be done.[35]

Acknowledging that there had been two objections to the French proposals, he pointed aptly to the contradictory nature of the objections, 'even though they were raised by the same objectors'.[36] On the one hand, there was the argument in favour of a supranational Europe; on the other, the refusal to undertake political action until Great Britain had been admitted to the Common Market. 'Yet everyone knows that Great Britain, in its capacity as a great State and a nation loyal to itself, would never agree to lose its identity in some utopian structure.'

Finally de Gaulle laid siege to the whole concept of political union through supranational integration:

> I would like, incidentally, since the opportunity has arisen, to point out to you gentlemen of the press – and you are perhaps going to be very surprised by this – that I have never personally in any of my statements spoken of a '*Europe des Patries*,' although it is always being claimed[37] that I have done so. It is not, of course, that I am repudiating my own; quite the contrary, I am more attached to France than ever, and I do not believe that Europe could have any living reality if it did not include France and her Frenchmen, Germany and its Germans, Italy and its Italians, and so forth. Dante, Goethe, Chateaubriand belong to all Europe to the very extent that they were respectively and eminently Italian, German and French. They would not have served Europe very well if they had been stateless, or if they had thought and written in some kind of integrated Esperanto or Volapük. . . .
>
> I should like to speak more particularly about the objection to integration. The objection is presented to us with the words, 'Let us merge the six states into a supranational entity; this way things will be most simple and practical.' But such an entity cannot be founded without there being in Europe today a federator with sufficient power, authority and skill. . . .
>
> These are ideas that may, perhaps, beguile certain minds, but I

35. *Major Addresses*, press conference of 15 May 1962, pp. 174–5.

36. Here, the reference is plainly to Spaak and the Dutch.

37. Here, the reference is probably to the Dutch *Algemeen Handelsblad* article, which was widely quoted.

certainly do not see how they could be carried out in practice, even if there were six signatures on the dotted line. Is there a France, a Germany, an Italy, a Holland, a Belgium, a Luxembourg, that would be ready – in a matter that is important for them from the national or the international point of view – to do something that they would consider wrong because this would be dictated to them by others? . . . There is no way, at the present time, for a foreign majority to be able to constrain recalcitrant nations. It is true that, in the 'integrated' Europe, as they say, there would perhaps be no policy at all. This would simplify things a great deal. . . . But, then, perhaps, it would follow the lead of some outsider who did have a policy. There would perhaps be a federator, but the federator would not be a European.[38]

The diatribe against the integrationists hit hard against de Gaulle's internal 'European' opposition, but they had hardly been the noisiest opponents of the Fouchet Plan. Monnet's Action Committee had actually supported the French initiative as a first step toward the kind of Europe they desired.[39] The attack on integration, with the implicit reference to surrender to American policy, was undoubtedly aimed at Spaak and his 'integrationist' supporters. The one opponent de Gaulle had not singled out was the Dutch, who had adroitly contributed more to the defeat of the Fouchet Plan than either of the others. Jean Monnet himself acknowledges this fact critically in his own analysis of the Fouchet negotiations:

I find it difficult to say who was responsible. General de Gaulle was certainly very much responsible, because of his attitudes which gave rise to misunderstandings and wounded feelings, in France itself and in neighboring countries. But public quarrels do not explain the failure; they merely prolong it in words. The failure was inscribed, at the outset of the discussions, in the very manner in which they were undertaken. No *grand dessein*, if any existed, had the time to take shape, and everyone entered immediately into the defensive search for reciprocal concessions. De Gaulle made important ones, which one admired, without suspecting that he would withdraw them once he thought he no longer needed to offer them to the small countries. For the moment, he was dealing with Luns, Minister of Foreign Affairs of the Netherlands, and with his Belgian colleague, Wigny, who suspected him of nursing, first for France, and for France and Germany with the complicity of Adenauer, plans for domination of the continent. Doubtless, de Gaulle seemed to lend credence to such suspicions

38. *Major Addresses*, pp. 175–7.

39. Cf. Monnet, *Mémoires*, pp. 512–13.

through some of his statements, but I believed that one should not lose one minute in scrutinizing the secret motives of one side or the other. To act on the basis of the supposed intentions of your *interlocuteur* is, whatever political strategists may say, the surest means to miss your goal. *Did Luns and Wigny even have a goal? I don't know*.[40]

But de Gaulle had himself, alas, contributed in good measure to the defeat of the Fouchet Plan, above all by his high-handed move in unilaterally changing the draft text. For one so eager to promote political co-operation, he showed himself remarkably insensitive to the sensibilities of the small powers, and in the process encouraged their suspicions instead of persuading them of his good faith. As a consequence, the atmosphere of the negotiations worsened steadily. After months of negotiating and significant French concessions, de Gaulle appeared to be delivering a non-negotiable ultimatum. Yet, he then proceeded to come around to the same concessions he had abrogated. It is probable that even without de Gaulle's *coup de théâtre* the Dutch would have rejected the plan in the end. But de Gaulle's gesture gave their obstructionism a seeming justification. Success in diplomacy requires not only a realistic assessment of the problem, but also the skill to win over others to one's views.

De Gaulle's press conference was received as a declaration of war. He could not have been more specific, nor more bitingly sardonic, in setting forth his views on supranational integration. The MRP cabinet members, with perhaps some lack of sense of humour,[41] summarily resigned as a gesture of outrage at his put-down. It was actually a regrettable gesture. The one thing that both de Gaulle and the federalists shared was their real attachment to political unity, though they differed over the means. Had the 'Europeans' been more pragmatic, they might have adopted a minimalist/maximalist stance in regard to de Gaulle's proposals, affirming confederation as a first step to the goal of federation.[42] Instead, too intent on fighting the domestic heretics, both

40. Monnet, *Mémoires*, p. 513. Emphasis added.

41. Apparently de Gaulle could not resist the lure of the spicy *bon mot*. He had already spoken of that deliciously named international lingua franca of yesteryear, *Volapük*, back in November of 1953: 'On n'est pas un Européen si l'on est apatride . . . Chateaubriand, Goethe, Byron, Tolstoï, pour ne parler que des romantiques, n'auraient rien valu du tout en volapük ou en espéranto.' Quoted in Massip, *De Gaulle et l'Europe*, p. 34.

42. Ludwig Erhard took precisely this point of view in an interview with Maurice Schumann, published in *Réalités*, no. 213 (octobre 1963), pp. 5–7.

Gaullists and 'Europeans' forgot about the real infidels, the Dutch.

De Gaulle's press conference contained one interesting silence. From the time he had first set forth his plan for political union until the breakdown of the negotiations on 17 April, each time there had been a showdown, the French had eventually, though grudgingly, shown themselves willing to compromise, and to insert this or that phrase to assuage the European and Atlantic sensibilities of their partners. Their first priority had clearly been to reach some agreement on political co-operation. In the end, the negotiations had failed over the issue of the timing of the British entry into the EEC. Had de Gaulle wished to resume the negotiations, therefore, he had apparently only to offer some compromise over the question of the British entry. Yet, at his press conference, he maintained a circumspect silence on precisely that issue. It may well be that he had already made up his mind to reject the British entry. But what is perhaps more probable is that he was then still uncertain about the issue of the British entry – both in regard to their position on the critical question of the common agricultural policy, which was of top economic priority for the French; and, equally important, in regard to their political and military commitments to Washington. Under these circumstances, he was not willing to offer a compromise that would risk both undermining the chances of success on agriculture, and surrendering the direction of a future European political union to American policy.

In the meantime, there was still another road open – to proceed together with Italy and Germany toward an embryonic Fouchet-type union, in the hope of eventually enticing the others to abandon their intransigence. De Gaulle accordingly put forth his proposal for 'FRALIT' (France–Allemagne–Italie) in early July 1962, at a meeting with his ever-faithful colleague, Adenauer. But the Italians, who had played the role of mediator throughout the Fouchet negotiations, now feared being caught between France and Germany, and were, in any case, taken up with the 'opening to the Left' on their domestic political scene. They, therefore, opted out of de Gaulle's revised plan. That left Germany. The Franco-German spectacular of the last half of 1962, with all its attendant fanfare, was in fact a monumental wrapping for the fizzled-out Fouchet Plan. In its ersatz form, it became the Franco-German Treaty.

CHAPTER FIVE

The Franco-German Honeymoon: *une Image d'Epinal?*

You have begun, we are merely continuing your work.

De Gaulle to Robert Schuman. André Passeron, *De Gaulle parle: 1958–1962*, Paris, Librairie Plon, 1962, p. 433.

It is true, in a sense, that the Franco-German rapprochement begun under the Fourth Republic was essentially 'continued' under the Fifth. But it is also true that the Fourth Republic's European policy, of which Franco-German reconciliation became the cornerstone, often represented a reluctant concession, a *faute de mieux*, in response to American pressure, as cold war diplomacy fostered an evolution in US policy toward Germany from occupation to partnership. In that sense, de Gaulle's concern for Franco-German rapprochement can be viewed as the transformation of a casual date into a flowering courtship. The years from 1958 to 1962 stand out in retrospect as a period of increasing Franco-German convergence, with the signing of the Franco-German Treaty of Friendship in January 1963 as the symbolic high-water mark. The courtship was promising, but the marriage proved, unfortunately, something of a flop.

Germany had, of course, long both fascinated and frustrated de Gaulle. His reflections at the end of the war wavered between a determination to guarantee French security by breaking up the German Reich permanently into its rival constituent elements, on the one hand, and the dream of a Pax Europaea, of reconciliation across the old continent, on the other.[1] In the meantime, the establishment of a federal regime in Western Germany, and of the German Democratic Republic in the East, had substantially

1. See chapter 2.

removed the possible threat of a unified Reich. Then, the first chancellor of the new West German Government was that ardent Roman Catholic Francophile from the Rhineland, Konrad Adenauer.

No statesman was more attached to Franco-German reconciliation than Konrad Adenauer. Even before Schuman's proposal of the Coal and Steel Community, in an interview with the American journalist Kingsbury Smith on 9 March 1950, Adenauer had proposed the unification of France and Germany, beginning with a customs union and parliament, along the lines of the Zollverein established in Germany following the Napoleonic wars. He reiterated that proposal several times, but drew no response from his Fourth Republic counterparts. Charles de Gaulle, however, took note of Adenauer's proposal at a press conference on 16 March 1950:

> For thirty years, I have been following with interest and consideration Konrad Adenauer's actions and proposals. On several occasions, I thought I detected in what that good German says a sort of echo of an appeal to a ruined, disrupted, and bleeding Europe, which calls its children to unite.[2]

De Gaulle and the 'good German', Adenauer, did not meet personally until 14 September 1958, when de Gaulle invited the aging Chancellor to his country retreat at Colombey-les-deux-Eglises. No one has painted the outcome of that encounter more eloquently than Adenauer himself:

> Premier de Gaulle – and I say this very frankly – in no way matches the image which one might have of him from reading the newspapers in recent months. He is a quite different person from what he has been represented by the foreign press as well as our own. He is open-minded; he is not a nationalist; and he is well acquainted with foreign affairs. He is expecially well aware of the significance of Franco-German relations for these two countries, for Europe as a whole and for the shaping of international relations in general. No special topics whatever were taken up in detail in this private conversation. Instead, we discussed the fundamental principles which today spiritually guide the German people, because we are both of the opinion that day-to-day policy, in the last analysis, after all, rests on these basic principles. We also extended our discussion of these problems to include the intellectual climate of the entire world. . . .

2. *Rassemblement*, 25 mars 1950.

There is no point in my talking about a great many details. I would rather like to confine myself to a general impression of the entire discussion, an impression which I have retained and which I believe is shared by all members of the German delegation.

This impression was excellent. We did not conduct political negotiations about pending, urgent issues, but rather tried to determine where we agreed in our views of the great events of our times. And this I consider the significant thing about these lengthy talks: We discovered that we completely agreed with each other and that this mutual understanding would bring about agreement on specific questions which are presently pending or which will come up in the future.[3]

That Adenauer was impressed by de Gaulle is certainly an understatement. The meeting at Colombey formed the foundation of a firm confidence and friendship between the two statesmen – a relationship fostered at least as much by temperamental affinity as by common outlook on world affairs.

Charles de Gaulle and Konrad Adenauer had in common a certain autocratic aloofness in dealing with their subordinates. De Gaulle's cool and distant manner illustrated precisely what he had recommended to *le chef* in *Le Fil de l'épée*, while Adenauer maintained such a tight rein and distance from his subordinates that his style of administration was dubbed 'Kanzlerdemokratie'. Both men shared a love of broad *tours d'horizon* of policy, a penchant for sweeping general ideas over and beyond precise 'details', which they preferred to leave to their subordinates. One sees this clearly all through Adenauer's report of his first meeting with de Gaulle; indeed, that penchant for generalities and disdain for specific issues occasionally proved not a little responsible for the thorny misunderstandings over precisely what the two men had 'agreed' on. De Gaulle was more at home in history, more subtle in analysis, more articulate than Adenauer, but Adenauer appreciated and admired precisely those characteristics in de Gaulle. While differing in their personal religious expression both Adenauer and de Gaulle were Roman Catholics, a factor of considerable ceremonial importance in moments like the spectacular *Te Deum* in the cathedral at Rheims, in 1962, which seemed to consecrate in the popular mind the secular rapprochement between the two nations. Religion also drew the two men

3. For complete text of the Chancellor's report, see *News from the German Embassy* Washington, DC, vol. II, no. 12, 20 September 1958.

together in other than ceremonial ways. Both shared in the humane values, the admiration for lofty heroism and courage, the universalism, that were the finest heritage of the Roman Catholic tradition. Charles de Gaulle, the *littéraire manqué* with his taste for the *bon mot*, and Konrad Adenauer, who never felt more at home than in his rose garden and who spoke a German flavoured by the accent and the grammatical idiosyncrasies of his native Rhineland, in a way, supremely represented for one another the characteristics of their two nations.

But over and beyond the personal characteristics which drew the two statesmen together, what was above all important was their common political concerns. Both were men whose careers had been shaped by the experience of the war, both had suffered humiliation at the hands of the British,[4] and both were primarily interested in foreign policy.

At their first meeting at Colombey in 1958, de Gaulle and Adenauer made a kind of gentlemen's agreement on foreign policy. According to de Gaulle,

> What Germany asked of France . . . was to help her internationally to recover the respect and confidence that would reestablish her international status, to contribute to her security vis-à-vis the Soviet bloc, notably with respect to the threat hovering over Berlin, and finally to accept her right to reunification. For my part, I pointed out to the Chancellor that France had nothing in regard to her own unity, security or status to ask of Germany in return for so many requests, though she would certainly contribute to the recovery of her secular aggressor. France would do so – and with what merit! – in the name of the understanding to be built between the two peoples, as well as the unity and peace of Europe. In order to justify her support, however, certain conditions had to be met on the part of the Germans. These were: acceptance of the postwar borders as a *fait accompli*, an attitude of good will concerning relations with the East, the complete renunciation of nuclear weapons, and imperturbable patience regarding reunification. I must say that the Chancellor's pragmatism made agreement with my position possible in these matters.[5]

4. Adenauer reports acidly, in his personal biography in the German edition of *Who's Who*, that he was removed from office as Bürgermeister of Cologne in 1945 by the British on the grounds of 'incapability': 'v.d. Amerikanern eingesetzt, v.d. Brit. Militärreg. weg. Unfähigkeit entlassen', *Wer ist Wer?*, Berlin, Arani Verlag, 1967, p. 6.

5. De Gaulle, *Mémoires d'espoir*, pp. 186–7.

De Gaulle had agreed, in sum, to support certain broad principles of West German foreign policy, but he was far from subscribing across the board to the Bonn party line on the German question. Despite his commitment to rapprochement with West Germany as the cornerstone of his European policy, de Gaulle did not hesitate to spell out publicly the limits of his endorsement of West German policy objectives. At his press conference on 25 March 1959, in response to a question concerning the Soviet threat to Berlin, de Gaulle set forth his German policy unequivocally. 'Germany, as it is,' he began, 'in no way threatens us.'

> We shall therefore support nothing which would be such as to lead the German people to despair or to compromise its peaceful future or to wreck the hope on both sides of the Rhine.

On the future of Berlin:

> We hold it necessary in the first place that America, Britain and France should not agree to allow anyone to put obstacles in the way of the comings and goings of their troops to and from Berlin. . . . As regards the fate of the city itself, we note that those of its inhabitants who have the opportunity to express their views are unanimous in wishing it to stay Western. For this reason and for others, we would not allow West Berlin to be given up to the Pankow regime.

On the question of recognition of the GDR:

> Furthermore, we are not prepared to recognize this regime as a sovereign and independent state because it could not have been born and could not exist except by virtue of an implacable dictatorship. . . . We cannot put on the same level, on the one hand, this arbitrary construction, and on the other, the German Federal Republic, where citizens say, read, and hear what they like, come and go as they please and, in complete freedom, elect their representatives and their government.

On German reunification:

> The reunification of the two parts into a single Germany, which would be entirely free, seems to us the normal destiny of the German people, provided they do not reopen the question of their present frontiers to the west, the east, the north and south, and that they move toward integrating themselves one day in a contractual organization of all Europe for cooperation, liberty and peace.

On relations between the two Germanies:

> But, pending the time when this ideal can be achieved, we believe that the two separated sections of the German people should be able to multiply the ties and relations between themselves in all practical fields. Transport, communications, economic activity, literature, science, the arts, the goings and comings of people, etc., would be the subject of arrangements which would bring together the Germans within and for the benefit of that which I would call 'Germanness,' and which, after all, is common to them, in spite of differences in regimes and conditions.[6]

That de Gaulle's position substantially paralleled Bonn's policy on the question of the defence of Berlin and recognition of the GDR is clear. But on the issue of German reunification, the French policy went far beyond what Bonn was officially prepared to accept. The French policy set forth effectively a specific and long-range programme, a veritable Charter of the Two Germanies. And it did not pass unnoticed in West Germany: it raised a formidable hue and cry.

In the first place, de Gaulle served notice to the Germans that they must not open the question of their postwar borders – thereby implicitly according recognition to the much contested Oder–Neisse Line as the border between Germany and Poland – while the Bonn Government officially maintained that the final determination of the frontiers of a future reunified Germany must await a general peace settlement. Many groups within the Federal Republic contested the validity of the Oder–Neisse frontier, and the official government position therefore represented a deliberately ambiguous, dilatory formula. Secondly, while acknowledging the justice of the German desire for reunification, de Gaulle had in effect postponed it into the tomorrow of history by setting as its condition the eventual reuniting of the European continent in peace and freedom. Many German political leaders might privately have agreed with de Gaulle, but none would have said so publicly in 1959. And thirdly, his sermon on the future of Germany flatly advocated ending the official West German policy of a *cordon sanitaire* around the East German state, in favour of an expansion of contacts in non-political fields between the two Germanies. Far from rubber-stamping

6. *Major Addresses*, pp. 42–3.

the official West German policy, then, de Gaulle had in fact set forth a map of his own,[7] only part of which was acceptable to the Bonn Government.

The antagonism provoked by de Gaulle's public pronouncement on the German question was in effect just one example of the very substantial differences in outlook between the two governments despite the desire for rapprochement. German security, viewed through the prism of French policy toward Nato, proved a still more constant bone of contention in Franco-German relations, both under Adenauer and his successors. Whereas de Gaulle chafed at the subordination to American political leadership implicit in the Nato defence structure,[8] Adenauer, on the contrary, bemoaned what he regarded as the waning of American interest in Nato:

> Adenauer was also critical of NATO, but because, in his view, America was not *sufficiently* concerned with it.[9]
>
> For him, the sole concern in regard to security consisted, integration or no, in keeping the United States solidly attached to Europe.[10]

For Adenauer, Nato symbolized the assurance of the American guarantee to secure the defence of Europe against the Communist threat. The entire policy of his government had been built about this solution to West Germany's security needs. To question Nato, therefore, amounted in effect to calling West German security into question. De Gaulle's long-range intentions in regard to the Alliance cropped up time and again as an obstacle in relations between Bonn and Paris, even when they were both otherwise committed to a common goal. Indeed, according to Couve de Murville's account, German wariness of de Gaulle's intentions regarding Nato accounted for the long delay through the autumn of 1960 in convening the first European conference on political union; for de Gaulle had proposed in his discussions with Adenauer at Rambouillet to include defence among the objectives of the future union, thus implicitly undermining Nato. The deep crisis in relations over that issue was nurtured in good measure by the difficult test of domestic leadership de

7. The controversial policy advocated by de Gaulle in 1959 paralleled substantially the Ostpolitik pursued by the Brandt government over a decade later.

8. See chapter 3.

9. Couve de Murville, *Une Politique étrangère*, p. 247. Emphasis added.

10. Couve de Murville, *Une Politique étrangère*, p. 245.

Gaulle faced at the forthcoming referendum on Algeria. The German attitude, in fact, changed abruptly following de Gaulle's overwhelming success at the 8 January 1961 referendum, and accordingly, the conference eventually convened on 10 February. The renewal of de Gaulle's mandate, together with diplomatic assurances of France's fidelity to the alliance, apparently accounted for the shift.[11]

The long-protracted Berlin crisis provided the backdrop for still another crisis in Franco-German relations – one which reveals the capital importance of the US role in relations between the two states. Once again, what was basically at issue was the American commitment to provide for German security. De Gaulle had adopted a hard line in regard to Berlin from the outset, and the failure of the 1960 Paris summit conference had served to reinforce his position. As talk of neutralizing Germany gained favour in Britain, and the Chancellor's suspicions of the Kennedy Administration's willingness to make concessions to Moscow at Germany's expense deepened, Adenauer relied increasingly on de Gaulle to defend German interests.

The building of the Berlin Wall in August 1961 dealt a shattering blow to Adenauer's government. His CDU party lost its absolute majority at the autumn elections, forcing him to sacrifice his pro-French foreign minister, Heinrich von Brentano, to the more Atlanticist, pro-British Gerhard Schröder, in return for a coalition with the Liberal Free Democratic Party (FDP). The resulting tug of war over foreign policy had become patently evident by the December 1961 meetings in Paris between Adenauer and de Gaulle and their foreign ministers. It was, to put it mildly, a strained encounter.

The Kennedy Administration, supported by the British, had entered into contacts with Moscow regarding the Berlin situation. De Gaulle, true to his hard line on Berlin, refused resolutely to participate, on the grounds that the only prospect for agreement entailed concessions on both sides, and since he, for one, was unprepared to agree to any concessions, the talks were pointless. In contrast to the intransigent simplicity of the French position, the complete disarray of the West German Government was already indicative of the rift in the governing CDU Party that

11. See Couve de Murville, *Une Politique étrangère*, p. 248. See also chapter 4, p. 60, above.

would plague West German politics throughout the 1960s. Indeed, according to Couve de Murville's piquant account, while Adenauer was urging de Gaulle to participate in the talks in order to protect West German interests, i.e. to prevent the US concessions to Moscow which he feared, Schröder, while no less critical of French non-participation, was vehemently lecturing Couve on the prospects of tearing down the Berlin Wall and the consequent necessity of negotiating, and hence of following the US lead:

> Adenauer's suspicions were nonetheless alerted, for he had no confidence in what he called, with some disdain and not unjustly, the amateurism of Washington's diplomacy. That France remained resolutely distant and was not therefore in a position to counter the possible concessions of their powerful ally caused him deep dismay. . . .
>
> Schröder's criticism of the French position was, indeed, no less lively, but for altogether different reasons. Not that he was in the least inclined to envisage concessions – quite the contrary, he spoke of tearing down the wall, as if it were in the realm of possibilities. What he refused to accept was that the French were not following American policy, while Germany – in his view, the party most concerned – had subscribed to it since his arrival at the foreign ministry (Brentano, only in October, had taken precisely the opposite position).[12]

In the end, the Franco-German crisis wound down as West German suspicions of the US increased, and the US in turn lost interest in negotiations, which, as de Gaulle had correctly asserted, could only end in unacceptable concessions.

These intermittent crises in relations between Paris and Bonn during the first years of the Fifth Republic offer some instructive insights. What had in fact drawn the Bonn Government toward rapprochement with Paris was not so much the pre-established 'deal' between Adenauer and de Gaulle, as Alfred Grosser has suggested,[13] but above all a shift in American foreign policy in the late fifties and early sixties. In the first place, the Berlin crisis, which resulted in the building of the Wall on 13 August 1961, had revealed to the Germans that the era of the Berlin blockade was over. The United States would no longer automatically spring to the defence of West German interests as it had in the

12. Couve de Murville, *Une Politique étrangère*, p. 251.

13. Grosser, *French Foreign Policy under de Gaulle*, pp. 66–7. See above, p. 81, for the terms of the agreement.

past, but seemed on the contrary inclined to make concessions to the Soviet Union – particularly in relation to Berlin and German reunification. De Gaulle, however, remained steadfast in his public support of the West German hard line on both issues.[14] Secondly, the new American defence doctrine of 'flexible response' seemed to threaten the security of the Federal Republic by making even the American nuclear commitment less certain. The West Germans preferred the assurance of early deployment of nuclear weapons in response to an attack on their borders. And finally, American-German relations had steadily deteriorated since the death of Secretary of State John Foster Dulles, who had made Adenauer the principal partner of United States diplomacy in Europe. Relations between Kennedy and Adenauer were very poor. Close advisers of Adenauer make no secret of the fact that Adenauer held Kennedy personally responsible for the 'wall of shame'. Nor was Adenauer's lack of confidence in Kennedy's support of Bonn unfounded. On the eve of the departure for Moscow of a US mission headed by Averell Harriman, in 1963, writes Kennedy's biographer, Arthur Schlesinger, Kennedy suggested some possible concessions to the Soviets: 'The President added, "I have some cash in the bank in West Germany and am prepared to draw on it if you think I should." '[15]

By the summer of 1962, the West German Government was in a desperate position with regard to its foreign policy. On the one hand, with the Berlin crisis still smouldering,[16] relations with the United States were cordial but distant, characterized by suspicion and mounting mistrust, on the part of the Germans, in the validity of the American commitment. On the other hand, even though the Fouchet negotiations had failed, relations with France were excellent. Encounters between the Chancellor and the French President were characterized by precisely that con-

14. De Gaulle's hard line on Berlin was based on French national interest. So long as the Soviet Union continued to threaten Europe, the defence of West Germany represented, in geographic extension, the defence of France. Germany was 'à l'avant-garde du monde libre'. (Speech in reply to welcome by President Lübke at Bonn airport, 4 September 1962, *Notes et études documentaires*, no. 2.947, Paris, Documentation Française, 21 décembre 1962.)

15. Arthur Schlesinger, *A Thousand Days*, London, Deutsch, 1965; Boston, Houghton Mifflin, 1965, p. 904.

16. The last act of the Berlin crisis was the Cuban missile crisis, in October 1962, which was widely interpreted in Europe as the confirmation of US strategic and diplomatic superiority.

fidence which was lacking in West German–American relations. The firmness of the French toward Moscow, at a time when the Americans seemed prepared to yield German interests in exchange for *détente*, further drew West German foreign policy toward de Gaulle. For his part, checkmated by the Americans in his bid for a voice in international policy and by the Benelux countries in his proposal for a West European political union, de Gaulle was now prepared to proceed *à deux* with his friend Adenauer to consolidate a Franco-German foundation for the kind of Europe he sought none the less to build. It was time for another *grand geste*.

Adenauer's official state visit to France in July 1962 bore all the hallmarks of de Gaulle's attention to emotional symbols. As West German flags waved over the Champs-Elysées, in Bordeaux, in Rouen, in Rheims, de Gaulle welcomed Konrad Adenauer on the steps of the Elysée Palace, and hailed the promise of the New Europe, spurred by the reconciliation of the age-old enemies:

> It was a *grande cause*, indeed, that gave rise to our quarrels. Germany and France, seeking to impose their domination upon one another, in order thereafter to extend that domination to their neighbours, were in truth pursuing, each for its own purpose, the old dream of unity which has haunted souls on our continent for twenty centuries – in the ambitions of Charles V, of Louis XIV, of Napoleon I, of Bismarck, of Wilhelm II, even of Clemenceau (yes, even him!), and in the passion which a regime of criminal oppression exploited during the last war to lead the German people astray – the grandiose memories of the Caesars, of Christendom, of Charlemagne![17]

Let there be no mistake: Adenauer's ceremonious visit symbolized the final chapter, the sentimental *dénouement*, of Bainville's *L'Histoire de deux peuples*. Together, the old General and the professional civilian, Adenauer, would review the French and German troops at Mourmelon; and while the celebrated Gothic angel smiled down upon them, side by side, they assisted at a jubilant *Te Deum* in the ancient Rheims cathedral that towers like a beacon above the blood-drenched battlefields nearby. In Rheims cathedral, where French kings had been crowned for centuries, the reconciliation of France and Germany was solemnly consecrated. Radio, television, magazines and newspapers followed the two statesmen wherever they went, recording before a spell-

17. Text in *Le Monde*, 4 juillet 1962.

bound public this unique moment of history. It was deeply moving.

Two months later, the scenario was repeated on the other bank of the Rhine. On a six-day whirlwind tour of Germany from 4 to 9 September, de Gaulle covered 2,000 kilometres, made fifteen speeches, and slept in an incredible variety of beds designed especially to accommodate his long frame.[18] Everywhere he went, he was acclaimed with outbursts of enthusiasm. And no wonder. He spoke to the crowds in a carefully practised German and using no notes. 'Sie sind ein grosses Volk!' he thundered. It was a public absolution.

'Le Général de Gaulle a été l'objet d'un véritable plébiscite,' concluded *Le Monde*,[19] and, indeed, that seemed to be precisely the point of the whole *mise en scène*. De Gaulle had included in his original proposals for a European union a provision for a popular referendum on Europe. If that alternative were barred by the German constitution, there was certainly more than one way to solicit popular acclaim. The two visits were part of an elaborate spectacular designed to rally popular support behind the policy de Gaulle and Adenauer were about to embark on. The Fouchet negotiations had foundered on the rocks of an atmosphere of suspicion and mistrust. The Franco-German mission was launched in an atmosphere of popular enthusiasm. It would set the example of co-operation for the future Europe and perhaps drag along their recalcitrant European allies. 'What is essential is not the political conversations, but rather the visit itself . . .', commented Couve de Murville in a television interview.[20] The content of de Gaulle's fifteen speeches in Germany, nevertheless, is of signal interest in uncovering what hopes he held for the future Franco-German co-operation, and what he thought it could accomplish.

Two speeches are of particular interest: the address at the reception given in de Gaulle's honour by President Lübke at the Brühl palace, and the address before the officers of the Bundeswehr

18 The newspapers were especially fond of pointing to the bed three metres long, intended for 'Karl der Grosse' (the German name for Charlemagne), and to the fact that in Munich he was especially provided with the bed of Elector Charles-Albert of Bavaria, who subsequently became Emperor Charles VII. See for instance, *Carrefour*, 5 septembre 1962.

19 *Le Monde*, 11 septembre 1962 ('General de Gaulle has won a veritable plebiscite').

20. *Le Monde*, 7 septembre 1962.

Academy in Hamburg. In his speech at the reception in Brühl, de Gaulle set forth, with his customary rhetorical lyricism, the advantages of Franco-German unity at present and the hopes it presented for the future.

> *L'union pourquoi?* Union, first of all, because we are together and directly threatened. In the face of Soviet ambitions of domination, France knows what peril her body and soul would run, if Germany were to succumb before her; and Germany is not unaware that her fate would be sealed if France ceased to stand behind her.[21]

That de Gaulle chose to focus on the Soviet threat as the first reason for Franco-German solidarity is significant. Certainly, that argument was low on the list of de Gaulle's own priorities, while the others he mentioned subsequently figured as far more important to him personally. But it was *the* crucial issue for the West Germans, and the many conversations between de Gaulle and Adenauer, from 1958 until then, bear witness to that constant preoccupation of the Germans – the fear of isolation in the face of the Soviet threat.[22] The less clear signals from Washington had exacerbated that issue. Indeed, the day after de Gaulle's speech, when Adenauer's turn came to take the rostrum at another dinner in honour of de Gaulle at Petersburg, he referred to de Gaulle's speech at Brühl the day before, and, significantly, the *only* point he singled out was solidarity against the communist threat:

> Mr President, you delivered in Brühl yesterday a speech which merits being read and reread. . . .
>
> . . . President de Gaulle declared that our two countries are the countries of the free world which are exposed to the most menacing danger: that France and the French people know that they cannot safeguard their freedom against communist pressure if Germany succumbs to that pressure. The contrary is also true: we cannot safeguard our freedom, or resist communist pressure without the support of France and the other free countries of western Europe. . . . That is why, if we wish to protect France and the rest of western Europe against the communist pressure from the East, it is absolutely indispensable, I

21. Text in 'Visite officielle du Général de Gaulle, Président de la République, à la République Fédérale d'Allemagne, 4–9 septembre 1962', *Notes et études documentaires*, no. 2.947, Documentation Française, 21 décembre 1962, p. 6.

22. See Konrad Adenauer, *Erinnerungen: 1953–63*, Stuttgart, Deutsche Verlag-Anstalt, 1968, pp. 14–185.

have been firmly convinced for years, that France and Germany *co-ordinate their policies in order to erect a solid rampart against that communist pressure.*[23]

The rest of de Gaulle's ranging vision of a New Europe Adenauer apparently never truly grasped, or, if he did, it did not stir his political imagination. For him, Franco-German solidarity meant a bulwark against communism, seen as the external threat.

De Gaulle's vision went considerably beyond that. In the three other reasons for Franco-German union proposed in his Brühl speech, one catches a glimpse of what de Gaulle had in mind:

> Union, next, because the alliance of the free world – in other words, the reciprocal engagement of Europe and America – can only preserve its assurance and solidarity in the long run if there exists on the old continent a nucleus of power and prosperity of the same order as that constituted by the United States in the new world. Now, such a nucleus could have no other base than the solidarity of our two countries.[24]

The *Europe européenne* de Gaulle sought to promote on the foundation of Franco-German *entente* was above all a centre of power capable of acting independently of and counterbalancing the United States – of providing a European voice in world affairs and, indeed, in its own destiny. The bilateral Franco-German co-operation would provide a pole of attraction for their recalcitrant partners who had balked at the Fouchet proposal. To the extent that de Gaulle's ambition for Europe challenged the existing pattern of US–European relations, it was widely interpreted as anti-American. The Leftist French news weekly, *L'Express*, for instance, commented:

> If the anti-Soviet aspect of General de Gaulle's public statements has been emphasized by all commentators, the anti-American aspect of his enterprise, the attempt to disengage Europe from the Atlantic Alliance, has till now gone virtually unnoticed. . . .[25]

But the disengagement was not that clear – at least, not over the short term. The point was to establish a separate European identity, to introduce positive movement over the long run into a

23. Quoted in 'Visite officielle du Général de Gaulle', p. 9. Emphasis added. Communist pressure, for France, was more a domestic issue than an external threat.

24. 'Visite officielle du Général de Gaulle', p. 6.

25. *L'Express*, 6 septembre 1962.

stalemated postwar division – as well as submission – of Europe. De Gaulle continued:

> Union, further, in the perspective of a *détente*, then, of international understanding, which would permit all of Europe to re-establish its balance, its peace, its development, from the Atlantic to the Urals – once the ambitions of domination of an outdated ideology have ceased in the East. The imperative precondition for this is a living and strong European community in the West, i.e. basically that French and German policy be one and the same.[26]

The vision of a Europe in which the bonds of Yalta are broken once and for all – that permanent longing of de Gaulle – here revised and inserted in the context of the prospects opened by Franco-German rapprochement. Following the Franco-German example, Western Europe reunited would not only constitute a 'nucleus of power' *vis-à-vis* the United States, but also a pole of attraction for the rest of Europe now straining under the domination of 'an outdated ideology'.[27] And then, united at last, the New Europe could return to its historic mission as the beacon of humanistic culture:

> Union, finally – I would even be tempted to say above all – because of the immense task of scientific, technical, economic, social, cultural progress which is incumbent on the whole world. In that task, the combined assets of Europe – and, first of all, of Germany and France – can and ought to be the major element in the success of mankind.[28]

De Gaulle's ambitions were anything but parochial. If they were based on long-range goals for the far distant future, that did not in the least deter him from pursuing them relentlessly. It had taken centuries to build the great Gothic cathedrals, he was fond of pointing out.

When de Gaulle addressed the officers of the Bundeswehr Academy in Hamburg, his reflections took a more pragmatic turn. He spoke of the relationship of power and weapons:

> The general movement of the world makes us realize that France and Germany are in every sense complementary, and that by combining

26. 'Visite officielle du Général de Gaulle', p. 6.

27. It is said that at a cocktail party, when questioned by a diplomat concerning his formula of the 'Atlantic to the Urals', de Gaulle smiled broadly and quipped, 'The rest belongs to China, doesn't it?'

28. 'Visite officielle du Général de Gaulle', p. 6.

what they are, what they have, and what they value, they can constitute the basis for a Europe whose prosperity, power and prestige would equal those of anyone.

But, in this Franco-German union which everything compels us to build, how important is and must be the solidarity of our arms! . . .

In both planning and development, in order to be viable, armaments now require – who knows that better than you? – the utilization of resources and of scientific, technical, industrial and financial capabilities whose limits expand every day. France and Germany will be far better able to assure themselves of these means of power if they combine their possibilities. That will be true, *a fortiori*, if their neighbours also contribute their resources.[29]

This open-ended invitation left room for multiple interpretations. Was it a limited invitation to develop certain weapons together? Or was it eventually a broader invitation to pool their defence burden? Was de Gaulle gilding the lily – laying the groundwork for soliciting a contribution of German 'resources' to the French *force de frappe*? In return for what? In certain official circles in West Germany, it raised again the issue of a secret protocol between the West German Defence Minister, Franz-Josef Strauss, and his Fourth Republic counterpart, M. Bourgès-Manoury, in 1958, offering West Germany access to French nuclear technology in return for financial support.[30] But it was de Gaulle who had put an end to that project. He had made clear both publicly and in his first conversation with Adenauer his resolute opposition to any nuclear role for Germany. Military technology was a vaster domain than nuclear development, however.

De Gaulle attached great importance to promoting a common European effort in military technology, independent of the United States. That effort was certainly a central feature of French objectives during the Fouchet negotiations. De Gaulle had also made clear in his Rambouillet conversations with Macmillan in December 1962, according to Adenauer,[31] that a joint effort in military technology was a major issue in the question of the British entry into the Common Market. The underlying rationale for de Gaulle's focus on weapons development was the issue of autonomy. He considered defence policy as

29. 'Visite officielle du Général de Gaulle', pp. 15–16.

30. See Newhouse, *De Gaulle and the Anglo-Saxons*, pp. 16–18.

31. Adenauer recounts de Gaulle's report of the conversations. See *Erinnerungen*, pp. 204–5.

ultimately the most fundamental prerequisite for an autonomous foreign policy. Without modern weapons, or relying for its defence upon a paternalistic ally, Europe could find itself in precisely the deplorable diplomatic position that France was in in the 1930s – helpless behind its Maginot Line. It is worth noting, once again, what a watershed the misfortunes of the 1930s constituted for postwar political conclusions.

De Gaulle returned to Paris. 'L'Alliance des Capitalistes!', bellowed *L'Humanité*, the communist daily. But most of the other newspapers echoed *Le Monde* in their mixture of delight, and yet, at the same time, basic hesitation: 'In the person of de Gaulle, it is the French people who feel themselves, despite everything, flattered and satisfied.' But the closing paragraphs betray a more residual reservation:

> Did de Gaulle indeed notice the placard-carrying pickets, who wanted to pull him 'nach Berlin'? Did he take sufficient account of that old Germanic love, and of their lightly slumbering hopes – in short, of a certain militarism in the service of a manifest irredentism? Was it really necessary to remind the German army that nothing great is accomplished without the participation of the 'military factor', and the German youth that it must conquer, albeit by fighting if necessary? What would happen if Adenauer disappeared prematurely, and Germany disengaged herself from the tender links that she has made with de Gaulle? Should we exclude the possibility that he might then not hesitate to go to Moscow to solicit applause, in order to counter a resurgence of German militarism by 'la bonne et belle alliance' with Russia?[32]

In extending an invitation to partnership in military technology, de Gaulle's diplomacy plainly went beyond what public opinion at home was prepared to endorse.

As agreed at the meetings between de Gaulle and Adenauer during de Gaulle's trip to Germany, negotiations between the two countries were continued through diplomatic channels, in order to arrive at 'practical steps . . . to tighten effectively the links already existing in a large number of domains'.[33] Nine days after de Gaulle's return to Paris, on 19 September, a French memorandum was dispatched to Bonn, outlining procedures for

32. *Le Monde*, 11 septembre 1962.

33. Communiqué franco-allemand du 6 septembre 1962, in 'Visite officielle du Général de Gaulle', p. 22.

Franco-German co-operation along the lines of the ill-fated Fouchet Plan. Political co-operation should take the form of meetings of the foreign ministers every three months, meetings between the two heads of state every six months, and periodic meetings of other officials to regulate common technical problems. Military co-operation, while stopping short of integration, should aim at promoting joint research, production of standardized weapons, and intensification of the training of German forces on French soil. Cultural co-operation should aim at encouraging the teaching in each country of the language of the other – a proposal difficult of realization, in that under the German constitution, the Länder and not the Federal Government are responsible for education. Finally, economic co-operation should take the form of a 'harmonization' of the economic policies of the two countries within the framework of the existing European institutions – a fairly vapid formula.[34]

The eagerness reflected in the rapid drafting and dispatching of the French memorandum contrasted with the reluctance of the German reply. The Germans did not respond to the French memorandum until 8 November, nearly two months after the French move. The nature of the modifications they proposed clearly suggested the road of future difficulties. Whereas the French memorandum had proposed periodical meetings at fixed intervals among various officials, the Bonn counter-proposal was looser, accepting the principle of 'regular' consultations without further definition.[35] In other words, contacts would remain informal, without established dates and institutionalized procedures. Secondly, the principle of military co-operation was set within the framework of Nato. Both these modifications reduced in spirit the political import of bilateral co-operation, revealing the strained position of the Bonn Government, despite Adenauer's personal enthusiasm for the Franco-German partnership. Sensitive to the accusations of a 'Paris–Bonn Axis', Bonn moved to protect its EEC and Nato relationships by playing down its arrangements with de Gaulle. Faced with intense opposition within his cabinet, and the prospect of retirement in the autumn of 1963, the aging Chancellor was all the more eager to make the Franco-German reconciliation irreversible before then. There was indeed substantial division within the ranks of the CDU over

34. *Le Monde*, 28 septembre 1962.

35. *L'Information*, 14 novembre 1962.

his pro-Gaullist orientation: in fact, the two strongest contenders in the contest of succession – Ludwig Erhard and Gerhard Schröder – were both Protestants, Atlanticists and hardly Francophiles. For that reason, Adenauer was intent on obtaining some form of solemn Bundestag endorsement of the protocol on co-operation he was determined to sign. When his legal advisers informed him during his visit to Paris in January that only a *treaty* could be submitted to the Bundestag for formal approval, the text of the Protocol on Co-operation was hastily transformed between 21 and 22 January into a Treaty of Co-operation, which was duly signed by Adenauer and de Gaulle in Paris on 22 January 1963.[36] It was hardly de Gaulle's kind of treaty, for it committed them effectively to nothing more than a loose procedure of consultation.[37]

The treaty itself was divided into three parts: Organization, Programme and Final Provisions. The first section provided for a veritable labyrinth of consultations and contacts, ranging from the ministers of sports and youth to the diplomatic missions and consulates of the two countries, the foreign ministers, the defence ministers, high officials, and finally the two heads of state as well, who were to meet 'whenever this is necessary and, in principle, at least twice a year'.[38] They were enjoined to 'meet', but what they were to accomplish was not specified. The section entitled 'Programme' constituted the heart of the treaty. It dealt with foreign affairs, defence, and education and youth. In the domain of foreign affairs, the two governments pledged themselves to consult with one another 'prior to any decision, on all important questions of foreign policy', and specified in particular: questions relating to the European Communities, East–West

36. 'The Chancellor wished to give the agreement the most solemn form possible. He intended thereby to emphasize its fundamental importance. Above all, he wished to bind his successors by a legal act which would guarantee at all costs the permanence of Franco-German co-operation. This would be the final act of his political career, and he intended to mark it. Thus, it was finally decided to transform the initial memorandum into a *bona fide* treaty, which would be submitted to the Parliaments of both states.' Couve de Murville, *Une Politique étrangère*, p. 257. For the French text of the treaty, see *L'Année politique 1963*, pp. 404–6. For the English translation, see Appendix 4.

37. Ironically, the Franco-German Treaty was the only treaty signed by de Gaulle as President of the Fifth Republic.

38. *The Common Declaration and the Treaty between the French Republic and the Federal Republic of Germany, dated January 22, 1963*, New York, French Embassy, Press and Information Service, 1963.

relations, Nato and other international organizations, and 'important sectors of economic policy . . . within the framework of the Common Market'. In the realm of defence, the parties agreed to 'endeavour to harmonize their doctrines with a view to arriving at mutual concepts', to increase the exchange of armed service personnel, to co-ordinate their armaments programmes, to co-operate in the area of civil defence if possible. In the field of education and youth, the treaty provided for the promotion of the study of French and German as foreign languages, the establishment of academic equivalences between their two systems in order to facilitate educational exchange, and co-operation in scientific research. Finally, it established a Franco-German Youth Office, with an autonomous administrative council at its head and a joint fund at its disposal to provide for the exchange of students, young artists and workers. In the closing section of the treaty, France and Germany pledged to 'keep the Governments of the member States of the European Communities informed on the development of Franco-German co-operation'. One can hardly resist Alfred Grosser's well-formulated conclusion: 'It was a treaty based on wishful thinking. In general, a treaty establishes procedures or agreements; here, we find established the *desire* to arrive at agreement, which supposes that agreement did not exist at the time of signature.'[39]

The spirit of the treaty had in fact been violated before it was even signed. At his press conference on 14 January 1963, de Gaulle summarily served notice of his intention to veto the British entry into the EEC and, true to his usual style, he dropped the news like a bomb. His 'partner' Adenauer received the word along with everyone else. For his part, Adenauer had agreed in talks with American diplomats in early January to participate in the newly proposed Multilateral Force. Despite the agreement on prior consultation then pending, Adenauer, too, did not pause to consult his French 'partner' before reaching his decision.

While the disagreements that were to mark the subsequent years had, thus, already begun to surface by the time the Franco-German Treaty was signed in January 1963, the treaty none the less marks symbolically the culmination of the process of Franco-German reconciliation. As the instrument of policy intended by de Gaulle, its failure became almost immediately apparent. This

39. Grosser, *French Foreign Policy under de Gaulle*, p. 74.

was partly because Adenauer's successors were more open to the Anglo-Saxon world than Adenauer. But far more important in driving a wedge between the two countries was the intrusion of an actively antagonistic American diplomacy.

Franco-German rapprochement had been fostered largely by a temporary let-up in direct American involvement in Western Europe at the end of the Eisenhower Administration and the beginning of the Kennedy Administration, while problems of military strategy and confrontation with the Soviet Union dominated the stage in Washington. The re-emergence of an active American diplomacy in Western Europe during the last half of 1962, pushing for its own version of 'Europe', posed a challenge to de Gaulle's European diplomacy, and initiated the tug of war between Washington and Paris that was to characterize the entire Kennedy and Johnson years. That struggle served to immobilize West German foreign policy, and it cut deeply into West Germany's domestic politics as well.

The treaty had been signed, but it had not yet been ratified. In a revealing interview with the German periodical *Der Monat* on 29 January 1963, in Brussels, just after Couve de Murville had formally sealed England's fate, the anger and deep-seated frustrations of Adenauer's two apparent successors, Finance Minister Ludwig Erhard and Foreign Minister Gerhard Schröder, found their target:

Erhard: Es ist noch nicht das letzte Wort gefallen. Das habe ich den Engländern schon gesagt.
[We have not heard the last of this – I have already told the British that.]

Hohmann: [Erhard's Press spokesman] Es ist damit zu rechnen, dass in der gleich stattfindenden Pressekonferenz die Frage aufgeworfen wird, was jetzt aus dem deutsch-französischen Freundschaftsvertrag wird.
[We must consider that the forthcoming press conference will call into question what will now become of the German–French Friendship Treaty.]

Erhard: Der kommt nicht mehr zustande, das werde ich den Leuten erklären.
[That will come to nothing. I want to make that clear to people.]

Schröder: Herr Erhard, ich begreife Ihre Erregung, aber so können wir das leider nicht machen.

[I understand your excitement, but unfortunately we can't do it that way.]

Erhard: Wieso? Der Vertrag ist noch nicht ratifiziert und existiert damit rechtlich nicht.
[Why not? The treaty is not yet ratified and consequently does not exist legally.]

Schröder: Aber Herr Erhard, der Vertrag ist unterzeichnet und Sie selbst waren in der Kabinettssitzung neulich mit der Ratifizierung einverstanden.
[But Herr Erhard, the treaty has been signed, and you yourself agreed to its ratification at the recent cabinet meeting.]

Erhard: Ich habe nicht dafür gestimmt.
[I did not vote in favour of it.]

Schröder: Aber Herr Erhard, als ich den Text der Vorlage an den Bundestag vorgelesen hatte, fragte ich, ob alle Herren damit einverstanden seien.—Haben Sie daraufhin etwas gesagt?
[But Herr Erhard, when I read the text of the proposal before the Bundestag, I asked whether everyone was in agreement. Did you say anything about it then?]

Erhard: Hm. . . .
[Hm. . . .]

Schröder: (beim Verlassen des Raumes zu Erhard) Beruhigen Sie sich, Herr Erhard, der Vertrag wird ratifiziert, aber einfach nicht angewendet.[40]
[(while leaving the room, to Erhard) Calm down, Herr Erhard, the treaty will be ratified, but simply not carried out.]

40. Quoted in *Der Spiegel*, XXI, no. 12 (13 März 1967), p. 14.

CHAPTER SIX

Washington Steps In

In politics and strategy, as in economics, monopoly naturally appears to him who enjoys it as the best possible system.

De Gaulle, press conference, 14 January 1963

The year 1962 indeed deserved the epithet *l'année diplomatique* on both sides of the Atlantic. In Europe, it was the year of the failure of the Fouchet Plan, of the spectacular Franco-German courtship, and of the concerted effort at negotiating a British entry into the Common Market; in Washington, it was the year of the Cuban missile crisis and the Trade Expansion Act, of the Nassau Accords, and of the launching of a 'new' American policy toward Europe, based on the notion of Atlantic partnership. Popularized in a best-seller that graced every Washington coffee-table by mid-1962, the 'Grand Design',[1] as Kennedy's policy came to be known, was in spirit the diametric antithesis of de Gaulle's plan to 'Europeanize' Europe. It represented an effort to deal with the various economic, political and military strains in American–European relations by 'Atlanticizing' the solutions:

> Its essence is a creative harmony between the United States and Europe for economic, military, and political purposes. It would bring together in a working Atlantic Partnership two separate but equal entities. On the one hand would be this country with its special ties to Canada, Latin America and the Pacific, notably Japan. On the other would be Western Europe with its special ties in Africa and the Dominions of the Commonwealth. Between them, the two entities would command the overwhelming majority of the world's technical skills,

1. Joseph Kraft, *The Grand Design: from Common Market to Atlantic Partnership*, New York, Harper Brothers, 1962.

financial resources, consuming power and productive capacity. By cooperative arrangement, the two partners would first adjust mutual differences, and then, while combining forces to hold Communist aggression in check, apply their manifold strengths to the harmonious development of the Southern continents.[2]

In its first stages, Kennedy's Grand Design bore the stamp of Kraft's subtitle: 'from Common Market to Atlantic Partnership'. Its primary focus and appeal lay in its offer of a solution to the threat to US trade interests posed by the new Common External Tariff of the Six. The threat of an 'inward-looking' European Community was the more acute in that the already critical US balance of payments deficit was bound to suffer from an increase in industrial tariffs in Western Europe, while exclusion of agricultural exports would compound the already grave structural problems of American agriculture. Were US products to be priced out of the world's second richest and most dynamic market? The very success of the Common Market in wiping out internal tariff barriers ahead of schedule and negotiating within GATT from a position of strength seemed to suggest hard times ahead for those outside. Faced with that dire prospect, it was argued, the US had no alternative:

> If Atlantic Partnership is rejected . . . the handwriting is on the wall. The static sector of the American economy will continue to produce goods and services, in diminishing demand, at steadily higher prices. The dynamic sectors will continue to grow, but at a reduced rate, because markets abroad will be increasingly protected against American goods. Government, more and more paralyzed by subsidy requirements, obliged to fight inflation with inadequate tools and still bound by the negative majority, will be short of means to invigorate the economy. At the same time, foreign commitments will be on the rise. Unable to find markets for their goods, Japan, Latin America and many of the underdeveloped countries in Asia and Africa will beat more insistently on the door of the American treasury. The European countries will almost certainly drift off into a nuclear defense of their own, denying this country any sharing of security burden, offering for exploitation by the Communist bloc a split of gigantic proportions, and virtually foreclosing any chance of limiting the spread of nuclear weapons. The nation will thus find itself with a declining base of domestic strength, and a steadily widening horizon of overseas obligations. Sooner or later the toll will be taken in domestic upheaval or foreign catastrophe –

2. Kraft, *The Grand Design*, pp. 22–3.

perhaps both. The United States will have to default on power; resign from history.[3]

As an inventory of administration nightmares, Kraft's panorama of doom would be hard to beat. One pauses to wonder how the Common Market, so long extolled by the same American diplomats now evangelizing for the Grand Design, could overnight have metamorphosed from a golden harbinger of European unity into the apocalyptic spectre Kraft evokes. Perhaps the most remarkable note is that these wide-ranging catastrophic consequences would apparently be triggered, in his scheme, by economic factors alone. The tocsin had sounded. There was no choice: it was Atlantic Partnership or *le déluge*.

Set against that grim future there is the alternate possibility of Atlantic Partnership; a partnership in growth, plugging the United States into the dynamism of Western Europe and the Common Market: the Old World called in to redress the balance of the New.[4]

President Kennedy sent to Congress on 25 January 1962 recommendations for the Trade Expansion Act, granting the President authority over a five-year period to negotiate across-the-board tariff reductions. This marked step one in the economic implementation of the Grand Design. The US had chosen its strategy, and it had again reaffirmed that its European partner would be the emerging Community institutions of the Six. Considering who the advocates of the Grand Design were,[5] it is not surprising that the US should have chosen to advertise its support of Jean Monnet's Europe; yet, one cannot help but be struck by the aggressiveness of this choice, coming as it did right in the midst of the most critical phase of the difficult Fouchet negotiations, which could have taken Europe down a very different political road from Monnet's. That was in fact precisely the point.

From Marshall Plan on, United States postwar diplomacy had continually supported efforts aimed at European federation on an

3. Kraft, *The Grand Design*, pp. 119–20.

4. Kraft, *The Grand Design*, p. 120.

5. These included among others: Dean Acheson, William Fulbright, David Bruce, John McCloy, Douglas Dillon, Robert Bowie, McGeorge Bundy, Paul Nitze and, above all, Under Secretary of State George Ball, who had been Jean Monnet's right-hand man in Washington for fifteen years. Ball brought in with him Robert Schaetzel, Stanley Cleveland and Arthur Hartman; see Kraft, *The Grand Design*, pp. 24–6.

economic and political level, while promoting the integration of European defence forces within Nato. This policy was motivated by the desire to strengthen Western Europe against the common threat from the communist East. It was predicated on the assumption of a community of perceived interests between the United States and Europe, and it was also assumed that that spirit of harmonious co-operation would continue into the indefinite future. Thus, the notion of Atlantic Partnership was always an implicit ingredient of United States support for the cause of European integration, for it was never considered that a united Europe would be inward-looking, protectionist, or politically antagonistic to American objectives. But all of that now seemed threatened by the recent direction of events within Europe. There was, first, the economic threat of a protectionist European external tariff. Second, and still more critical, was the challenge to United States political leadership posed by de Gaulle's determination to steer Europe in the direction of greater independence from the United States. Finally, there was the thorny politico-military problem of the allegedly 'divisive' effect on Nato of the British and French national nuclear forces, to which both countries clung insistently *and for the same reasons*.

Ranged against that challenge to the whole spirit of United States postwar diplomacy, the policy of Atlantic Partnership was, simply put, a reassertion of United States influence – an effort to pull things back into line with the American vision of the future of Europe. The concept of Atlantic Partnership was proclaimed with the fervent spirit of a theology more than a policy. It was underpinned by a series of dogmatically held convictions that were rarely, if ever, subjected to examination. Chief among them was the anti-Gaullist shibboleth: de Gaulle wanted *l'Europe des patries*; he had apparently not realized that the nation-state had become obsolete. Enlightened statesmen, on the contrary, all understood that the only possible future for Europe lay in functional integration, in Jean Monnet's supranationalism as the road to federalism. De Gaulle was a troublesome old King Lear. His plan for Europe was presumed to be inimical to long-range US interests, which were in turn presumed to be identical with Europe's real interests by definition. In his official report to Kennedy on de Gaulle's objectives, Arthur Schlesinger, Jr, the President's *ad hoc* expert on French policy, concluded on the basis of an incorrect English translation of de Gaulle's memoirs that the General's objective was to establish 'primacy' for France in Europe. The original French text read 'sécurité'.[6] The slip-up was typical enough of the impassioned crusade against de Gaulle.

The corollary to the philippic against the Gaullist vision of Europe was the hypothetical spectre of reawakened German military ambitions. This was a major justification for opposing the British and French nuclear forces. Again, this presumption of 'German aspirations for equality' in the nuclear field was an article of faith. It was widely presumed and broadcast by partisans of the Grand Design, but no evidence was ever adduced in support of their contention.[7]

In keeping with the quasi-religious fervour underlying the policy of Atlantic Partnership, it was ceremoniously and dramatically proclaimed to the world on that high feast day of the American civil faith, the Fourth of July. President Kennedy's Declaration of Interdependence, delivered symbolically enough at Independence Hall in Philadelphia, was an impassioned statement of his Administration's West European policy:

> We do not regard a strong and united Europe as a rival, but a partner. To aid its progress has been the basic object of our foreign policy for seventeen years.
>
> We believe that a united Europe will be capable of playing a greater role in the common defense, of responding more generously to the needs of poorer nations, of joining with the United States and others in lowering trade barriers, resolving problems of commerce and commodities and currency, and developing coordinated policies in all economic, political and diplomatic areas.
>
> We see in such a Europe a partner with whom we can deal on a basis of full equality in all the great and burdensome tasks of building and defending a community of free nations.
>
> It would be premature at this time to do more than indicate the high regard with which we view the formation of this partnership. The first order of business is for our European friends to go forward in

6. See Schlesinger, *A Thousand Days*, p. 868; and compare with Charles de Gaulle, *Mémoires de guerre*, vol. III, Paris, Librairie Plon, 1959, p. 179. I am indebted to Joseph Joffe for this observation concerning the incorrect translation of this key word in the English edition.

7. See, for instance, Robert R. Bowie, 'Strategy and the Atlantic Alliance', in Francis O. Wilcox (ed.), *The Atlantic Community*, New York, Praeger, 1963, p. 207; and Livingston T. Merchant, 'Evolving United States relations with the Atlantic Community', *ibid.*, p. 106.

forming the more perfect union which will some day make this partnership possible.[8]

Beneath the rhetorical flourishes, the concept of Atlantic partnership was really quite simple – and hardly 'new'. It was based on the *future* 'equality' and 'interdependence' of America and 'a united Europe', and the hope that the European 'partner' would therefore cheerfully accept *now* to share a portion of the American burden in defence, foreign aid and the promotion of free trade. The Declaration of Interdependence, which inspired no end of metaphorical representations, was therefore a cautious statement. It did not promise either equality or real partnership in the present, but quite explicitly set them forth for some distant day when Europe had achieved its unity, which alone would make full partnership possible. 'A great new edifice is not built overnight,' Kennedy concluded.[9] The Declaration of Interdependence was a calculated gesture. If the Europeans were to buy the concept of Atlantic Partnership, the United States might exchange the promise of future equality for less resistance on the part of the Europeans to American policy in the present. The speech inspired more of a stir in America than in Europe where, ironically enough for the anti-Gaullist phobias of the promoters of the Grand Design, attention was riveted on the official visit of Konrad Adenauer to France, from 2 to 8 July 1962. According to Adenauer's account of his conversations with de Gaulle, Kennedy's speech went unnoticed.

Nowhere was the mixture of economic and political motives underlying the Kennedy Administration's Grand Design more evidently exposed than in its ardent support of Britain's entry into the Common Market. The American Ambassador in Bonn confided to Adenauer that Macmillan had originally greeted the idea as politically impossible for the Conservative government, and proposed instead an economic agreement between Britain and the United States, but that Kennedy had rejected that proposal and insisted that England must enter the Common Market.[10] Schlesinger presents the Administration's rationale for promoting British entry unambiguously:

Kennedy fully understood the economic difficulties British entry would bring to the United States. But these were, in his mind, over-

8. Full text quoted in the *New York Times*, 5 July 1962.

9. *New York Times*, 5 July 1962.

10. Adenauer, *Erinnerungen*, pp. 164–5.

borne by the political benefits. If Britain joined the Market, London could offset the eccentricities of policy in Paris and Bonn; moreover, Britain, with its world obligations, could keep the EEC from becoming a high-tariff, inward-looking, white man's club.[11]

Britain would thus assure a Common Market more responsive to United States interests.

Kennedy never lost an opportunity to press his more reticent British colleagues forward. When Hugh Gaitskell came to Washington early in 1962, Kennedy apparently mobilized half the Cabinet to convince him of the necessity of Britain's joining the Market. Macmillan's turn came in April 1962, when Kennedy informed him candidly that the United States was backing the British entry basically 'for political, not for economic reasons', though he went on to insist that Britain must not make economic arrangements 'at America's expense'.[12] The Atlantic Partnership of the Kennedy Administration was, thus, premised on the hope of a Common Market community sympathetic to American policies and interests: the British membership was intended to secure that hope, against the wayward ways of de Gaulle and Adenauer. For the time being, however, the French and the Germans were busy honeymooning; it was the British who were caught in the pinch of American policy in 1962.

While the State Department was promoting its version of an Administration policy toward Europe based on interdependence and partnership, the Defense Department, under McNamara, was engaged in an all-out war against national nuclear deterrents, proclaiming the virtues of an Atlantic military community united under central command, and based on the American deterrent – meaning, in practice, the continued *dependence* of Western security on American nuclear control. McNamara spelled out the strategic arguments in favour of what was shortly dubbed the 'McNamara Doctrine' in speeches at the Nato ministerial meeting in Athens in the spring of 1962, and at Ann Arbor, Michigan, in June. He took direct aim at the notion of independent national nuclear deterrents: 'Limited nuclear capabilities, operating independently, are dangerous, expensive, prone to obsolescence, and lacking in credibility as a deterrent,' he concluded summarily.[13]

11. Schlesinger, *A Thousand Days*, p. 845.
12. Schlesinger, *A Thousand Days*, p. 846.
13. Robert S. McNamara, *Address at the Commencement Exercises, University of*

McNamara's invective was aimed at the French national force, but his argument could just as easily have been applied to the British deterrent as well, despite official reassurances in response to British protests. Indeed, Schlesinger reports that Kennedy had privately confided to Macmillan in February 1962 his fear that 'a British effort to maintain its own deterrent through the sixties might both confirm de Gaulle in his own course and hasten the day when the Germans would demand nuclear weapons for themselves'.[14] This comment provides compelling evidence that the Administration's opposition to national nuclear forces was not based solely on McNamara's strategic arguments, but also on political considerations. The *force de frappe* was the bogey man, and, once again, the fear of alleged German demands provided the spectre over the horizon – what Schlesinger so eloquently calls the fear of stirring 'Valkyrian longings in German breasts'.[15] The American effort to square the circle, by retaining effective nuclear control while promoting a 'sense of nuclear participation' among her Nato allies, gave rise to a host of schemes, the most illustrious of which was the proposal of a 'multilateral force' within Nato. If one ponders the account of Arthur Schlesinger, the MLF affords a case study of how a morass of bureaucratic non-communication resulted in a foreign policy that was only vaguely supported by the President.

Though couched in military terms, the multilateral force was in fact the brainchild of Harvard University Professor Robert Bowie, whose spiritual home was the State Department, not the Pentagon. The MLF was first proposed in the early 1960s in the context of the thorny debate over non-proliferation and nuclear participation within Nato. A combination of factors had prompted a crisis of confidence in the credibility of the American deterrent in the early 1960s. Crucial among them was the end of United States non-vulnerability. Paired with that, in the European view, was the new strategic doctrine of flexible response, espoused by

---

Michigan, Ann Arbor, Michigan, June 16, 1962, Department of Defense, Office of Public Affairs, News Release no. 980–62, 16 June 1962.

14. Schlesinger, *A Thousand Days*, p. 849.

15. Schlesinger, *A Thousand Days*, p. 856. This myth persisted despite evidence that as late as 1964, even after the Germans were *encouraged* to support the MLF, empirical studies of the attitudes of the German political elite concluded: 'Our own and other data indicate that most German leaders do not consider NATO nuclear sharing either necessary or desirable.' Karl Deutsch *et al.*, *France, Germany and the Western Alliance*, New York, Scribner's, 1967, p. 148.

Defense Secretary McNamara to increase American military options, but first put forth by General Maxwell Taylor in his book *The Uncertain Trumpet*.[16] Taylor's book attracted rather more notice in political circles in Europe than in the United States, doubtless because he seemed to be suggesting that American security came first, and that the United States might not spring automatically to the nuclear defence of Europe in all cases.[17] The Unites States, he argued, needed a more flexible series of responses to limited Soviet moves in Europe, short of nuclear war. A deterrent strategy based on massive nuclear retaliation in response to limited military challenges in Europe was not credible. Intended to increase the credibility of the US commitment to defend Europe, in Western Europe the doctrine of flexible response had precisely the opposite political impact. Therefore, when McNamara gave official sanction to Taylor's doctrine, and Kennedy went further by appointing Taylor Chairman of the Joint Chiefs of Staff in August 1962, European fears compounded. Bonn's Defence Minister, Franz-Josef Strauss, was so alarmed that he had whole passages of Taylor's book translated and distributed among German leaders. The issue of *who decides?* in questions of nuclear strategy was thus escalated to the forefront of alliance politics.

The problem for Washington then became how to assuage its allies, how to give them a *sense* of nuclear participation, of control over their own fate, without surrendering United States control in fact. The MLF was that sort of scheme. As such, not surprisingly, it failed from the outset to generate any interest among the Nato allies. It was essentially a political sop, and it was viewed as such. As first proposed, the MLF would have consisted of a mixed-manned seaborne force under 'multilateral control', though what that amounted to specifically always remained vague. Though it had little support abroad, the MLF became the political darling of the Atlanticists within the State Department, who welcomed it as another potential ingredient of Atlantic partnership; and it enjoyed a thoroughly undistinguished career, until it was pulled like a rabbit out of the diplomatic hat, in December

16. Maxwell Taylor, *The Uncertain Trumpet*, London, Stevens & Sons, 1960; New York, Harper Brothers, 1959.

17. See, for instance, Pierre Gallois, *Paradoxes de la paix*, Paris, Presses du Temps Présent, 1967, pp. 34 ff.

1962, at Nassau, to paper over the colossal diplomatic blunder, when American cost-effectiveness calculations and inattention to the domestic political context of an ally culminated in the unilateral public disclosure of the cancellation of the Skybolt missile project, on which Britain's Conservative government had pinned the future of its national nuclear force. The incident thoroughly humiliated the Macmillan government, engendering a serious crisis of public confidence at home, and a crisis in Anglo-American relations as well.

At the root of the crisis lay a fundamental divergence of priorities. In the wake of the 1956 Suez crisis and the retrenchment of British influence in the world, Macmillan had turned necessity into policy by committing his government to working in a 'special relationship' with Washington. At the same time he shored up flagging national pride with the heady symbol of Britain's independent nuclear force. In reality, the RAF bombers were rapidly becoming obsolete, as missile technology displaced dependence on vulnerable bombers equipped with nuclear weapons. Unable to go it alone down the enormously costly road of missile research and development, the British Government sought and obtained from the Eisenhower Administration a promise to provide the RAF with the air-to-surface Skybolt missile, then being developed by the US Air Force. In the American strategic repertory, Skybolt was a stop-gap measure, intended to pinpoint destruction of enemy ground installations, clearing the path for SAC strategic bombers. For the British, it was a last-ditch hope to extend by a decade the effectiveness of their strategic deterrent, in that Skybolt could be released from a bomber 800 miles from the target, while the Russians were at least ten years from developing a system to counter weapons released from such long range. Hence, what hope remained for their independent deterrent had at best a very limited horizon. The Anglo-American bargain was all the more appealing to the British in that the US alone was to underwrite the cost of development and production of Skybolt. That was where the trouble began. As the costs of the Skybolt project escalated alarmingly each year, the Eisenhower Administration – and following it, the Kennedy Administration as well – began to question the usefulness of Skybolt, though basic doubts over the project were initially neutralized by pressure from the Air Force and its

Congressional allies. By 1962, however, there were some hard facts that Secretary of Defense McNamara could no longer overlook. In the first place, there was continued difficulty over the guidance system of the Skybolt, with no assurance of solution in sight, but certainty that the costs of the project would continue to soar. In the second place, the surface-to-surface Minuteman missile was ahead of schedule in development and represented a more sophisticated strategic fallback that would eventually replace manned bombers in any case. Under these circumstances, in the autumn of 1962, McNamara reached the decision to recommend to Kennedy cancellation of Skybolt. Early in November, Skybolt was accordingly cancelled, subject to consultation with the British.

The task of consultation fell to McNamara, who unfortunately delayed his trip to London several weeks in order to combine it with a scheduled Nato ministerial meeting in Paris. The inevitable happened: by the time McNamara arrived in London, news of the Skybolt cancellation had already leaked out in the international press and had escalated to a level of frenzy in London. McNamara's task was rendered all the more difficult in that the State Department was firmly opposed to a substitute offer of the sea-to-surface submarine-borne Polaris missile in exchange, on the grounds that it would prolong the life of the British deterrent into the seventies, sink the chances of British entry into the Common Market, and, most importantly, encourage others to go the independent route of de Gaulle. McNamara arrived, therefore, empty-handed, but prepared for a British bid for Polaris. Richard Neustadt, in his excellent analysis of the Skybolt affair,[18] goes to great pains to emphasize the extraordinary – and to say the least surprising – reticence of both Defence Minister Thorneycroft and Prime Minister Macmillan to ask squarely for the Polaris in exchange, either after the public announcement of Skybolt's cancellation or earlier, amidst multiple unambiguous indications to them in private that Skybolt was in trouble. Apparently, they were convinced that their American counterparts had their best interests at heart and would do nothing to embarrass them or compromise their government's position domestically. Unfortunately, their naïve faith was hardly vindi-

18. Richard Neustadt, *Alliance Politics*, New York, Columbia University Press, 1970. I have followed closely Professor Neustadt's account of the crisis.

cated. As Neustadt would have it, McNamara and Kennedy were truly 'puzzled by the crisis',[19] and were at a loss to explain why the British had not 'done their homework' and communicated their needs to them.

What is, however, still more puzzling is the puzzlement of Kennedy and McNamara. It is perhaps not so surprising that McNamara and Thorneycroft should have misread each other's perceptions and priorities in the months preceding the crisis, not even so surprising perhaps that Macmillan did not telephone Kennedy to express his concern amidst mounting rumours of Skybolt's impending demise. What is astounding, however, is that the State Department and the British Embassy in Washington failed so completely to communicate to their respective governments the critical importance of Skybolt for the Macmillan government and for relations between the two countries. The Skybolt episode seems to have been handled in Washington almost purely as a technical matter, as witnessed by the nonchalance with which McNamara delayed informing the British of the decision, even once it was finally reached. The State Department seemed to be concerned only that the British should not obtain Polaris, and not at all with the crisis its closest ally would face should Skybolt be scrapped. Nor did the situation improve.

The meeting between Kennedy and Macmillan in Nassau was not scheduled hastily in the heat of crisis, but was actually a routine semi-annual consultation between the two governments. It nevertheless took place under the worst possible conditions. To begin with, at a time when sensitive diplomacy was of the essence, to say the least, the American Secretary of State, Dean Rusk, remained inexplicably behind in Washington.

The Kennedy Administration was committed to non-proliferation and opposed to autonomous nuclear programmes, but it had also to salvage the badly damaged political reputation of its closest ally. By the time Kennedy arrived in Nassau, he saw two available options. One was to turn the Skybolt project over to the British and to offer to pay half the cost. But after all that McNamara and Kennedy had said to the press about the deficiencies of Skybolt, Macmillan could obviously no longer treat that as a meaningful symbol to hold off his critics. A second alternative

19. Neustadt, *Alliance Politics*, p. 49.

was to offer Polaris on condition that the British deterrent remain 'integrated' under the effective control of Nato. 'Macmillan responded with an eloquent soliloquy. . . . Its point was buried in a reference to the Queen's prerogative of using British weapons independently at moments of supreme emergency.'[20] Macmillan held out staunchly for the independence of the British deterrent.[21]

The outcome of the Nassau meetings was a clear victory for Macmillan, in that he succeeded in convincing Kennedy to provide submarine-borne Polaris missiles in place of the discredited Skybolt, and had further successfully resisted Kennedy's efforts to force the pure and simple integration of the British deterrent within Nato. More importantly, from the British standpoint, with Polaris he had prolonged the life of Britain's independent deterrent beyond the obsolescence of the RAF bombers. The Nassau Agreement squared the circle ostensibly, providing for independence *and* integration. The British would obtain Polaris missiles from the US. They would build the nuclear submarines to launch them and also the nuclear warheads to equip them, with technical assistance from the US. In return, under Article 6 of the agreement, they pledged their deterrent to Nato in a '*multinational* force', comprising allocations of national contingents to the Nato Command, but retained the right to withdraw their national force in case of emergency. This effectively guaranteed the continued independence of the British nuclear deterrent based on the Polaris. In Article 7 of the agreement, both governments pledged additionally to work toward a Nato *multilateral* force (MLF), a mixed-manned surface fleet operation, without the critical escape hatch of the right to emergency withdrawal. The British would be free to allocate their Polaris missiles to either force. Finally, it was also decided to offer the Polaris to France under the same conditions, in the hope thereby of enticing de Gaulle back to a Nato where both independence and integration could now presumably coexist.

For the Europeanists within the State Department, the Nassau Agreement obviously represented a severe setback for their Atlantic community plans. But they lost no time in latching on to the MLF clause as their hope for a comeback. Once again, the

20. Neustadt, *Alliance Politics*, p. 53.

21. See Harold Macmillan, *At the End of the Day: 1961–1963*, London, Macmillan; New York, Harper & Row, 1973, pp. 355 ff.

banner of German exclusion was brandished in order to promote an energetic push for the MLF, which was expanded for a time to include Polaris submarines, until the determined opposition of Admiral Rickover forced a retreat back to a surface fleet. In a patent effort to woo West German diplomacy away from de Gaulle's European ambitions, George Ball was dispatched to Bonn in early January 1963 in order to sell Adenauer on the MLF. The MLF, which began as a politico-military scheme intended to contain nuclear proliferation, became thenceforth the hapless symbol of Atlantic community, and, as such, the major diplomatic instrument in an all-out ideological struggle against the Gaullist vision of Europe. The diplomatic battleground was above all West Germany.

De Gaulle's response to the Skybolt episode and the Nassau invitation to participate in a Nato Polaris scheme came, characteristically, in the form of a press conference a few weeks later, on 14 January 1963, just four days after George Ball, in his role as apostle of the Atlantic Community, had addressed the Nato Permanent Council in Paris on the subject of the MLF and Polaris, before departing to Bonn. In one fell swoop, de Gaulle dealt a *coup de grâce* to the economic and military underpinnings of the Grand Design. Arguing that 'the nature, structure, and economic context of England differ profoundly from those of the other states of the Continent',[22] de Gaulle went on to explain why the British application for membership in the Common Market was about to fail. The crux of his argument was that the British entry would entail perforce the admission of the other EFTA states as well, each with its particular conditions of entry. The result would be so much to weaken the cohesion of the present Common Market that 'in the end there would appear a *colossal Atlantic community under American dependence and leadership* which would soon completely swallow up the European Community'.[23] What

22. *Major Addresses*, p. 213.

23. *Major Addresses*, p. 214. Emphasis added. This issue of Europe's being swallowed up by an Atlantic community under US leadership has continued long after de Gaulle to pose a problem in relations between France and her European partners. At the twentieth anniversary of the signing of the Treaty of Rome, in March 1977, the question concerned the insistence of the EEC smaller states that the EEC Commission represent the Community at the forthcoming summit conference in London. *Le Figaro* editorialized: 'At bottom, the problem is well known, whether the Heads of State speak clearly about it or not. On the one hand, most of the Europeans and the Americans desire the institutionalization and the "globalization" of EEC–US

de Gaulle was rejecting was indeed the American policy itself – it was for no other reason that the Kennedy Administration had so tirelessly promoted the British entry.

The spectre of that 'community under American dependence and leadership' was, moreover, in de Gaulle's view, evident in the Nassau Agreement, where Great Britain, in the guise of safeguarding its independent nuclear force, was, in fact, anchoring its future nuclear development entirely to the United States:

> Britain may purchase from America, if it so desires, Polaris missiles which are, as you know, launched from submarines specially built for that purpose and which carry the thermonuclear warheads adapted to them for a distance of 1,100–2,000 miles. To build these submarines and warheads, the British receive privileged assistance from the Americans. You know . . . that this assistance was never offered to us and you should know, despite what some report, that we have never asked for it.[24]

The necessity of European autonomy *vis-à-vis* the United States was confirmed for de Gaulle by the *dénouement* of the Cuban missile crisis, which served as the prelude to Nassau. De Gaulle interpreted the missile crisis both as the undisputed acknowledgment of American superiority in the nuclear field, and also as proof of the fact that the two superpowers would indeed play the nuclear poker game over the heads of the middle-level powers of Europe.[25] Neither England nor France was consulted in advance of the American move. This did not surprise de Gaulle, but it convinced him all the more that the task of the moment for Europe lay in fighting off staunchly and relentlessly the hegemonial domination of the two superpowers who threatened to seal the fate of Europe by freezing its present divisions. In aligning British policy with the United States proposals at Nassau, Macmillan had, in de Gaulle's view, committed the sin of Anglo-Saxonism. He had shown in the crunch that his government's priorities were not yet 'European'; indeed, that he was quite prepared to serve as the willing vehicle for American Grand Designs, and lesser ones.[26]

---

relations (plus Japan); on the other, France fears – and has long feared – being drowned by this system in an Atlantic Community under American leadership.' 'La France seule face à ses partenaires', 26–7 March 1977.

24. *Major Addresses*, pp. 218–19. 25. *Major Addresses*, p. 217.

26. De Gaulle surprised Macmillan at Rambouillet with what Macmillan viewed as a 'curious remark'. He recalled that 'at one stage of the war, Mr Churchill had

De Gaulle never took very seriously the proposed multilateral force, which he early in the game privately baptized the 'multilateral farce'. As a military strategist himself, he judged it operationally ineffective and fraught with hopeless contradictions; and as an astute political analyst, he correctly sized up its essentially political *raison d'être*, commenting provocatively: 'In politics and strategy, as in economics, monopoly naturally appears to him who enjoys it as the best possible system.'[27] Since he judged the MLF scheme of so little strategic consequence, de Gaulle made clear immediately that France had no intention of participating in it. He could not really see why anyone would be interested in it at all, but if the Germans or British favoured supporting such a scheme, he had no objections. He did, however, heap his very considerable scorn upon the plan at every opportunity in private contacts with his German counterparts.

Macmillan had advanced warning that de Gaulle planned to reject the British application. Two days before Macmillan went to Nassau to bargain for the substitution of Polaris for Skybolt, he met de Gaulle at Rambouillet. The atmosphere grew steadily cooler as the two men discussed defence and the British entry. De Gaulle later related to Adenauer that he had sensed very clearly that Macmillan was about to propose the Polaris deal to the Americans, but that Macmillan had remained absolutely silent, if anything implying that the Americans were probably about to invite the British to participate in the Polaris programme.[28] In any event, de Gaulle found it altogether paradoxical that the British should seek to set up a special relationship with the Americans in the field of atomic weapons without first considering a joint effort with their prospective European allies, and his comments concerning the British application for membership accordingly stiffened. Adenauer reports that de Gaulle went so far as to suggest outright to Macmillan that if the Americans were no longer interested in building Skybolt, the British might solicit European co-operation on the programme. But Macmillan remained silent.[29] De Gaulle found the reaction

said to him that he would always choose Roosevelt rather than de Gaulle'. Macmillan, *At the End of the Day*, p. 353.

27. Press conference of 14 January 1963, *Major Addresses*, p. 217.

28. Adenauer, *Erinnerungen*, p. 205. This conflicts with Macmillan's contention that he brought the subject up with de Gaulle. See Macmillan, *At the End of the Day*, p. 348.

29. Adenauer, *Erinnerungen*, p. 202.

characteristic of the well-established British commitment to maintain at all costs their special relationship with the United States, even if exchanging Skybolt for Polaris effectively meant their complete dependence on the United States in nuclear affairs.

Macmillan's own account of the Rambouillet meeting strikes a note of bewilderment at de Gaulle's pessimism concerning the British application and Europe's political future. He is at a loss to explain the General's reserve, yet he records his own discussion of the Skybolt episode in these words:

> But of one thing I wished to assure the General – we were determined to maintain our independent deterrent. I would explain to the President that, if Skybolt broke down, I must have an adequate replacement from the United States, such as Polaris. . . .[30]

In other words, that Britain would continue to rely on America. Macmillan found de Gaulle melancholy over the failure of the Fouchet Plan. If the Six could find no practical basis for concerting policy, 'on what subjects could an enlarged Europe with Britain possibly have a policy?'. 'The truth was that the European countries did not dare to do anything without the United States.'[31] 'For France,' Macmillan reports de Gaulle's conclusion, 'it was important that the Common Market should remain unchanged for the present – there was no hurry.'[32] Macmillan was perplexed by de Gaulle's pessimism, even as he failed to perceive the relationship between his own preoccupations with the British–American special relationship, on the one hand, and de Gaulle's preoccupation with the political will to unite Europe, on the other. Macmillan had shown his colours as an Anglo-Saxon first, and a purely nominal European, at Rambouillet.[33] Clearly, Macmillan had no reason for optimism concerning the British application's chances of success thereafter.

After de Gaulle's press conference, in any case, the fate of the negotiations should have been clear. Erhard's disarming astonishment, when Couve de Murville formally closed the discussions at the end of the month in Brussels, revealed a rather extraordinary lack of political awareness.[34]

The year 1962 was indeed one of intermittent crises, false

30. Macmillan, *At the End of the Day*, p. 347.
31. Macmillan, *At the End of the Day*, p. 350–1.
32. Macmillan, *At the End of the Day*, p. 352.
33. See chapter 10, p. 182.
34. See chapter 5, pp. 98-9.

promises and open-ended new departures. In Europe, the most spectacular event was doubtless the preparation of the Franco-German Treaty, but it was also the year the ill-fated Fouchet Plan was laid to rest, the year that negotiations on the British entry into the Common Market fanned false hopes for success. In America, the Grand Design was launched with fervour and fanfare by those who were sure that they knew better than the Europeans what was in the real European interest. The strain of the American diplomatic offensive was felt most acutely, quite naturally, in West Germany, whose political life, for obvious reasons, was most dependent on the United States, and where the rift between Paris and Washington was paralleled in short order by a split within the governing Christian Democratic Party.

CHAPTER SEVEN

The Wilting of the Rose: Bonn between Two Chairs

I am firmly convinced that this Treaty will later be pointed to by historians as one of the most important and worthy Treaties of the post-war period; and I am firmly convinced that it will serve the needs of both peoples, the needs of Europe, and world peace.

Adenauer, *Erinnerungen*, 23 January 1963

When George Ball arrived in Bonn as an apostle of the MLF in January 1963, he found an Adenauer eager for any assurance of the American commitment to Germany. Indeed, the Chancellor's exasperation with the uncertainties of American policy runs as a *leitmotiv* through all his conversations with de Gaulle, as he himself reports in his memoirs:

When one compares the year 1963 with the years 1961, 1960 or 1959, one is struck by how much greater world insecurity is today than before. . . .

I am very disturbed by the United States. I do not know what course of defence they plan to follow, when everything changes so rapidly there. The uncertainty began with McNamara's public statements concerning conventional weapons. Next came the Bahama Agreements which are full of loopholes. . . . Ball's explanations before NATO did not satisfy me. . . .

Who knows what plans America will have tomorrow? To be sure, America does not want to disappoint anyone; but then no one knows what the Americans will be thinking tomorrow. . . .

At all costs we must not let go of America's hand; we must, instead, imbue them with a sense of responsibility. I see in the present situation no other possibility than to inspire the Americans by a display of trust, so that they may assume a sense of responsibility for Europe based on trust.[1]

1. Discussion with de Gaulle in Paris, 21 January 1963, in Adenauer, *Erinnerungen*, pp. 199–200.

As cold war rigidities gave way to the less fixed modes of diplomacy, in the early 1960s, Adenauer viewed the signs of change in American foreign policy with a sense of desperation heightened by his conviction that West German security depended totally on American protection. American acquiescence in the building of the Berlin Wall provided stinging evidence of the more reserved stance the Kennedy Administration had adopted toward Europe. The combined effect of all the recent reappraisals, plus the sense of remoteness from the hub of discussion, centred clearly in Washington, left Adenauer basically uncertain of the firmness of the American commitment to defend Europe. De Gaulle's point of view differed from Adenauer's in that he did not share the Chancellor's uncertainty about America's basic commitment to the defence of Europe. De Gaulle's misgiving was that an American defence of Europe would take place on American – and not European – terms, with the Americans deciding the time, the place, and the weapons to be used as best suited to their own self-defence, and not necessarily in the perceived interest of the Europeans.[2] American priorities and European priorities were not identical. That was part of the political rationale for the *force de frappe* – to foreclose American options. Adenauer obviously did not have the alternative of constructing his own nuclear force. But he was sufficiently desperate to reach out for whatever straw in the wind the Americans had to offer.

The MLF, garnished with the rhetoric of Atlantic Community and the hope of closer relationship with the United States, thus fell upon fertile diplomatic soil in Bonn. It was not the strategic significance of the plan that interested the West German Government so much as the political assurances they thought they would reap from participation in the plan, which Washington seemed, moreover, to be urging with unusual fervour. The problem for Adenauer was that the MLF was no longer simply an American non-proliferation scheme designed to buoy European confidence in Nato. It had indeed become an instrument of battle, but not against the Russians:

If de Gaulle meant to make West Germany choose between France

2. Meeting on 4 July 1963, in Adenauer, *Erinnerungen*, p. 227. This objection is reminiscent of the US–French conflict over the liberation of Strasbourg in 1945. See also de Gaulle's comments on the Cuban missile crisis at his press conference of 14 January 1963, *Major Addresses*, p. 217.

and the United States, the MLF in Washington's view was the way to make it clear that Bonn would find greater security in the Atlantic relationship. To strengthen this point, Kennedy decided in mid-January to visit Germany on a spring trip to Europe.[3]

The MLF had become a device to bring the Germans back into line and to thwart their temptation to support de Gaulle's European policy. A state visit by Kennedy would provide a powerful counterpoint to de Gaulle's nefarious influence.

The spring of 1963 marked the first all-out campaign in the MLF crusade. President Kennedy had authorized a small mission headed by veteran diplomat Livingston Merchant to assess the situation in the various European capitals in regard to the MLF. By the time the group departed, however, the 'small mission' had escalated into a delegation of forty, travelling in their own private jet; and the whole operation had turned into a massive sales campaign to promote the MLF in the capitals of Western Europe.

Not surprisingly, the Merchant Mission was above all successful in Bonn. The West German Government proved indeed such a receptive client that it eventually agreed to foot the bill for 40 per cent of the cost of the project. It was thought that this might encourage the more recalcitrant British to rally to the cause, but they instead maintained a studied reserve toward the scheme and refrained from commitment, despite persistent American efforts to win support. Finally, on the eve of Kennedy's trip to Europe, the Profumo scandal broke out, and sealed the fate of whatever hopes Washington entertained of an immediate British decision on the MLF. With the Labour Party resolutely hostile to the plan, and Macmillan's Conservative government – on which the only hope for the scheme rested – completely discredited, it became apparent that no British decision on the MLF would be forthcoming. In Italy, the legislative elections produced such a chaotic internal political situation that it proved difficult even to form a government. With the Italians in complete disarray, and the French on record as opposed, the choice thus lay between proceeding *à deux* with the West Germans, or tabling the scheme temporarily. Kennedy chose the latter course.

The direction of American diplomacy in Europe was, moreover, about to shift, yet again, in any case. During the summer of

3. Schlesinger, *A Thousand Days*, p. 872.

1963, the Nuclear Test Ban Treaty was signed. It signalled the first step in practical *détente* between Moscow and Washington. Despite Washington's best efforts to portray the MLF to Moscow as a non-proliferation scheme, the Soviet Union remained intractably opposed to any scheme that would afford even a suggestion of a nuclear role for Bonn. Indeed, the Soviet Government delivered a sharp diplomatic protest note to that effect on 8 April. Thereafter, Russian opposition to the MLF constituted a major obstacle; for top US priority lay unquestionably in reaching agreement with Moscow on non-proliferation.

But the Merchant Mission had been successful in Bonn beyond its fondest dreams. The West German Government was completely sold on the MLF; nor did British and Italian difficulties dampen its enthusiasm for the scheme, with all it promised of a renewed assurance of the American guarantee and a voice in Alliance nuclear affairs. The point had not been lost on Adenauer that, since the death of Dulles, United States diplomacy had ceased to view Bonn as its principal European partner; indeed, not only did Adenauer feel as if he had lost his privileged status in Washington's eyes, but his fears were compounded by the apparent withdrawal of American diplomatic interest from Europe during the first two years of the Kennedy Administration. He therefore welcomed the MLF as an overture from Washington, and was not in the least reticent to proceed with it *à deux*.

Kennedy's visit to West Germany and Berlin in June was intended to dissipate the magic of de Gaulle's seduction and to bolster German–American relations. It was in every way a well-researched production. Kennedy's political stock rose many points within German political circles as a result of his 'Ich bin ein Berliner' speech. Comparing the visits of Kennedy and de Gaulle, *Die Welt* commented:

> General de Gaulle appealed to the German people last July, and the German people responded wholeheartedly when de Gaulle placed Germany once again within European history and freed her from the past. But the General did not go to Berlin, and he spoke only reservedly of German unity. President Kennedy . . . must have understood quickly that he could only win the heart of the German people by speaking of what concerns them – the unity of the German people and the freedom of their capital.[4]

4. *Die Welt*, 29 June 1963.

De Gaulle had refused to go to Berlin and had spoken unpopular, hard facts about German unity. Kennedy was quite prepared to fan the fires of nationalist hopes, no matter how unprepared he was to defend them in practice.

McNamara's visit to Bonn in August 1963 provided still another opportunity to boost West German–American relations, and the Bonn Government rallied by signing a joint tank agreement and by voicing again its enthusiasm for the MLF. The tank agreement represented a symbolic setback for the French, for discussions aimed at developing a joint French–German tank had ended in an impasse just that spring. With Adenauer about to retire and Strauss discredited by the *Spiegel* affair,[5] the *Gaullisten* within the CDU/CSU coalition held no sway against the powerful trio of Erhard, Schröder and von Hassel, all staunch supporters of US policy. It was therefore not difficult for Washington to drive a wedge between Bonn and Paris, and to thwart de Gaulle's efforts to lead Europe according to his own designs.

But Kennedy was not willing to proceed on the MLF alone with the West Germans. In October 1963 it was decided to shelve the MLF, by relegating it to a committee called the Working Group, until after the American and the British elections in 1964 when, hopefully, the British would be in a better position to endorse the project. A further setback came in early December, when the Assembly of the Western European Union formally rejected the MLF proposal by a vote of 32 to 29, with 5 abstentions.

The result of the MLF campaign was, not surprisingly, to paralyse effective Franco-German co-operation. In that respect, it accomplished its diplomatic objective brilliantly. Throughout 1963, none the less, French diplomacy remained basically reserved in regard to the MLF. There was no effort to pressure Bonn into rejecting it, nothing in any way comparable to the independent effort on the part of the American Nato delegation to whip up support for the MLF in West German circles, even when Washington was officially playing down the scheme. The discretion of the French position was, of course, facilitated by the coolness of the British, and therefore the unlikely prospects for the project's success. This initial policy of apparent non-concern was in marked contrast to the militant French opposition to the project by the autumn of 1964.

5. See next page.

The sun was shining on German–American relations in the autumn of 1963, but the Franco-German rose had wilted.

De Gaulle's veto of the British application for membership in the Common Market on the eve of Adenauer's visit to Paris for the signing of the Franco-German Treaty placed the Chancellor in an extremely delicate position at home. The very timing of the two events reinforced the apparent alternative: de Gaulle or Europe? There is no indication from Adenauer's public statements or memoirs that he himself disapproved of either de Gaulle's reasoning or his action, but then he held no personal brief for the British entry anyway. But the northern, Protestant wing of his party, represented by Schröder and Erhard, were as hostile toward de Gaulle's policies and style as they were eager to welcome England to the European club, while both the liberal FDP and the Socialists were categorically in favour of the British entry and suspicious of de Gaulle. It therefore proved near impossible thenceforth for Adenauer to bill the Franco-German Treaty as a step toward the building of Europe.

But it was not only the public splash occasioned by de Gaulle's press conference that created problems at home for Adenauer. His influence had already been substantially eroded in the aftermath of the unfortunate *Spiegel* affair of November–December 1962. The arbitrary and dramatic midnight arrests of editor Rudolf Augstein and his collaborators on *Der Spiegel*, the most widely read German weekly news magazine, on the dubious grounds of publishing military secrets, led to the resignation of the FDP cabinet members. Before the affair was over, Adenauer had been forced to drop from his cabinet his powerful ally and close collaborator, Defence Minister Franz-Josef Strauss, head of the Bavarian CSU Party and Adenauer's chief coalition partner. Strauss's ouster cast discredit on the *Gaullisten* within the CDU, of whom he was an outspoken leader, and also upon Adenauer himself, who was finally obliged to set the date for his own retirement in the autumn of 1963. The whole episode thus played into the hands of Adenauer's intra-party rivals, Ludwig Erhard and Gerhard Schröder, by relegating the Chancellor thenceforth to a lame-duck status, and by banishing his strongest supporter. Adenauer's position was in every way the opposite of de Gaulle's; for in December 1962 the Gaullist UNR had carried a majority of the seats in the legislative elections. De Gaulle's parliamentary hand was thus strengthened even as his partner's was irretrievably weakened.

Two days before the first reading of the Franco-German Treaty in the Bundestag, on 24 April 1963, Ludwig Erhard was formally elected as Adenauer's successor. The choice of Erhard, Atlanticist and outspoken critic of de Gaulle, was surely a portent of things to come. Adenauer regarded the ratification of the treaty as the culmination of his life's work. But his moment of glory was about to be stolen. The American Embassy in Bonn had been hard at work behind the scenes mobilizing its supporters into action.

When the Bundestag came to vote on the first reading, it coupled its approval of the treaty with a resolution reminding the Government that the treaty should be applied 'in keeping with the objectives that the Federal Government has for years shared with its allies', and it stipulated among them: German reunification, the inclusion of Britain in a united Europe, and support of Nato. Every party had some condition or stipulation to propose to modify the no longer popular treaty. The SPD proposed a clause to stipulate that Franco-German negotiations must take place within the context of the Nato and EEC treaties. Not to be outdone, finally, the FDP came through with the suggestion of a formal preamble to the treaty, delimiting narrowly the scope of the treaty and reaffirming the commitments and objectives of the Federal Republic's foreign policy. The preamble was a clear product of American diplomatic pressure. Adenauer was incensed by the proposal of the preamble, and agreed to it only reluctantly at the urging of the French diplomats in Bonn and leaders within his cabinet, who assured him that the treaty would fail without that concession. Among the commitments the preamble reaffirmed was the close co-operation between Europe and the United States, German reunification, the admission of Britain to the EEC, and an integrated Nato command.[6] Once Adenauer agreed to the preamble, the hapless treaty encountered no further obstacles. The preamble was approved on 9 May, and the formal ratification took place in the Bundestag on 16 May.

The ratification no longer bore the faintest resemblance to a great historical moment. *Le Monde* editorialized aptly: 'If everyone has indeed agreed to apply the treaty according to the letter,

6. Text of preamble in *Le Monde*, 10 mai 1963.

there is no hiding the fact that no one intends to apply it in the spirit . . . of General de Gaulle.'[7] De Gaulle had hoped for the rapprochement of the two states to be sealed by the historic rapprochement of their great peoples. He hoped to set an historic example for the building of Europe. What he got instead was party politics.

The French debate over ratification was a shabby replay of the West German one. The opposition attempted in vain to mount its own campaign in favour of a preamble. In the end, the Government held strong, and ratification was voted by 325 to 107, with 42 abstentions. But de Gaulle no longer held great hopes for the treaty's future. Shortly before the first working meeting in Bonn under the terms of the new treaty, on 4–5 July, he mused publicly at a reception for deputies at the Elysée that treaties, like young maidens and roses, have their day. Parodying Victor Hugo, he quipped, 'Hélas, que j'en ai vu mourir de jeunes filles!'[8]

The romance of the rose continued its rhetorical career during de Gaulle's visit to Bonn, when Adenauer, reacting to the press reports of de Gaulle's comment, offered his own personal experience as a rose gardener. 'The rose is the most perennial of plants,' he assured de Gaulle. 'It has thorns . . . but it survives every winter. . . . This friendship between France and Germany is like a rose bush, which always blossoms, then buds again and blooms still more, and superbly survives the harshness of winter.'[9]

'Vous avez raison, Monsieur le Chancelier,' de Gaulle continued:

> The treaty is neither like a rose nor even a rose bush; it is like a whole rose garden. A rose blooms but a single morning. Young maidens, too. But a rose garden lasts a very long time, *quand on le veut*.[10]

The whole question of the treaty's future hinged on the last pithy phrase. In the absence of commitment, the Franco-German garden would wither at best. The rhetoric could no longer mask the very real strains in relations between the two countries.

The first working meeting under the new treaty took place in the wake of de Gaulle's withdrawal of the rest of the French fleet from Nato, a step he had boldly announced in his habitual

7. *Le Monde*, 26 avril 1963.

8. *L'Année politique 1963*, p. 280.

9. Federal Republic of Germany, Presse- und Informationsamt der Bundesregierung, *Erste deutsch-französische Arbeitsbesprechung, Bonn*, 1963.

10. *L'Année politique 1963*, p. 280.

manner, without consulting his German 'partner'. The meeting thus took place in a less than receptive atmosphere. There were none the less modest accomplishments. In the area of defence, the two governments agreed to support a forward defence strategy within Nato, to encourage the exchange of troops, and to collaborate on the development of the vertical take-off military cargo plane, Transall, a project which in fact dated back to 1959. The latter decision represented no small success for French diplomacy, which had been engaged all spring in an effort to promote such Franco-German military co-operation, and which had suffered a discouraging setback when, following the visit of Roswell Gilpatrick in February, Adenauer had announced plans to step up the purchase of American weapons.[11] The American firm, Lockheed, was also engaged in an all-out campaign to promote its Hercules C-130 transatlantic cargo plane in Germany, and its efforts did not cease with the Transall announcement. The Transall project, joining the French firm, Nord Aviation, and the German firms, Hamburger Flugzeugbau and Weser Flugzeugbau, represented a market of about fifty planes to be purchased by the French army and about 110 by the German army.[12]

The major accomplishment of the meeting was the establishment of a Franco-German Youth Office to promote various exchange programmes between the youth of the two countries.[13] The Youth Office, generously financed with an annual budget of 50 million francs, set up its offices in Adenauer's native Rhineland village of Rhöndorf, with a branch office in Paris. It came subsequently to be viewed as the most outstanding success of the treaty; at the very least, its activity represented one of the treaty's most enduring and concrete accomplishments.

There were disagreements in Bonn, too, though perhaps the most telling fact was not the success or failure of this or that particular proposal so much as the absence of spirit, the contrast between the vast ambitions for the building of Europe which had inspired the treaty and the absence of political will to accomplish

11. *Libération*, 15 février 1963.

12. *Le Monde*, 12 octobre 1963. The Transall project was eventually abandoned in 1967.

13. Future CDU Chancellor Kurt-Georg Kiesinger, Minister-President of Baden-Württemberg, was one of the architects of the youth exchange programme in his capacity as Commissar of the Federal Republic for cultural co-operation within the context of the Franco-German Treaty.

them. In his account of the Bonn meeting, Adenauer dwells exclusively on East–West problems – Kennedy's visit to Germany in June, relations with the Soviet Union, and finally Nato and the recent withdrawal of the French fleet. De Gaulle offered him the following justification:

> For France and also for Europe, it was absolutely necessary that France should recover and become once again what she had been, namely a major power. If France did not recover her power, then she would collapse, and what remained would amount to nothing. In order to recover her power, however, it was essential for France to feel that she was bearing her own national and international responsibilities, and above all to take on her own defence – naturally, within the framework of the Alliance. In this perspective, NATO was catastrophic, precisely because it destroyed what he called national responsibility. I had already witnessed what had happened to the French army in Algeria. If he, de Gaulle, were to hand this army over to the Americans, then there would no longer be any French army at all. . . . Therefore, the Alliance was not being called into question in the least, and France remained an ally of the Americans and all the other powers united in the Atlantic Alliance. But the Organization of that Alliance would not allow France to reject its accent on integration.
>
> I replied that I understood almost all the General's basic motives. I had nonetheless to point out very clearly that every setback within NATO strengthened Khrushchev. I was forever preaching to my people that it was of primary importance that every foreign policy move be viewed with an eye to whether or not it strengthened Russia. The withdrawal of the French fleet would certainly be interpreted by the Russians as a sign of NATO's inner weakness. The question remained, which was more important. . . . I could not say whether the grounds that de Gaulle had just cited were so strong as to warrant the consequence they entailed – that the Soviet hope in the disintegration of the West was strengthened.[14]

Adenauer's sober words set in sharp relief the essential simplicity of West German foreign policy in its intense obsession with security and anti-communism, as against the more subtle and complex concerns of French policy. As de Gaulle progressively loosened France's ties to Nato, therefore, relations between the two countries were bound to grow ever more sharply strained.

Indeed, when de Gaulle came to discuss the outcome of the Franco-German meetings at a news conference on 29 July, he

14. Adenauer, *Erinnerungen*, pp. 228–9.

placed the discussions and the treaty in an altogether different light:

> The Bonn meeting strengthened the feeling in the minds of those taking part that French–German co-operation should during the present year affirm itself in an essential area: the economic organization of Europe, the complete and effective setting up of the Common Market. It is quite clear that this is, we might say, the testing ground of the Treaty.[15]

De Gaulle was politicking. 31 December 1963 had been agreed upon as the deadline for the completion of the agricultural arrangements for the Common Market. With the Germans now dragging their heels, and the general 'Kennedy Round' tariff negotiations scheduled for the spring of 1964, de Gaulle was more than ever determined to wrest an agreement from his reluctant partners before the end of the year. Limited agreement had been reached on cereals, pork, poultry and eggs, wine, fruit and vegetables in January 1962; what remained an obstacle was rice, beef and dairy products.[16] Final agreement had likewise yet to be reached on the delicate issue of the financing of the European agricultural fund (FEOGA), which was functioning on a temporary basis for three years. The economic stakes were high; indeed, the value of beef and dairy production in France and Germany alone exceeded that of all EEC metal-working industries, including shipbuilding and the automotive industry. They accounted for 42 per cent of West Germany's agricultural production and 32 per cent of France's.[17] Central to the completion of the agricultural common market was the good will of the West German Government, which would perforce foot the bill for the French agricultural surpluses under a European financing scheme.

Konrad Adenauer made a sentimental farewell journey to Rambouillet on 21 September 1963, shortly before he officially stepped down as chancellor. If the policy of co-operation between France and West Germany were founded strictly on the personal friendship linking de Gaulle and Adenauer, as many observers contended, that theory was about to be put to the acid

15. Press conference of 29 July 1963 in *Major Addresses*, p. 239.

16. For a detailed discussion of the 1962 agreement, see *L'Année politique 1962*, pp. 382–3.

17. European Communities Information Service, *Newsletter of the Common Agricultural Policy*, no. 8 (December 1963–January 1964).

test, as avowed Atlanticist Ludwig Erhard became the new West German chancellor on 11 October.

As new chancellor, Ludwig Erhard, accompanied by Foreign Minister Gerhard Schröder, paid a courtesy visit to de Gaulle on 21 and 22 November. De Gaulle took special care to spare nothing in welcoming Erhard to Paris. Dismissing protocol, he attended a luncheon at the German Embassy. Doubtless, he was attempting to charm Erhard in an effort to offset the latter's reputation of hostility toward him. Erhard saw his role as one of 'honest broker'. A pragmatist by nature, a man of the middle politically committed to economic liberalism, Erhard's deepest hope was to heal the French and American rift. He would avoid at all costs falling between the two stools tendered by Paris and Washington. This corresponded, moreover, to the most obvious common sense, given the West German internal political context. As chancellor of a CDU–CSU coalition deeply divided between its Atlanticist and its Gaullist wings, he had little choice but to attempt the role of conciliator.

Foreign Minister Gerhard Schröder was more detached and resolute in his thinking. He had long since made his choices public. At a meeting of the CDU foreign affairs commission, a month before the trip to Paris, he declared:

> Gaullist policy . . . has destroyed completely the idea of European unification on a supranational basis, and more and more one is left to believe that the General is seeking French hegemony within a grouping of European states. In studying the recent speeches of the General, the question arises whether we should not re-examine again the problem of Franco-German relations.[18]

Schröder was trenchantly opposed to Gaullist policy, an ardent partisan of the British entry and of Atlantic Partnership. Furthermore, on a personal basis, he and French Foreign Minister Maurice Couve de Murville did not get on at all well. Relations between the two men were not merely reserved; they were politely, but openly, hostile.

The meetings between de Gaulle and Erhard focused on two issues: Atlantic relations, on which there was no agreement between the two governments, and EEC relations, which account

18. Quoted in *L'Express*, 31 octobre 1963.

for four of the seven substantive paragraphs in the final communiqué:

> A discussion in depth of European problems took place. This concerned essentially economic issues, in accordance with the agenda adopted last May 9th, to which both governments are equally attached.
>
> General de Gaulle and Mr Erhard recognized the importance for France, for the Federal Republic as well as for the Economic Community itself, of the adoption within the timetable agreed upon of the agricultural and financial arrangements still pending, and they agreed to deploy all efforts necessary to assure the success of the negotiations in Brussels. . . .
>
> The President of the Republic and the Chancellor of the Federal Republic also proceeded to an exchange of views on the very important proposals which the Common Market Commission has just set forth concerning the establishment of a common level of cereal prices within the European Economic Community.
>
> Both governments hope that the setting in operation of the above-mentioned timetable of May 9th will make it possible to carry on the work which has begun, not only on economic grounds, but also on political grounds, and thus to promote the construction of a united Europe.[19]

Unmentioned in the final communiqué were Nato and the question of the British entry. Erhard rationalized the latter on the grounds that it was not a pressing question of the moment. On the issue of relations with the United States, however, Erhard made his position clear in public declarations. On the night of his arrival in Paris, he stated at a dinner in his honour at the Quai d'Orsay:

> I believe, Mr Prime Minister – and this is my credo – that co-operation between our two peoples is essential if we wish to make of Europe something other than a vague geographic notion, if we wish that the political import and value of our two great countries should grow. Only then will we be able to bring all our weight to bear on the scale, with a view toward a close Atlantic Partnership.[20]

And to keep the public record straight, at the end of his stay, he again declared at a press conference: 'The common and reciprocal action of Europe and America offers the best guarantee that the great tasks can be resolved within the Atlantic Alliance and com-

19. 'Communiqué franco-allemand publié à l'issue de la visite en France du chancelier Erhard (Paris, 22 novembre)', in *L'Année politique 1963*, pp. 421–2.

20. Quoted in *Le Monde*, 22 novembre 1963.

mitments honoured toward the rest of the world. . . . I cannot imagine any other policy.'[21]

De Gaulle had, therefore, mixed success with Erhard. With a little more than a month to go until the 31 December deadline, he was above all interested in assuring West German commitment to working out an agricultural agreement. That much had been obtained, or at least promised. For the time being, therefore, he said nothing publicly about Erhard's Atlanticist heresies. He would wait until after the difficult agricultural negotiations had ended for that.

21. Quoted in *L'Année politique 1963*, p. 316.

CHAPTER EIGHT

Of Cabbages and Commissions

When the Common Market was created, it would have been fatal to us, burdened as we were by our agriculture, if we had joined the Six without guarantees.

André Malraux, *Felled Oaks: Conversation with de Gaulle*, translated by Irene Clephane, New York, Holt, Rinehart & Winston, 1971, p. 97

For all de Gaulle's public bravado, the deteriorating relations between France and West Germany posed a critical challenge to French diplomacy. The problem was in part the very dynamism and strength of West Germany. The formidable growth of the West German economy made it likely that West German diplomacy would not remain indefinitely in the weak and passive mood it was in currently. The German challenge to France in the offing was therefore one of competition for leadership. It was no longer the old anti-German phobia, but rather the potential political weight of West Germany that posed the principal challenge.[1] France therefore needed the Common Market, quite beyond idealism, for the same concrete rationale Schuman had used to sell the plan to the French in the first place – to anchor West Germany to France, with the result that the French would continue to exercise some control over their distressingly powerful neighbour.

The prospect of effective long-term control over West Germany was not the only political advantage the Common Market offered the French, however. It was also destined, from the French Government's point of view, to prod the sluggish French economy forward into the industrial age, to metamorphose traditional

1. See de Gaulle, *Mémoires d'espoir*, p. 196.

industries through the stimulus of international competition. Modernization of French industry would indeed require a metamorphosis, and the Common Market would serve as a driving force:

> Another essential concern was international competition, because this offered a lever to stimulate our business sector, to force it to increase productivity, to bring the business world together and push it to do battle abroad; hence my decision to promote the Common Market which was still just a collection of paper. . . .[2]

While the adaptation of French industry posed a manageable challenge to the French Government, the problem of agriculture proved a persistent thorn in its side. How could the last vestiges of rural, agrarian society – the peasants with their fragmented landholdings and backward ways – be brought into the modern age?

> How could we maintain on our territory more than two million farms, three-quarters of which were too small and too poor to be profitable, but on which, nonetheless, nearly a fifth of the French population still continued to live? How, in this day and age, could we leave the agricultural profession to stumble along, without the benefit of technical training, organized markets, and the support of a rational credit system required for it to be competitive?[3]

The answer was obviously for the government to intervene to ease social transitions while facilitating the efficient reorganization of agriculture, including both drastic reduction in the number of farms and vast increases in production. With surpluses in agricultural production, the French Government was faced with the quandary of exporting farm products at low world-market prices, then of underwriting a huge bill for economic subsidies to farmers, 'subsidies so enormous that they would cripple its finances'.

> I must say that if, on resuming control of our affairs, I immediately embraced the Common Market, it was as much because of our position as an agricultural country as for the progress it would impose on our industry. To be sure, I was well aware that in order to include agriculture effectively within the community, we would have to work vigorously on our partners, whose interests were not the same as ours in this domain. But I believed that this was, for France, a *sine qua non*

2. De Gaulle, *Mémoires d'espoir*, p. 143.
3. De Gaulle, *Mémoires d'espoir*, pp. 165–6.

of her participation. For, in a community theoretically free of customs duties and national taxes, where the fruits of the earth were alone denied free access, in a grouping of consumers where domestic agricultural products did not enjoy preferential treatment over those from outside, our agriculture would prove to be a burden that would relegate us, relative to the others, to a position of chronic inferiority. In order to impose on the Common Market, as its framework developed, what we considered necessary in this respect, *we were thus obliged to put up a literally desperate fight*.[4]

De Gaulle was thus absolutely determined from the outset to secure economic compensation to France for the obvious advantages which accrued, above all, to West German industry through the progressive lowering of commercial and industrial customs barriers among the Six. The establishment of an agricultural common market, financed on a Community-wide basis, would assure that the affluent West Germans would help defray the expense of supporting French agriculture. It would do so mainly by providing urgently needed outlets within the Community, especially in West Germany, for the endemic French agricultural surpluses. In addition, a European agricultural fund would protect the prices established for the European market against lower priced competition from outside by levies on imports, and would subsidize the export of surpluses outside the community. The issue of a common agricultural policy was, thus, of capital importance to the French Government.

For the West German Government, the domestic pressures against a common European agricultural policy were intensified by the fact that the farmers were major constituents of the governing Christian Democratic coalition. A Community-wide price system meant, in effect, forcing West German consumers to pay higher food prices by penalizing imports from outside, and lowering the income of the farmers, who stood to see their subsidies reduced at the same time as competition from the French posed basic questions of their survival. The agricultural common market would in essence be a device for spreading to the Community the burden of protecting French agriculture, of insulating it from external competition through price supports and export subsidies for surpluses. With crucial stakes resting on the outcome, the issue of agricultural policy lined up as major parties in

4. De Gaulle, *Mémoires d'espoir*, p. 167. Emphasis added.

the debate France, as the largest exporter, and West Germany, as largest importer of agricultural products within the Community.

De Gaulle held one trump card. He could afford to push the West Germans hard on the agricultural question precisely because there was no doubt of the fundamental commitment of both major West German political parties to the EEC. When the chips were down, there were few concessions the West Germans were not prepared to make in return for the assurance that the European institutions would continue, for they were committed both to political federalism and the economic features of the EEC. That certitude was in effect the only diplomatic card de Gaulle held in hand, and he exploited it adroitly at every turn. Consequently, despite the real and inevitable conflicts over agricultural policy, both governments remained fundamentally committed to the European communities, though for somewhat different reasons, and with different long-term intentions.

There remained the question of what price de Gaulle would be willing to pay in return for an agreement on agriculture. The stillborn Fouchet Plan had set forth de Gaulle's version of progress toward European political union. But meantime, spurred on by the Common Market Commission, the partisans of supranational integration – including Chancellor Erhard – had not in the least given up hope that circumstances might eventually constrain de Gaulle to make some concessions to their vision of a federalist, supranational Europe, expanded to include Britain.[5] They found in the issue of the agricultural common market the lever they thought might be effective in implementing their goal. In return for progress on the agricultural question, de Gaulle might be cornered into some political concessions.

But de Gaulle proved a formidable poker player. French diplomats engaged in hard-nosed negotiations, making whatever technical concessions were necessary to assure immediate success; and when they had finished, de Gaulle fulminated in press conferences against the supranationalist 'illusions' of his partners, championed in so many ways by the Commission. The agricultural negotiations stand out as a game of grim determination on de

5. Macmillan himself notes the paradoxical contradiction in the push for both federation and British entry. The British position was closer to de Gaulle's confederal stance than to the supranationalist programme. See Macmillan, *At the End of the Day*, p. 112.

Gaulle's part to reach economic agreement, and of equally grim determination on the part of his European partners to corner him into political acquiescence. De Gaulle repeatedly brandished the threat that France would quit the Common Market if agreement were not reached on agriculture. It was probably not true, if only because the EEC also served an important political function in French policy toward Germany. But the fact that he had taken such resolute action in regard to Nato left his real intentions sufficiently ambiguous for his partners not to desire to call his bluff. In any case, the French threat, as an expression of de Gaulle's determination, did undoubtedly serve to prod the Six along toward gradual establishment of the agricultural common market.

The crisis atmosphere which hovered over the Community's future following de Gaulle's veto of the British application in January 1963 was not of long duration. This was because the concern of France's partners to push the Community forward was stronger than their irritation with French high-handedness. There were two important carrots to encourage them back to the negotiating table – the prospect of accelerating the customs union tariff cuts three years ahead of schedule, and the need for a Community position for collective bargaining at the forthcoming Kennedy Round trade negotiations. The West German Government was particularly eager to win agreement on these two points. For that reason, West German Foreign Minister Gerhard Schröder took the initiative at a Council of Foreign Ministers meeting, on 1 and 2 April 1963, in proposing a plan that would win French acceptance by tying progress on agriculture to agreement on other issues. The deadline set for agreement on a framework for agricultural policy was 31 December 1963.

It was easier to agree to agree on agriculture than to come to terms with the specific issues of common prices and financial arrangements, which put the French Government on the line at the bargaining table, opposite the West Germans, in what were sure to be difficult negotiations. The task involved setting Community-wide prices, well above world free-market levels, and protecting them through tariffs and export subsidies financed by the whole Community. De Gaulle was braced for the push, and rose to the verbal offensive on agriculture at his press conference in July, warning dourly that the Community's future hinged on meeting the agricultural deadline. In November, the Commission exploited the inevitable Franco-German tug of war by interjecting its own proposal, the so-called 'Mansholt Plan' – an ambitious package that would have jumped toward immediate adoption of a single target price for cereals, rather than phased adjustments toward a single price, culminating in full Community financing of agriculture by 1970. There was no indication by the time the Council of Foreign Ministers finally met in Brussels, on 18 December, that any agreement could be reached. Tension and apprehension characterized the meeting.

The bargain that was finally struck, after a marathon all-night session, was hailed as the 'miracle of Brussels', an epithet more revealing of the dreaded apprehensions of deadlock than a commentary on the actual agreement. The West Germans finally yielded, in principle, but the principle was to postpone the clash. What was agreed to was mostly new deadlines. On the critical issue of the Mansholt Plan for unifying cereal prices, consideration was postponed until the spring. The issue of cereal prices was obviously the central stake, in that all other prices hinged to some extent on that denominator. Hence, the 'package deal' worked out in Brussels did not, in effect, give much away. It provided just enough progress for de Gaulle to save face and for the Commission to receive a mandate for the Kennedy Round trade negotiations. All substantive price questions were effectively postponed. Agreement on new deadlines took the place of substantive agreement.

What was agreed on was broad lines, a general framework, for beef, dairy products and rice, with transitional arrangements extending to 1 January 1970, after which all prices would be aligned, in a single Community price. It was further agreed in principle that, by 1970, the Community would take over the subsidizing of agricultural exports, with subsidies to be financed partly by levies on imports from third countries and partly by direct contributions of member governments. This meant, concretely, that Community levies on West German imports from third countries would be used to subsidize the sale on world markets of French farm surpluses. But the specific mechanics of the complex financial framework that entailed remained to be worked out – i.e. who should pay what, how much, and under what circumstances?

Two critical issues, therefore, still remained to be settled: (1) what the common price levels would be, and (2) the functioning of the common agricultural fund. The question of the common price level for cereals, which in turn determined the level of other agricultural prices, was to dominate the scene throughout 1964. The issue of working out a financial framework for the common fund resulted in the crisis of 1965.

The Brussels agreements were billed as a victory for the French, despite the fact that the working papers submitted by the Commission took consistently stronger positions than those the French were urging. The French, in fact, made several important concessions during the course of the negotiations.[6] On the issue of West German subsidies, they yielded to the principle of a gradual phasing out of government intervention rather than an immediate shift in policy. They agreed to end French chicken subsidies. They accepted a longer time schedule for completion of the agricultural market than that advanced by the Commission or promoted by French negotiators at the outset. All these were concessions to the West Germans. In return, the West Germans had agreed to a general framework and timetable for agricultural policy, but to nothing specific. They had obtained a green light for the Kennedy Round tariff negotiations ahead. Under the threat of crisis, the French and West Germans had brought their divergent interests into acceptable balance. But once the agricultural hurdle was past – to everyone's great relief – both sides attempted to manipulate the situation to their own advantage.

With the weight of de Gaulle's implicit threat to dissolve the Common Market over the agricultural showdown lifted, Erhard returned to his mission as apostle of European political unity. Caught in the power struggle between his ardent Atlanticist foreign minister, Gerhard Schröder, and the intrigues of the West German 'Gaullist' faction, Chancellor Erhard was maintaining at best a precarious control over his internally torn party. The strain of intra-party factionalism and the prospect of elections not too far over the political horizon made the West German Chancellor particularly anxious to consolidate his position as acknowledged champion of the popular cause of European unity in order to bolster his credit at home. Erhard very much needed diplomatic

6. For an excellent discussion of the negotiations, see *L'Année politique 1963*, pp. 320–6.

success symbols to shore up his fragile position domestically, and thought he had found that possibility in taking up the tattered banner of European political unity. He therefore met in late January Italian Premier Aldo Moro, and signed a joint communiqué pledging his government to defend the true and orthodox faith: 'Both governments are convinced that the future Europe must be democratic, integrated, aligned with the Atlantic Alliance, open to Great Britain.'[7] The challenge was obviously thrown to de Gaulle.

Having won agreement on the principles and timetable for decision on the agricultural question, de Gaulle also was now free to address himself again to the future direction of Europe. Three days after the Moro–Erhard communiqué, at a press conference on 31 January 1964, de Gaulle took up Erhard's challenge. After commending the loyalty and solidarity of the West German Government in accepting the agricultural agreements, he pointedly denounced those who would 'either deliberately . . . place Europe under the dependency of America, or maintain it in the realm of brilliant topics of political discourse . . .'.

> No European union, they say, unless through integration under supranational leadership. No European union, if England does not belong to it. No European union, without its being incorporated in an Atlantic Community. Yet it is clear that not one of the peoples of Europe would allow its destiny to be handed over to an assembly composed mainly of foreigners. In any case, this is true for France. It is also clear that England, which is a great nation and a great state, would accept it less than anyone else. Finally, it is clear that to merge the policy of Europe in a multilateral Atlantic policy would be tantamount to Europe's having no policy itself, and in that case, we do not see why it would want to confederate.[8]

Forced to confrontation with the West German Chancellor over both agriculture and the political future of Europe, de Gaulle chose to bank on the possibility that the Erhard Government might fall and be replaced by that wing of the Christian Democratic coalition more favourable to his policies. He was apparently braced for an open confrontation with Erhard.

De Gaulle knew Erhard was vulnerable, and found his opportunity to discredit the Chancellor on his home ground in July 1964,

7. *Le Monde*, 28 janvier 1964.
8. Press conference of 31 January 1964, in *Major Addresses*, p. 255.

during a routine visit to Bonn under the terms of the Franco-German Treaty. The meeting proved a great setback for Erhard. No communiqué was issued at the end of the meeting. Erhard obtained only a vague promise to pursue further the discussion of European political co-operation – hardly the concrete result he desired just before the CSU congress in Munich, where he knew Franz-Josef Strauss was preparing to deride his diplomatic defeats. De Gaulle did not mince his words in criticizing Erhard's ultra-American loyalties. He especially saw no justification for Bonn's supporting American policy in Vietnam so wholeheartedly.[9] De Gaulle interrupted his official duties in Bonn to pay a very well-advertised private visit to his friend Adenauer, and deliberately emphasized his preference for relations with Adenauer by breaking protocol and keeping a fuming Erhard waiting twenty minutes, then half-apologizing with scantly transparent irony: 'J'ai été séduit, et donc prisonnier.'[10] It was an unambiguous public humiliation. Finally, in case Erhard missed the point, as the young translator was reading the perfunctory final summary of the meetings to the assembled delegations, de Gaulle interrupted irascibly:

> There is no use deceiving ourselves – the Franco–German Treaty of Co-operation has not yet developed as we had hoped. Constantly going over the same things is not enough; we must move ahead, notably in the military domain. There is a lot of talk about the Transall plane, but that dates back to 1960, and since the signing of the treaty nothing further has been done.[11]
>
> Europe will only be a reality when France and Germany are truly united. Whatever our intentions and our goals, we have not yet succeeded in accomplishing that. But we believe that that union corresponds perfectly to the concerns of public opinion, and that the day will come when our two peoples will have a common foreign policy. Everything points in that direction.[12]

The tension mounted. In the days following the Bonn meetings, the major international press featured sensational reports of de Gaulle's having urged on Erhard that the West German Government contribute to financing the *force de frappe* as a joint French–

9. De Gaulle had publicly denounced the American intervention in Vietnam in August 1963. See *Major Addresses*, p. 241.

10. 'I was seduced, and thus a prisoner.' Quoted in *Le Monde*, 7 juillet 1964.

11. The Transall project was eventually abandoned in 1967.

12. Quoted in *Le Monde*, 7 juillet 1964.

German venture. West German observers interviewed were unanimous in attributing these 'leaks' to the Gaullist faction within the Christian Democratic coalition, which planted them for its own purposes. The German Gaullists would indeed have welcomed such a Franco-German venture, but there is no indication whatsoever that de Gaulle would have advocated such a scheme. Indeed, it represented substantially the unfulfilled hope of the secret protocol between CSU chairman and former defence minister Franz-Josef Strauss and his Fourth Republic opposite Bourgès-Manoury, which de Gaulle had subsequently rejected.[13] Still less would he have urged it on Erhard at a time when the agricultural agreements had already placed the Chancellor in a difficult position *vis-à-vis* the implicit West German subsidizing of French agriculture.

The Gaullist *fronde* within the CDU reached its culmination at the CSU congress in July. Heaping praise on de Gaulle, Strauss scornfully attacked Erhard's foreign policy. But Erhard returned promptly to Bonn and counter-attacked vigorously, defending foreign policy as the sole prerogative of the Chancellor and dismissing as 'unthinkable' the prospect of a two-power union with France.[14] Erhard emerged the victor. The executive meeting of the CDU, at which Strauss had intended to attack Erhard's foreign policy officially, was cancelled; and on 15 July the Cabinet officially endorsed the Chancellor's European policy.

De Gaulle's attempt to play internal politics had therefore failed. It remained for him to denounce Erhard's foreign policy publicly, as Strauss had unfortunately been unable to do. He lost no time. At his press conference of 23 July 1964, de Gaulle painted a bleak portrait of Franco-German relations. In reply to the question, 'Mr President, what results has the French–German Treaty produced in political, economic and military matters? Do you deem these results satisfactory, disappointing or simply insufficient?' De Gaulle replied by reviewing the whole historical evolution of postwar Europe, contrasting the old international system established at Yalta with the new system emerging as a result of the re-establishment of Europe as a power, the rise of China, and the internal failures and accommodations within the communist bloc. He then placed the Franco-German Treaty in the context of the Fouchet negotiations,

13. See above, p. 93.

14. *Die Zeit*, 17 Juli 1964.

taking particular care to emphasize that the treaty had been concluded 'sur la proposition du gouvernement allemand'. Why had the treaty ended in disappointment?

> Assuredly there is not, and there could not be any opposition, strictly speaking, between Bonn and Paris. But . . . one could not say that Germany and France have yet agreed to make a policy together, and one could not dispute *that this results from the fact that Bonn has not believed, up to now, that this policy should be European and independent*. If this state of affairs were to last, there would be the risk, in the long run, of doubts among the French people, of misgivings among the German people and, among their four partners of the Rome Treaty, an increased tendency to leave things as they are, while waiting, perhaps, to split up. . . .
>
> In wanting and in proposing the organization of a Europe having its own policy, France is sure of serving the balance, the peace, and the progress of the world.[15]

There was nothing particularly new in this line, except that de Gaulle was acknowledging the failure of the Franco-German Treaty, and blaming that failure squarely on the West Germans, who, along with the rest of his EEC partners, had not sufficiently grasped that Europe must be 'European' and 'independent'.

De Gaulle's press conferences were hardly geared to win friends. They had rather the effect of reaffirming both the worst prejudices of his opponents and the most solid convictions of his followers. While de Gaulle was apparently a master of persuasion in private conversations, his public style was not to persuade so much as to proclaim. Since his vision of the future was both so complete as an organizing principle for policy, and so diametrically opposed to that of his EEC partners, there was in fact scant room for compromise. He himself, in any case, was unprepared to yield on the essential directions of his European policy. Compromise had consequently to come from the other side, in the form of capitulation. It was the same high-handed style that had so irritated Churchill and Roosevelt during the war, although his fundamental insights had subsequently appeared proven by events. De Gaulle was quite prepared to stand alone, to be outnumbered and scorned, and yet to stand fast by his conviction

15. Press conference of 23 July 1964, *Major Addresses*, vol. II, p. 23. Emphasis added.

that he was right and all the others wrong, while awaiting vindication by *la force des choses*.

The others were not so willing to entrust the future to historical destiny. They saw the agricultural negotiations as a golden opportunity to force de Gaulle's hand, albeit to counter coercion with coercion, in order to promote their vision of an integrated Europe under a federal executive, responsible to a European parliament. But, for a while at least, it was difficult to distinguish the faithful from the heretics where agriculture was concerned.

Barely had the ink dried on the much hailed 'miracle of Brussels' of December 1963 when the West German Government showed its true colours concerning application of the agricultural agreements signed eleven months earlier and scheduled to enter into force on 1 January 1964. Invoking the safeguard clause, Bonn notified the Commission that the agreements concerning fruits and vegetables would not be enforced within the Federal Republic in regard to apples, because of market dislocations. The Commission adroitly side-stepped the confrontation, while affirming strict adherence to the agreement, by accepting the West German derogation in principle, but setting approximate deadline of 12 January for the full application of the agreement. The Commission's decision was upheld on appeal to the Council of Foreign Ministers, over the protest of the West German Government, which desired a longer deadline. The Apple War terminated.[16]

In February, the more recent December 1963 agreements were put to the test. The West German Government again invoked the safeguard clause, this time in order to close its borders to eggs coming from its EEC partners – principally the Netherlands. The Commission this time ordered the West German Government to open its borders immediately, on the grounds that the fall in egg prices was due to increased internal production more than to the influence of imports. On appeal to the Council of Foreign Ministers, once it became apparent that the Council was again prepared to rule against the German position, Bonn withdrew its appeal and opened its borders.[17] Thus, twice within one month, the West German Government had tried and failed to subvert application of the agricultural agreements.

On the question of a common cereal price, Bonn chose simply

16. *L'Année politique 1964*, pp. 205–6.

17. *L'Année politique 1964*, p. 295.

to drag its heels interminably. In February 1964, West German Minister of Agriculture Werner Schwarz declared before the Bundestag that under no circumstances would German cereal prices be lowered for the year 1964–5.[18] With parliamentary elections due in 1965, the West German Government had no desire to alienate the farmers, who traditionally supported the CDU. Negotiations over the common cereal prices therefore dragged on into the autumn of 1964 with no progress yet in sight, despite the fact that, as a concession to Bonn, it had been suggested in May that the common price should not be applied until July 1966. Herr Schwarz continued his policy of resolute silence at the negotiations. This led the French Government to issue an ultimatum on 21 October 1964:

> Without prejudicing the continuing negotiations, General de Gaulle, Mr Pompidou and the Government have once again emphasized that France would cease participating in the European Community, if the Agricultural Common Market were not to be organized as it had been agreed that it would be organized.[19]

The combined pressure of French and American diplomacy finally had its effect. The American Government intervened to pressure the Erhard Government, when it began to fear that the French would not enter into the Kennedy Round trade negotiations in the absence of a prior European agreement on agriculture. But de Gaulle actually made the first concession. Shortly after the French ultimatum, France agreed to a compromise on the issue of the common EEC exception list for the Kennedy Round tariff cuts. It was clearly an overture to Germany.

On 30 November, West German Agriculture Minister Schwarz finally put forth a proposal: reduction of the price of wheat from 475 to 440 marks per ton, beginning 1 July 1967; 700 million marks in compensation to German farmers out of Community resources; the possibility of upward revision of the common price to take account of interim cost-of-living increases; and finally, despite Bonn's federalist rhetoric – a prelude to French policy round the bend – *exclusion of all decisions concerning agriculture from the majority vote procedure scheduled to replace the unanimity rule in the Council of Ministers as of 1 January 1966*. The Commission-

18. *L'Année politique 1964*, p. 220.
19. *L'Année politique 1964*, p. 295.

sponsored Mansholt Plan had proposed a wheat price of 425 rather than 440 marks per ton beginning 1 July 1966, rather than 1 July 1967 and with a compensation set at 560 million marks rather than 700 million.[20] The West German Government had moved, but not very much.

The showdown came at the meeting of the Council of Foreign Ministers in December. With the threat of French withdrawal heavy in the air, the ministers went through yet another all-night marathon negotiating session on 14–15 December, in their determination to hammer out an agreement.

In the end, the West German Government accepted the Mansholt price of 425 marks per ton, but held out for their date of 1 July 1967, and a provision for upward revision of the common price in accordance with rising cost of living. The terms of compensation to farmers represented a considerable West German concession. The amount finally agreed to be paid out of Community resources amounted to only about a half of the initial Mansholt proposal, but the West German Government was left free to supplement the Community compensation with its own.[21] This was important in that it allowed the West German Christian Democratic government effectively to offset the impact of the lower Community prices on its farmers, who represented an important political constituency – though entirely at its own expense.

Once the common price for wheat had been agreed upon, other cereal prices fell into line accordingly.[22] But faced with another difficult hurdle in the issue of financial regulations, the Council resorted to a by now old standby strategy, and set deadlines for agreement, instructing the Commission to propose financial regulations by April 1965, and setting 1 July 1965 as the deadline for final decision. One had faith that deadlines and marathons had in the past produced agreement. Hope was in the air that 1 July 1967 would indeed see the completion of a full customs union among the Six, including both industrial and agricultural sectors.

20. *L'Année politique 1964*, p. 317.

21. *L'Année politique 1964*, pp. 321–5.

22. By June 1973, the situation had changed so dramatically that, faced with acute cereal shortages on the world market, world prices had moved into line with the EEC price levels, and the Commission decided to end export subsidies for cereals. By July 1973, it recommended *export tax penalties* in a complete reversal of the original terms of negotiation over the common price for cereals. See *Le Monde*, 13 juillet 1973.

It should be clear by now that hand in hand with the French determination to complete the agricultural regulations on schedule went an equally unequivocal determination to avoid the political consequences of 'supranational' political integration. The rubric 'supranational integration' covered two essential and interrelated issues: (1) the role of the Commission, and (2) the transition from unanimity rule to majority vote for decisions of the Council of Ministers, set in the Treaty of Rome for 1 January 1966 – less than a year away. The French position on the latter issue was not, in fact, substantially different in practice from that of Bonn, as evidenced in Schwarz's insistence that agricultural decisions be excluded from future majority vote provisions.[23]

De Gaulle never missed an opportunity to denigrate the pretensions of the Brussels Commission to constitute an international 'executive', despite the very real support which the Commission had given to French positions throughout the agricultural negotiations. The Commission's situation was in fact fairly straightforward: its interest lay in promoting the further integration of the Community. Since the agricultural negotiations lined up the French as promoters of further integration against the reluctant West Germans, the Commission obviously tended to support French initiatives. This convergence of Commission and French positions was deeply resented in West Germany. So strong was the backing given by the Commission to the French that West German critics bitterly likened it to the collusion of the Emperor and the Pope.

The Commission did in fact play an extremely important role in formulating compromise proposals – incorporating the common denominators of a solution, and then acting as broker among the various parties. It was indeed an important political role, and not merely a technical role, as de Gaulle stubbornly billed it. De Gaulle's deliberate playing down of the Commission's role was part of his programme to discredit the notion of supranational integration. It was pure political invective:

> As always, the elements of a solution were formulated by the technicians. But then, to reach a conclusion, the decision, despite all the contradictory interests, could only come from the States. That is indeed what happened.

23. See above, p. 144.

The Brussels Commission having objectively accomplished work of great value and offering the negotiators, as they debated, carefully studied suggestions, the governments none the less found themselves obliged to take the decisive steps and assume their responsibilities. . . . However important the work and counsels of the Brussels Commission have been and must continue to be, we have seen clearly that the executive power and duty belongs to the governments alone. Thus, once again, is evidenced the tendentious impropriety of concept and phraseology by means of which a certain parlance entitles 'executive' a meeting, however qualified it may be, of international experts.[24]

De Gaulle's legalistic invective against the Commission was not gratuitous theorizing. Over the horizon of 1965 lay two important deadlines: 1 July 1965, the deadline for the completion of the agricultural fund regulations; and 1 January 1966, when, in accordance with the provisions of the Treaty of Rome, the Council of Ministers was to adopt the procedure of majority rule. Thus, a crisis in Community relations over the issue of majority rule was clearly in the offing for the end of the year. But the showdown came still sooner than that, precipitated by a shift in the strategy of the Commission.

The agreement on a common cereal price in December 1964 escalated everyone's hopes: de Gaulle's, that the financial regulations would be completed on schedule and the final implementation of the agricultural market achieved; Erhard's, that the moment was now ripe for a *relance* in the direction of political union, for which he could assume credit at the West German elections in the autumn of 1965; and the Commission's, that the prospect was now ripe for strengthening the power of Community institutions.

With the agricultural common market well on the way to becoming a reality, the Commission apparently thought the time was propitious for a confrontation with de Gaulle over the issue of Community institutions. More specifically, it appeared that France was by now sufficiently committed to the agreements that had been so laboriously negotiated on the agricultural common market, for the Community's bargaining position to be strengthened *vis-à-vis* de Gaulle's threat to pull out if things did not go according to his plans. With only the financial regulations remaining to be settled, therefore, the Commission prepared

24. Press conference of 31 January 1964, in *Major Addresses*, p. 253.

its proposals in time for the 1 April deadline, as instructed by the Council in December 1964. But the proposals the Commission finally presented to the Council, even in the words of a sharp critic of de Gaulle's policies, would have constituted a 'giant step towards economic union'.[25] They were a bold new departure rather than a consolidation of what had been agreed at the agricultural negotiations. As such, they were predictably to elicit enthusiasm from the supporters of stepped-up supranationalism and the wrath of de Gaulle.

The Commission played its game with a heavy hand. It could not have failed to realize that its proposals were, to put it mildly, controversial; and yet it chose to present them irregularly, even before the 1 April meeting of the Council, at a session of the European Parliament in Strasbourg. If the Commission really had hopes of persuading de Gaulle, rather then cornering him by a clumsy replay of his own tactics of coercion – but from a much more disadvantageous position – it should have played its hand with a great deal more political finesse and tact.

The proposals aired before the European Parliament contained three parts. Part I dealt with the interim functioning of the Common Fund until the single-market stage, which was proposed for 1 July 1967. Part II of the Commission's proposals dealt with the period after 1 July 1967, when the Community would have its own resources. Once a full customs union had been established, the Commission proposed, duties on industrial products should progressively become community property, over a period extending until 1 January 1972; agricultural levies should become community property by 1 July 1967. The total Community resources envisaged by the plan would have amounted to approximately $2·4 billion by 1972. Part III set forth a labyrinthine budgetary procedure intended to strengthen the role of the relatively eclipsed European Parliament in regard to the budget.[26] There was no common measure between the modest task the Commission was given back in December concerning financial regulations for agriculture, and the ambitious scope of this scheme, which included industrial revenues as well. The proposals would indeed have created a whole supranational executive and legisla-

25. Miriam Camps, *European Unification in the Sixties*, London, Oxford University Press, 1967, p. 46.

26. See *L'Année politique 1965*, pp. 231–2.

tive structure, with revenues completely independent of its member-states' control. It was a head-on challenge to de Gaulle.

During the foreign ministers' negotiations on 14–15 June, Couve de Murville took up the challenge. Picking up an inconsistency in the Dutch proposal to consider the Commission Plan as an indivisible whole, he argued that the Dutch were in favour of strengthening the European Parliament, but not of including customs duties on industrial products in the Community resources, whereas France was indeed in favour of customs duties eventually forming a part of the Community's resources. His counter-proposal was to delay the date of assigning both agricultural levies and customs duties to the Community until 1 January 1970. Until that date, France proposed that the agricultural fund continue to function by direct contributions from national parliaments.[27] Since there would be no immediate question of Community resources, there was consequently no need to expand the powers of the European Parliament. The issue to be settled by the 1 July deadline, therefore, was simply the distribution of national allocations to the Common Fund from 1 July 1965 on. What was clear was that France was willing to sacrifice the material advantages of full Community support of agriculture in order to avoid the political implications of the Commission Plan, which was supported in varying degrees by her five partners.

Between the foreign ministers' meeting of 14–15 June and the final meetings on 28–30 June, the French made a concerted effort to reach common ground with the West Germans. In the past agricultural negotiations, once a compromise had been worked out by France and West Germany, agreement had eventually been reached. The West Germans eventually conceded the 1 July 1967 date for the imposition of levies on agricultural imports, in return for French agreement to support full industrial customs union parallel to the agricultural union. Final agreement now hinged on acceptance of the French proposal for national financing of the Common Fund from 1965 to 1970 – i.e. financing by pro rata direct contributions from national parliaments rather

27. The French had originally favoured allocation of agricultural levies to the Common Fund, but France was unwilling to relinquish *control* over the Common Fund to supranational institutions. That was the crux of the challenge in the Commission's plan.

than by levies on agricultural transactions becoming community resources.

During the night of 30 June there was disagreement in all quarters. The Italians, eventually supported by the Dutch for different reasons, would not agree to extending national financing until 1970. They pushed instead for a maximum of two years before a showdown. Finally, in the context of a general atmosphere of pandemonium, the French–German accord broke down, as Foreign Minister Schröder began brandishing a Bundestag resolution calling for strengthening the powers of the European Parliament. No agreement could be reached. The final stumbling block proved to be the relatively trivial issue of the time period of the interim financing arrangements. But behind that issue lay three months of political confusion engendered by the Hallstein Commission's determination to push for an ambitious agreement beyond any foreseeable common denominators of success. Far from confronting opposed material interests, the final negotiations resulted in a hopeless morass of opposed principles, pent-up frustrations and fuzzy politics. The French Government withdrew its permanent representative to the Communities a few days later, and French representatives ceased participating in work groups. The policy of the 'Empty Chair' began.[28]

The style of de Gaulle's response to the crisis – withdrawing France's representatives and boycotting Community activities – was hardly geared to facilitate a rapid solution. Nor was his studied silence, despite a spate of renewed Community proposals, over the entire summer of 1965. Internally, the Government's action was extremely unpopular; yet, even with the presidential election scheduled for December, de Gaulle did not bend. By September, he had apparently drawn his conclusions from the crisis, and was prepared to announce his terms. On 9 September de Gaulle called a press conference.

The crisis in Brussels was 'sooner or later inevitable', concluded de Gaulle, not only because of the reluctance of France's partners to move forward toward the realization of the agricultural common market, but also because of 'certain basic errors or ambiguities that appear in the treaties on the economic union of the Six'. In the preceding agricultural negotiations, the

28. For an excellent (anti-Gaullist) account of the negotiations and their aftermath, see Camps, *European Unification in the Sixties*, pp. 38–80.

Community officials had acted competently, and had not attempted to infringe the responsibilities of the states. But there were well-known differences in view on how to bring about a united Europe:

In Brussels on June 30th, our delegation came up against a refusal with regard to the final drafting of a financial regulation in accordance with the commitments made. A little earlier, moreover, the Commission, suddenly emerging from its political reserve, had formulated on the subject of this regulation conditions intended to give itself its own budget, which would have amounted to as much as $4 billion, with the states handing over to it the levies and customs receipts that would have made it literally a major independent financial power.... The combination – premeditated or not – of the supranational demands of the Brussels Commission, of the support that several delegations declared themselves ready to give them and, finally, of the fact that some of our partners at the last moment went back on what they had previously accepted, forced us to bring the negotiations to a close.

I must add that in the light of this event, we more clearly measured the situation in which our country would risk finding itself if one or another provision initially provided for by the Rome Treaty were actually applied. Thus, in terms of the text, the decisions of the Council of Ministers of the Six would, beginning on January 1st, 1966, be taken by majority vote; in other words, France would be prepared to see her hand forced in any economic matter – therefore social and even political – and, in particular, what would have seemed gained in the agricultural area could be, despite her, placed at stake again at any moment....

Whatever the case, France, for her part, is ready to participate in all exchanges of views that would be proposed to her in this subject by the other governments. If necessary, she envisages resuming the Brussels negotiations, once the inclusion of agriculture in the Common Market is truly adopted and there is a desire to put an end to the claims that abusive and fanciful myths are setting against common sense and reality.[29]

De Gaulle could not have been more categorical. The conditions for France's resuming her participation included: (1) conclusion of financial arrangements for agriculture, (2) an end to the Commission's pretensions to play the role of a 'major independent

29. Press conference of 9 September 1965, in *Major Addresses*, vol. II (17 March 1964–16 May 1967), p. 96.

financial power', and (3) abandonment of the treaty provision on majority voting.

De Gaulle's attack on the Treaty of Rome proved a boon to Erhard, who reaped unexpected support from the wave of anti-Gaullism at the West German elections, with the CDU carrying 245 seats, as against 190 for the SPD and 67 for the FDP.

For his part, de Gaulle stubbornly resisted all efforts to induce France back to the bargaining table until after the French presidential elections in December, even though that strategy doubtless cost him dearly at the elections, where he was forced into a second ballot run-off against the candidate of the leftist coalition, François Mitterrand. Mitterrand had sung the whole litany of supranationalism during the campaign, advocating election of the European Parliament by universal suffrage, expansion of the powers of the Commission, and immediate resumption of negotiations. De Gaulle was finally re-elected with 55 per cent of the vote. The meagre outcome was certainly, in good measure, an indication of the popular support the European Communities had acquired in France. But there is no indication that de Gaulle was in the least personally influenced by that fact.

Shortly after the French elections, Couve de Murville finally agreed to attend a foreign ministers' meeting of the Six, provided, however, that it were held in Luxembourg, and not in the orbit of the Commission in Brussels. When the ministers met on 17–18 January, it became immediately apparent that the French Government had not retreated in the least. Couve de Murville arrived with a ten-point document detailing the French position on the curtailment of the powers of the Commission and the elimination of majority voting.[30] On the latter point, the French Foreign Minister made it clear during the ensuing discussions that the French were unprepared to make any concession: France intended purely and simply to reserve her right of veto in regard to Council decisions. No agreements were reached during this meeting, but a second meeting was scheduled for the end of the month, again in Luxembourg. The French intransigence on the issue of majority voting had drawn the other five together in a solid front, led, symbolically enough, by West German Foreign Minister Gerhard Schröder.

Couve de Murville returned to Luxembourg apparently deter-

30. See *Le Monde*, 19 janvier 1966.

mined to reach agreement on the major issues. What 'agreement' finally emerged was a masterpiece of Byzantine logic:

(1) When issues very important to one or more member countries are at stake, the members of the Council will try, within a reasonable time, to reach solutions which can be adopted by all the members of the Council, while respecting their mutual interests, and those of the Community, in accordance with Article 2 of the Treaty.
(2) The French delegation considers that, when very important interests are at stake, the discussion must be continued until unanimous agreement is reached.
(3) The six delegations note that there is a divergence of views on what should be done in the event of a failure to reach complete agreement.[31]

Thus, the Treaty of Rome was not changed, the confrontation of principle was not really resolved, but a pragmatic *modus vivendi* had been worked out in which opposing positions were recorded rather than reconciled. The French Government was on record in non-acceptance of majority rule, and all were on record in agreeing that they disagreed over the implications of that position.

Compromise was reached, however, on the controversial role of the Commission, which saw its ability to act independently restricted considerably, and its obligation to act in close co-operation with the Council affirmed. With the confrontation over supranationalism out of the way, agreement was quickly reached on a timetable for the financial regulations which were finally adopted on 11 May 1966.[32] Discussions were to begin on 15 February 1966 on the issue of membership in the enlarged Commission which was to result from the fusion of the three executives (Euratom, the Coal and Steel Community and the

31. Quoted in Camps, *European Unification in the Sixties*, p. 112.

32. The agreement provided that the Common Fund (FEOGA) would administer the financing of the common agricultural policy beginning on 1 July 1967, and that the Common Fund would be financed half by contributions from member states and half from agricultural levies on imports from third countries. By 1 July 1968, all agricultural quotas within the Community would be abolished, and common prices would be in effect for most products; on the same date, all internal industrial tariffs would be abolished and a common external tariff would be applied. The French contribution to the fund would amount to about 24 per cent of its budget, while France would receive about 45 per cent of the budget. Germany would contribute 31 per cent, but receive only 18 per cent because of the levies on imports from third countries. (Germany was a major agricultural importer from countries outside the Six.) See *L'Année politique 1966*, pp. 129–30.

Common Market) in 1966. De Gaulle was determined to have Walter Hallstein's head at that point, and he eventually did.

The crisis was over. The outcome represented substantially what the French had pushed for seven months earlier–if anything, the Luxembourg agreements went further than the French demands at the June negotiations. The agricultural common market was completed, and the issue of supranationality, which the Hallstein Commission had adroitly attempted to tie into the agricultural arrangements, had been dealt a resounding defeat. The Commission's challenge to de Gaulle had backfired.

The portrayal of Walter Hallstein in de Gaulle's memoirs is revealing both of the intensity of the confrontation between the two men, and of the stark opposition of their points of view:

> Walter Hallstein is the President of the Commission. He espouses the thesis of the Super-State ardently and dedicates all his very capable activity to endowing the Community with that character and appearance. He has made Brussels, where he resides, into his capital. There he is, decked out in the trappings of sovereignty – directing his colleagues, among whom he parcels out power; disposing of several thousand functionaries who are hired, assigned, promoted, remunerated by virtue of his decisions; receiving the credentials of foreign ambassadors; claiming the highest honours during his official trips; anxious, moreover, to promote an *assemblage* of the Six, in the belief that the force of events will bring about his imaginings. But in seeing him, in seeing him again, in noting his action, I believe that if Walter Hallstein is a sincere European in his way, it is because he is first of all a German who is ambitious for his fatherland. *For, in a Europe as he envisages it, there is a context within which his country could, without cost, recover the respectability and the equality of rights which Hitler's frenzy and defeat caused it to lose; and then acquire the preponderant weight which its economic capacity will doubtless have earned it; and finally, the dispute over its borders and its unity would be taken on by a powerful ensemble*, in keeping with the doctrine to which he gave his name when he was minister of foreign affairs of the Federal Republic. These reasons do not alter the esteem and the consideration I have for Walter Hallstein, but they account for the fact that the goals I am pursuing for France are incompatible with such projects.[33]

Beneath the conflicting ideologies involved in the confrontation over supranationalism, one sees limpidly in this impassioned indictment of Hallstein the political mainspring of de Gaulle's

33. De Gaulle, *Mémoires d'espoir*, pp. 195–6. Emphasis added.

intransigence. In a supranational Europe, West Germany would enjoy the political leadership that its economic preponderance would otherwise entitle it to, were it not for the disadvantages, both moral and political, of its wartime defeat. Supranational Europe would, hence, take up the German national agenda, advancing German claims with a diplomatic force that West Germany acting alone could not muster. The threat was not only, as de Gaulle often proclaimed publicly, that a federal Europe would perforce merely rubber-stamp American policy and have no autonomous policy of its own. The essence of the problem was the two-pronged threat posed by West German domination of a federal Europe: on the one hand, the irredentist foreign policy goals the West German Government remained officially committed to in regard to its eastern borders and its national unity; and on the other hand, the prospect that under West German leadership, ever vulnerable to security issues, Europe would indeed follow the Washington line. This negative stance in regard to West Germany's influence is a fundamental component of de Gaulle's adversary relationship with the kind of European institutions promoted by the partisans of supranationalism. The Franco-German rapprochement de Gaulle sought to substitute represented a serious commitment to working toward a convergent common foreign policy, a goal he repeatedly hammered at in negotiations with Erhard.[34] So long as French and German foreign policy objectives remained divergent, there would be no *Europe politique*.[35]

France had won the struggle over supranationalism and the agricultural common market in the end, but relations between France and West Germany had in the meantime deteriorated to an all-time low, with Schröder actually leading the forces of opposition during the Luxembourg negotiations. The test of will over agriculture was only one aspect of the deteriorating relations between the two countries.

34. See above, p. 140. See also, Pierre Drouin, 'Les Raisins du gâteau', *Le Monde*, 21 janvier 1971.

35. This same argument, applied to Britain, is apparent in the Soames affair. See below, chapter 9, pp. 168 ff.

CHAPTER NINE

L'Europe européenne?

> *I thus believe that in the present, as in ages past, European union cannot consist in the fusion of its peoples, but that it can and must result from their systematic rapprochement.*
>
> De Gaulle, *Mémoires d'espoir*, p. 181

Following his return to power in 1958, de Gaulle had tried without success to obtain a change favourable to France within the power relationships of the bipolar cold war international system. So long as the international context continued to be dominated by the postwar division of communist East versus non-communist West, the best hope of influence lay in improving one's relative position within the bloc. De Gaulle's multiple attempts to convince Eisenhower to concede a place for France in an international Nato directorate can be seen in that light. Kennedy's 1962 Atlantic Partnership initiative also fell basically still within the cold war context of the anti-communist unity of the West. It promised a let-up in American domination of Alliance relations – more of a 'voice' for Western Europe. From 1962 on, however, it appeared increasingly to de Gaulle that the door to movement within the international system itself might at last be ajar.

In cold war politics, Europe was both the stake and the crossroads of the world-wide confrontation between the two superpowers. The problem of 'European security', in the context of the Soviet political-military threat, was accordingly the *raison d'être* and the continuing cement of the Atlantic Alliance system, which was based on American military power and political leadership. The Cuban missile crisis, in the autumn of 1962, in which de Gaulle believed the Russians had finally acknowledged United States nuclear superiority, set the stage for a new phase in

French policy: an attempt to exploit a certain freedom of manœuvre within the international system – to exploit the potential for change.

The cold war international system, symbolized for de Gaulle by Yalta, meant a Europe whose division was sealed by the global rivalry of the two superpowers, a Europe which could do little more than gather beneath the umbrella of American protection, or suffer passively the domination of Moscow, as institutionalized in Nato and the Warsaw Pact. The Soviet recognition of American nuclear superiority during the Cuban missile crisis, coupled with the rise of China as a power, and a consequent softening of Moscow's position, had resulted in a new wind of *détente*. Open hostility had given way to a more relaxed atmosphere. A more autonomous policy on the part of Western Europe might now pave the way for a looser international system, promising not least the reconciliation of the divided continent. Released from the bonds of its oppression, a 'European Europe' might evolve – one in which multiple relations between the states of the continent, in an atmosphere of co-operation and rapprochement, would replace the rigidities and divisions imposed by their integration into blocs. Free since 1962 of the domestic shackles of the Algerian War, de Gaulle could now broaden the range of French policy, break out of the straitjacket of the postwar system.

In January 1964, de Gaulle accorded diplomatic recognition to the Chinese Government in Peking. The surprise move was resented acutely in Western circles, particularly in Bonn and Washington, where it was viewed as a blow to the unity of the West in its struggle against the world-wide communist threat.

Stepped up disengagement from Nato constituted another aspect of the French determination to contribute to the demise of the old system by pulling out of the United States orbit. In 1964, de Gaulle withdrew French naval officers from the integrated command; in 1965, he refused French participation in Nato manœuvres, and shortly thereafter announced that French forces would cease to be integrated within Nato by 1969, when the twenty-year initial engagement expired; in 1966, he evicted foreign forces stationed on French soil, announced the withdrawal of French troops, and served notice that the Nato Command must be removed from France by 1 April 1967. The French military withdrawal was invariably accompanied by a litany of loyalty to the principle of the *alliance*; what was rejected was allegedly the fact of subordination implicit in its command structure. So long as the Soviet threat had receded but not disappeared, de Gaulle repeatedly reaffirmed the importance of the alliance.

These moves could only have been viewed with delight by the Russians. Henceforth, France shared in two of the Soviet Union's long-standing policy goals for Europe: (1) to reduce United States influence, and (2) to prevent West German domination of Western Europe. The third Soviet goal – to obtain *de jure* acceptance of the postwar settlement in Eastern Europe – was not shared by de Gaulle. He hoped, on the contrary, to move beyond the cold war goals. Where de Gaulle looked for political movement, the Soviet Union sought to legitimate the *status quo*. But agreement on the two goals, plus the hope of softening the Soviet position through good relations, led to another new departure in French foreign policy in 1964 – bilateral rapprochement with Moscow and the states of Eastern Europe, under the rubric *détente*, *entente*, *coopération*.

The new French Eastern policy moved forward at a rapid pace. Economic and cultural ties were strengthened with Czechoslovakia, Yugoslavia, Hungary and Bulgaria, and especially with Rumania, which promised to play the analogue of the Gaullist role within the Warsaw Pact. In April 1965, Soviet Foreign Minister Gromyko was received in high style during a five-day visit to Paris. His visit was quickly followed by return visits to Moscow, first of Finance Minister Valéry Giscard d'Estaing, and then of Foreign Minister Maurice Couve de Murville in November. In June 1966, de Gaulle himself made a much heralded state visit to the Soviet Union, and signed a series of economic and cultural agreements.[1] The following year, he travelled to Poland and paid public tribute to the quintessential 'Polishness' of the disputed Oder–Neisse territories. Far from following the German lead on the outstanding issues of a postwar settlement, de Gaulle was taking the lead in the direction of accommodation, of acknowledging certain political realities in Eastern Europe in order to move beyond the old political impasses. In 1968, at the outbreak of the fateful student riots in Paris, de Gaulle was, revealingly

1. It will be recalled that de Gaulle had already signed a treaty of friendship with Stalin in 1944.

enough, in Rumania, still energetically barnstorming for his Eastern policy of reconciliation across the old continent.

French foreign policy henceforth diverged at nearly every point from West German policy. During the three years of Erhard's chancellorship, relations between France and West Germany grew steadily more strained, for Erhard was as convinced that the cold war was still a cardinal tenet of faith as de Gaulle was that the old system was at last giving way. Erhard saw the existence of a divided Berlin and an intractably hostile East German regime as concrete proof of the continued reality of the cold war. West German security, in the event of military threat, required American protection. Erhard was therefore a staunch defender of American leadership of Nato. Nor did he welcome de Gaulle's repeated preachments that the solution to German reunification lay in the far-off reconciliation of the whole European continent. Erhard continued to proclaim the old Nato shibboleth that reunification would come about through a Western 'position of strength' – the implication being that the East German state would collapse somehow through its own internal weakness. Indeed, even while his foreign minister, Gerhard Schröder, cautiously embarked on a limited version of Ostpolitik in 1964–5, establishing commercial missions in Poland, Czechoslovakia, Hungary and Rumania,[2] Erhard continued to brandish the rhetorical banner of the Communist Menace, and publicly supported every move of American foreign policy, from the MLF to Vietnam. Erhard was as determined to tie the United States solidly to West Germany through good relations as Washington was determined to tie West Germany safely to the United States to remove the possibility of her following de Gaulle. Hence, while it is true that West German Ostpolitik began to a limited extent under Erhard's chancellorship, Erhard unequivocally committed his administration to the old-fashioned virtues of total reliance on Washington and resolute isolation of the East German regime – which he always carefully referred to in public as the 'so-called German Democratic Republic' or the 'Soviet Occupation Zone'. Schröder's Ostpolitik sought to consolidate East German political isolation by a network of

2. Because of the 'Hallstein Doctrine' of excluding diplomatic relations to states which had recognized the Pankow regime, West Germany had no diplomatic relations with its communist neighbours.

bilateral economic links with its East European neighbours. Its ultimate objective continued to be the demise of the East German regime.

It was the opposition Social Democratic Party leader, Willy Brandt, who saw the opportunity to exploit Ostpolitik for improvement on the issue of reunification, in his policy of *Wandlung durch Annäherung*, or change through rapprochement. Rejecting the all-or-nothing policy of the Adenauer–Erhard governments, Brandt advocated a policy of 'small steps' leading gradually to improved relations between the two German states – moving little by little beyond confrontation to co-operation. Like the Schröder policy, however, Brandt's Ostpolitik initially took no account of the Soviet Union. It assumed that relations could be improved bilaterally, between West Germany and the states of Eastern Europe, including East Germany, independent of Moscow. The resounding defeat of that assumption was eventually to be dramatically demonstrated in the Soviet military occupation of Czechoslovakia in August 1968. Brandt was highly critical of de Gaulle's Nato policy, but his evolving Eastern policy began to sound more like de Gaulle than the so-called German *Gaullisten*.

However personally unpalatable de Gaulle found Erhard's policies, both in principle and in the fact, he none the less could not accomplish his own objectives without West German support. He needed West German support, at least residually, in order to implement his fond dream of European reconciliation. Without West German favour, there could be no European reconciliation, since Germany was the crux of the issue. Europe could only take its rightful place in history again if the Germans played their part. He, de Gaulle, could lead the way, by setting the example of rapprochement in the hope that others would follow. But at the very least, the West Germans must not do anything that would irrevocably seal their fate by alienating Moscow. That was the danger of the MLF.

By the late summer and autumn of 1964, the Russian campaign against the MLF had reached hysteria proportions, as American officials began encouraging the West Germans to suggest publicly that the United States was prepared to go ahead bilaterally on the MLF.[3] De Gaulle now sprang to the defensive. An American–

3. The United States move was Machiavellian, designed to pressure the British

German MLF, which he did not believe possible in 1963, began in 1964 to appear in the offing – posing a real threat of West German access to nuclear weapons and spelling certain disaster for his reconciliation policy. During the summer and autumn of 1964, de Gaulle mobilized every weapon in his diplomatic arsenal in order to deter the West Germans from the MLF road. French diplomats carried on a relentless propaganda campaign with their West German counterparts in Bonn, in Nato headquarters, and in Brussels; de Gaulle himself took the stage in press conferences and public statements, and even went so far as to play a behind-the-scenes game of internal politics by supporting the anti-Erhard faction within the CDU/CSU coalition,[4] who favoured close co-operation with the French in developing a European deterrent rather than footing the bill for the MLF. De Gaulle stepped up in intensity his insistence that Europe in order to be 'European' must be autonomous *vis-à-vis* the United States, must reject 'the division of the universe between two camps, respectively led by Washington and Moscow',[5] must 'unite in order to act'.[6] He warned Erhard that reunification and participation in the MLF were mutually exclusive. Speaking at a luncheon of the Association of Parliamentary Journalists on 5 November, Premier Georges Pompidou summed up the French Government position in regard to the MLF: 'Originally, in the mind of its promoters – that is, the American government – this project was something rather vague. . . .' It was supposed to give its participants, and Germany in particular,

> the feeling that they were not completely outside decisions concerning nuclear weapons. . . . Now, this project seems to have taken on lately a greater reality and a more aggressive consistency. If the multilateral force were to end in the creation of a sort of German–American military alliance . . . we could not consider that such an outcome would be perfectly compatible with the relations we maintain with the

---

Conservative government into commitment to the plan. With British elections due in the autumn of 1964 and the Labour Party on record as opposed to the MLF, American promoters of the scheme tried an oblique pressure tactic. In fact, there is no indication that the United States Government ever considered a bilateral arrangement with the West Germans. But de Gaulle believed the propaganda line. And so, probably, did the West Germans.

4. See above, pp. 198 ff.
5. Press conference of 23 July 1964, *Major Addresses*, vol. II, p. 22.
6. Speech in Strasbourg on the twentieth anniversary of the liberation of the city, quoted in *L'Année politique 1964*, p. 439.

Federal Republic under the terms of the Franco-German treaty.... Nor would this be in keeping with both the French Government and the Opposition conception of the defence of Europe.

In sum, we could ask ourselves ... if such a multilateral force would not be destructive for Europe, provocative for certain other countries, and finally directed more or less against France.[7]

But the French campaign proved in itself largely unsuccessful. What sealed the fate of the MLF was the fact that the Labour Party won the British elections in October 1964. They were on record as opposed not only to the MLF, but to the British deterrent as well.

In reality, the American Government was never prepared to go it alone with the West Germans on the MLF. It would have been difficult to sell the plan to Congress under any circumstances, let alone as a scheme to satisfy the supposed nuclear appetite of the Germans. By the end of 1964, in any case, American concern was turning increasingly away from Europe altogether, and toward escalation in Vietnam.[8] The MLF scheme was never officially repudiated by Washington. It simply faded from the scene at the end of 1964, never to reappear. The demise of the MLF represented the last official attempt at a 'hardware' solution to the problem of nuclear participation.

As French disengagement from Nato and rapprochement with Moscow progressed, French and West German diplomacy grew ever more antagonistically opposed over Nato relations and the future of Europe – defence and *détente*. De Gaulle was not merely undoing Nato, in Bonn's view. He was publicly advocating a radical new political approach to the future of Europe.

Shortly after his recognition of Communist China, de Gaulle turned to the question of the future of Germany at a press conference on 4 February 1965. Before proceeding to a detailed analysis of the German question, de Gaulle summed up France's general policy: 'to see to it that Germany henceforth becomes a definite element of progress and peace; on this condition, to help with its reunification; to make a start and to select the framework

7. *L'Année politique 1964*, pp. 301–2.

8. By the time the Erhard government fell in the autumn of 1966, the shift in priorities in Washington had left Erhard high and dry and bewildered in his policy of total commitment to Washington. Not surprisingly, the new Grand Coalition government was eager to build bridges back to de Gaulle.

which would make this possible'. But what framework? There was first of all the old cold war framework:

> The rivalry between East and West which was taking place on Germany's soil could only aggravate its political and territorial division. It is true that the Soviets, having in their zone imposed a regime modeled on their own, were trying to make believe that, sooner or later, Germany could be reunited under a system of the same kind. . . . For the Soviets to have had a chance of unifying Germany under a system like their own, they would have had to triumph in a world conflict. Now, despite the tension they were maintaining in Berlin, they were careful not to start such a conflict.[9]
>
> On the other hand, the United States, whose policy was at the time led by John Foster Dulles, could think that by strongly reinforcing NATO, the West could make Moscow withdraw and thus restore Germany's unity. But that was only a dream, unless someone made war – something which Washington and its allies were in no way disposed to do. . . . Twenty years have thus elasped without determining Germany's new destiny. Such indetermination, in such a region of the world and at such a time, obviously cannot go on forever. . . . It is clear that real peace, and even more, fruitful relations between East and West, will not be established so long as the German anomalies, the concern they cause and the suffering they entail continue.[10]

This framework, which de Gaulle was in the process of dismissing, was precisely the one Erhard and Johnson continued to reaffirm in their final communiqués, right up until September 1966.[11] De Gaulle, instead, proposed a new framework:

> This matter will not be settled by the direct confrontation of ideologies and forces of the two camps today rivaling each other in the world. What must be done will not be done, one day, except by the understanding and combined action of the peoples who have always been, who are and who will remain principally concerned by the fate of the German neighbor – in short, the European peoples. For them to envisage first examining together, then settling in common, and lastly guaranteeing conjointly the solution to a question which is essentially that of their continent – this is the only way to bring about, this is the only link that can maintain, a Europe in a state of equilibrium, peace and cooperation from one end to the other of the territory which nature has given it.[12]

9. As the Cuban missile crisis had demonstrated. See above, p. 114.
10. Press conference of 4 February 1965, *Major Addresses*, vol. II, pp. 84–5.
11. See below, pp. 166–7.
12. *Major Addresses*, vol. II, p. 85.

The new framework de Gaulle proposed was thus to be a European one. In operational terms, de Gaulle contended that there could and should be no lasting European settlement dealt out by the two superpowers over the heads of the Europeans – no repeat of Yalta. He likewise rejected the notion that a solution would be found through Nato.

Commentators immediately sounded the alarm over de Gaulle's deliberate exclusion of the United States from those responsible for a European settlement. In playing down the superpower confrontation over Europe, de Gaulle was indeed advancing a radical notion – that the Europeans themselves were ultimately responsible for, and eventually capable of, bridging the gulf of separation, of engineering a European political settlement and ultimately establishing a new system of European security. But de Gaulle was far from proposing a prototype of a European security conference, at which the states of Europe would presumably set a date for a summit conference to decide on Germany's fate. He saw the process as one of gradual evolution, and based on fundamental conditions:

> Certainly, the success of such a vast and difficult undertaking implies many conditions. Russia must evolve in such a way that it sees its future, not through totalitarian constraint imposed on its own land and on others, but through progress accomplished in common by free men and peoples. The nations which it has satellized must be able to play their role in a renewed Europe. It must be recognized, first of all by Germany, that any settlement of which it would be the subject, would necessarily imply a settlement of its frontiers and of its armaments in agreement with all its neighbors, those to the East and those to the West.[13]

What de Gaulle was in fact describing was a new international system, beyond the cold war, within which the 'rejuvenated old continent' could realize its 'world ambition . . . in the progress of the two billion men who desperately need it'.[14] It was the old dream.

The West German Government could hardly have been expected to respond with joy to de Gaulle's renewed insistence that reunification had to await something so improbable in the near future as the internal transformation of the communist system; but he had said that before. What was new was the

13. *Major Addresses*, vol. II, p. 85.
14. *Major Addresses*, vol. II, p. 85.

suggestion that Germany's fate should be meted out by her neighbours, and with permanent aspects of discrimination, notably in regard to armaments.[15] The omission of an American role in the proposed German settlement also aroused fears in Bonn that de Gaulle's recent policy of rapprochement with Moscow might operate at Germany's expense. Franco-Russian alliances were, after all, historically anti-German. Were the French preparing to go so far as to recognize formally the Oder–Neisse frontier or the East German regime? Would de Gaulle compromise political positions and interests considered vital by the West German Government? What was de Gaulle up to? All eyes in Bonn were, thus, riveted on de Gaulle's spectacular two-week visit to Moscow in June 1966.

The joint Franco-Soviet statement issued at the end of de Gaulle's visit was, however – to Bonn's great relief – a paragon of discreet diplomacy. All that was said regarding the German question was that the two governments had 'exchanged views'. De Gaulle had given away nothing. In fact, de Gaulle had resisted Kosygin's strong pressure to recognize the East German state because he was determined not to endorse the *status quo* as such.

The Soviets were apparently courting French favour, as evidenced by the small victories of rhetoric they accorded the French. In regard to European security, the Soviet Government agreed to a statement whose wording could only have originated at the Quai d'Orsay:

> The two governments agree that the problems of Europe should be, first of all, discussed within a European framework. They believe that the states of the continent should dedicate their efforts to create conditions necessary for the agreements which must be reached and, in particular, to establish an atmosphere of *détente* between all countries, both East and West. Such an atmosphere would indeed facilitate rapprochement and *entente* between them, and thus, the discussion and settlement of the problems confronting them. For both France and the Soviet Union, the first goal, within this spirit, is the normalization, and then the development of relations between all European countries. . . .[16]

15. The non-proliferation treaty, which Washington was shortly to urge on the West Germans, entailed precisely the same acceptance of permanent nuclear discrimination.

16. 'Déclaration commune franco-soviétique', *Sélection hebdomadaire du Monde*, 30 juin–6 juillet 1966.

Détente, *entente*, *coopération*. For West Germany, of course, 'normalization of relations' could not be accomplished without abandoning the Hallstein Doctrine, the veritable cornerstone of Bonn's foreign policy.[17] The Soviet Government considered this a primordial objective; for the Erhard government, on the other hand, this was a non-acceptable alternative.

The old Nato party line held that the key to *détente* in Europe was German reunification, and that no real peace in Europe was possible without a prior German settlement. The fragile Soviet bloc could not hold out in the end against the strength and magnetic attraction of the West. The strength and unity of Nato, therefore, would ultimately compel the Soviet Union to agree to a settlement on Germany favourable to the West. *Détente* would come about following the reunification of Germany by free elections, in that order. But now, de Gaulle was step by step withdrawing from Nato, weakening its unity, and actively courting the Russians – in short, reversing the priorities, giving East–West *détente* priority over German reunification. The West Germans obviously had a certain stake in the old scheme – not primarily because of the political importance of reunification, but above all because the old policy guaranteed its security and placed West Germany at the centre of alliance concerns. It amounted to an extraordinary bargaining lever in advancing the interests of West German foreign policy. In the old scheme, security and eventually reunification were both dependent on the American guarantee: the simplest logic therefore dictated out-and-out West German support of American policy. The West German Government had no desire to see American involvement weakened – on the contrary.

The MLF episode had not been ended by Bonn, but by Washington. Despite the embarrassment that the metamorphosis of the MLF into the nebulous McNamara Committee caused his government, Chancellor Erhard none the less reaffirmed his government's policy of unflinching reliance on Washington and full support for American foreign policy across the board. In return, the final communiqués of the meetings between Chancellor Erhard and US President Lyndon Johnson always dutifully reiterated the tried and true party line on German reunification:

17. The Grand Coalition government proceeded to do precisely that less than one year later, when it established diplomatic relations with Rumania.

President Johnson reaffirmed the objective of the reunification of Germany as one of the most significant goals of American foreign policy. Chancellor Erhard stressed the human suffering which results from the continuing artificial division of Germany, and the President and Chancellor agreed that a solution of the German problem on the basis of self-determination was essential in the interest of humanity as well as of lasting peace in Europe. They emphasized the right and duty of the Government of the Federal Republic of Germany, as the only freely elected Government of the German people, to speak and to stand for their interests until the German nation has been made whole. They agreed that the freedom of Berlin must be preserved and that the problem of Berlin can be resolved only within the framework of the peaceful reunification of Germany.[18]

This apparent convergence of West German and American policy under Erhard was paralleled by great strains at all levels in French–German relations – strains that worsened as French European policy moved actively toward *détente*.

Once the high hopes of the Franco-German treaty had foundered on the rocks of West German internal politics and American intervention, de Gaulle had revamped his policy toward West Germany. On the one hand, he pushed the West Germans unabashedly for concessions on a common EEC agricultural policy, alternately by threat of withdrawal and by holding out now and then some ambiguous promise of progress on political unity; and on the other hand, he struck out resolutely on his Eastern policy of *détente*, *entente*, *coopération*, in the hope that the West Germans would eventually see the light and follow his example. All in all, French policy toward West Germany throughout the Erhard years consisted in dragging West Germany along as much as possible, while attempting to neutralize the potential negative effects of what de Gaulle viewed as American obstructionism – such as the MLF and the policy of Atlantic Partnership.

De Gaulle considered his *détente* policy as a policy of movement, designed ultimately to alter the existing *status quo* in Europe. In de Gaulle's view, his policy differed from *détente* between the two superpowers precisely in that the price for improved relations between the United States and the Soviet Union would assuredly be acceptance of the *status quo* in Europe. French policy was based

18. Joint communiqué, 27 September 1966, *Department of State Bulletin*, LV (17 October 1966), pp. 583–4.

on de Gaulle's belief that through economic and cultural interpenetration among the states of Europe, a new atmosphere of co-operation would replace the old atmosphere of suspicion and hostility. Economic ties would not alone solve political problems, but political attitudes would surely evolve in an improved atmosphere of limited but concrete co-operation.

De Gaulle's European policy did not change fundamentally during the remainder of his tenure of office, despite dramatic setbacks such as the Soviet occupation of Czechoslovakia in August 1968.[19] There were, however, indications that, shortly before his resignation in early 1969, he had reassessed the implications of the Prague crisis and was exploring a policy shift in his conversation with British Ambassador Christopher Soames.[20] None the less, to obtain the moderate political evolution in Europe that was the long-term objective of French policy, there was no real alternative to an active *détente* policy, whatever the setbacks. Thus, despite the apparent failure of his policy in the Prague crisis, de Gaulle continued to dedicate the full efforts of French foreign policy toward the goal of *détente* in Eastern Europe. He remained fully committed to the goal of 'normalizing' relations between the states of Europe as the means to an ultimate settlement of the 'German anomalies'. During his last years in office, it was American policy toward Europe, and finally, West German policy, which changed in orientation.

The fall of the Erhard government in the autumn of 1966 over economic policy coincided with a dramatic shift in priorities in American policy toward Europe. Under-Secretary of State George Ball and the European specialists at the State Department had contended, and continued to argue forcefully, that West European political union must be the first priority of American policy toward Europe, that West Germany must be securely anchored to the West until political union is achieved. The MLF, the Atlantic Partnership scheme, and the struggle against de Gaulle were all part of the State Department world view, which, curiously enough, had favoured a 'hardware' solution to the nuclear sharing problem within Nato, rather than a consultative solution – which, paradoxically, was eventually advocated by the Pentagon. But by the summer of 1968, other voices were being heard – among them former Secretary of the Treasury Douglas

19. See below, pp. 171 ff.

20. See below, chapter 10, pp. 173 ff.

Dillon, Defense Secretary Robert McNamara, Presidential Security Advisor McGeorge Bundy, and Senator Frank Church – demanding a change in United States priorities.

> They want to trade the mixed nuclear force for a treaty against the spread of nuclear weapons, if possible. They want to encourage Bonn, as Mr. Bundy suggested at a Congressional hearing yesterday, to accept the Oder–Neisse boundary with Poland; to renounce the 1938 Munich Pact . . . , to establish diplomatic relations with the Eastern European nations, and finally to renounce nuclear weapons for all time.
>
> In effect, they are asking the Administration to accept publicly the premise that a gradual process of East–West accommodation is the only possible approach to a German settlement and to sever its alliance with the most conservative forces in Bonn.[21]

The advocates of change in American policy were beginning to sound very much like de Gaulle indeed. Writing in the October 1966 issue of *Foreign Affairs*, Senator Frank Church, a member of the Senate Foreign Relations Committee, remarked:

> I am personally convinced that the State Department errs in preaching that reunification will come about by 'the adhesion of the East German people to some . . . system of Western unity' – in other words, by appending themselves to a united Western Europe.
>
> What seems far more likely is that a German settlement will be reached as a last stage in a gradual healing of the breach between the two parts of Europe. And the price the German people will have to pay for reunification will surely include abstention from nuclear arms. By preserving the option of Bonn's participation in an improbable Western European deterrent force, are we not jeopardizing the possibility of German reunification as part of a Central European settlement?[22]

On 27 September 1966, Lyndon Johnson and Ludwig Erhard signed a traditional final communiqué, reaffirming all the usual shibboleths from Atlantic Partnership to Bonn's right to represent the entire German nation.[23] Ten days later, on 7 October, President Johnson delivered an address entitled 'Making Europe Whole: an Unfinished Task', in which he firmly committed

21. Max Frankel, 'U.S. Policy on Europe: Pressure Builds to Give East–West Détente Priority over German Unity', *New York Times*, 22 June 1966.

22. 'U.S. Policy and the "New Europe"', *Foreign Affairs* 45 (October 1966), p. 56.

23. See above, pp. 166–7. It was scant compensation for the fact that Washington's attention had shifted so markedly that, through a slip-up in protocol, no one was on hand to welcome Erhard at the airport on his arrival.

United States policy to a new set of priorities in Europe. 'Our purpose', the President began,

is not to overturn other governments, but to help the people of Europe to achieve:

- a continent in which the peoples of Eastern and Western Europe work together for the common good;
- a continent in which alliances do not confront each other in bitter hostility, but provide a framework in which West and East can act together to assure the security of all.

In a restored Europe, Germany can and will be united.

This remains a vital purpose of American policy. It can only be accomplished through a growing reconciliation. There is no short-cut.[24]

Johnson's policy of 'building bridges to Eastern Europe' included an important expansion of trade made possible by extending commercial credits, liberalization of travel, negotiation of a civil air agreement between the United States and the Soviet Union, and exchange of cloud photographs from weather satellites.

Further, it is our policy to avoid the spread of national nuclear programs – in Europe and elsewhere. That is why we shall persevere in efforts to reach an agreement banning the proliferation of nuclear weapons. . . .

If changing circumstances should lead to a gradual and balanced revision in force levels on both sides, the revision could . . . help gradually to shape a new political environment.

The building of true peace and reconciliation in Europe will be a long process.[25]

With the French military withdrawal from the Nato integrated command barely over, the issue of the stationing of French troops in West Germany still locked in difficult negotiations, the British wavering over withdrawal of the army on the Rhine, the West Germans were now confronted with Johnson's proposal of mutual balanced force reductions (MBFR). Talk of United States force levels pointed in only one direction – gradual withdrawal of United States forces from West Germany. The growing crisis in West German–American relations – the fear of isolation and abandonment in the face of Soviet political pressure – left the Bonn Government with nowhere to turn, but back to Paris and to some new initiatives of its own.

24. Quoted in *Department of State Bulletin*, LV (17 October 1966), p. 623.
25. *Department of State Bulletin*, LV (17 October 1966), p. 625.

The new Grand Coalition government of Christian Democratic Chancellor Kurt-Georg Kiesinger[26] and Socialist Foreign Minister Willy Brandt set out to mend the broken fences of the Franco-German Treaty, and to work together with the French Government on initiatives to improve relations with Eastern Europe. Both Kiesinger and Brandt were firmly committed to reconciliation with France as a primordial goal of West German policy.

As foreign minister of West Germany, Gerhard Schröder had been from the outset committed to non-application of the Franco-German Treaty.[27] While he had opposed the preamble for procedural reasons of legal formality, the preamble certainly represented the substance of Schröder's policy. By 1967, when the Grand Coalition took office, de Gaulle had moved from his policy of privileged partnership with West Germany as the prototype of West European political co-operation toward priority to *détente* with the East. Consequently, while he welcomed the Kiesinger government's dedication to resume cordial relations, he none the less resolutely continued down the road toward his vision of *l'Europe européenne*, through *détente*, *entente* and *coopération* with the East. What remained of the Franco-German Treaty was its pragmatic, operational side – the framework of regular meetings between various ministers and the heads of state. Gestures of Franco-German good will abounded throughout the winter and spring of 1966–7. But in the end, although there was limited progress on Ostpolitik,[28] disagreement continued over the issue of the British EEC application, over the pro-Arab French Middle-Eastern policy, over West European political unity, over the non-proliferation treaty – which the French urged the West Germans to sign – and, finally, over international monetary policy. No concerted policy emerged.

The Czech crisis of August 1968 dealt a sobering setback to French Eastern policy in that it demonstrated all too brutally that the Soviet Union was in no way prepared to allow gradual

26. It will be recalled that Kiesinger had participated in the negotiations setting up the Franco-German Youth Office. See above, p. 126.

27. See above, pp. 98–9.

28. The Grand Coalition government resisted French pressure to establish contacts with East Germany and to recognize the Oder–Neisse Line. Its Ostpolitik was still basically aimed at isolating East Germany. It was not a policy of full commitment to *détente*.

internal 'liberalization' to challenge its political control over Eastern Europe. A critical factor in the Czech crisis was, some thought, Prague's enthusiastic response to the Grand Coalition government's Ostpolitik, which appeared to score significant victories in Czechoslovakia, with the political effect of isolating East Germany and challenging Soviet interests directly. Bonn's policy at that time did not seek to counterbalance progress in bilateral relations with Eastern Europe with improved West German–Soviet relations.[29] Furthermore, within West Germany, Socialists were publicly exulting over the Dubček regime's 'new economics' as the prototype for the socialism of the future. The Czech situation was, thus, uniquely loaded in potential for political confrontation. The combined effect of the West German role in Czechoslovakia and the snowballing pace of internal loosening up produced a challenge to the political and strategic *status quo*. Moscow's response was to re-establish control by armed intervention in a brutal display of the limits of *détente*.

De Gaulle roundly condemned the Soviet action in Czechoslovakia. In his interpretation, the intervention demonstrated that 'the Soviet Union had not abandoned the *politique des blocs*' imposed on Europe by the Yalta agreements, in which the great powers had divided up spheres of influence in Europe.[30] With or without the Yalta shibboleth, it was certainly true that the strategic demarcation line between the Soviet Union and the United States divided Europe in two, and, to that extent, de Gaulle was correct in his assessment that *la politique des blocs*, in the form of the strategic balance between the two superpowers, was at stake in the Czech crisis.

De Gaulle none the less remained firm in his commitment to France's role as champion of *détente* in Europe. At a press conference on 9 September 1968, he addressed himself at length to the question of French *détente* policy in the perspective of the Czech crisis:

The events within the communist bloc having Czechoslovakia both

29. With the fall of the Grand Coalition government in September 1969, the new chancellor, Willy Brandt, following the French lead, entrusted Egon Bahr, as his personal representative, to improve relations with Moscow. Progress was thereafter rapid in re-establishing political relations with Poland, East Germany, and eventually Czechoslovakia.

30. 'Déclaration du 21 août 1968', in *L'Année politique 1968*, p. 271.

as their theatre and their victim appear worthy of condemnation to us, above all because they are absurd within a perspective of European *détente*. I want to say that her people's enthusiasm over the beginnings of liberation; and then their moral unity *vis-à-vis* the occupier; and finally their repugnance in accepting the return to subjection – taken together with the reprobation expressed everywhere in the West of our continent at the prospect of a return of the cold war – all demonstrate that, although our policy may appear momentarily unfounded, it is in conformity with basic realities in Europe; and consequently, it is a good policy....

It is too late for any ideology, notably communism, to win out over national feelings. Taking account of the general aspiration toward progress and peace, it is too late to succeed in dividing Europe forever into two opposed blocks....[31]

De Gaulle did not, therefore, alter the fundamental commitment of French policy to a new European order based on 'rapprochement ... through bilateral or multilateral relations'[32] with the states of Eastern Europe. Yet, clearly, his hope for movement had been thwarted. As Michel Debré put it so eloquently before the foreign affairs commission of the National Assembly on 29 August 1968: 'It is not because there has been an accident on a road that one should close the road to traffic.'[33] De Gaulle saw evolution as a long road – Czechoslovakia had proved that it might be longer than some hoped – yet he remained convinced that the Soviet Union could not indefinitely sustain the strain of military occupation to prevent political evolution, and that *détente* would ultimately replace the rigid confrontation of blocs in Europe.

There were, none the less, indications that de Gaulle had begun to reassess French European policy in the wake of Prague, at least in emphasis. The Soviet response to what amounted to the success of Western *détente* policy – slamming the door to political evolution and demonstrating Moscow's readiness to have recourse to armed intervention to impose its political will – suggested the wisdom of seeking again to strengthen the position of Western Europe through concerted action. With the British EEC application still pending, British Ambassador to France Christopher

31. *L'Année politique 1968*, p. 279.

32. See remarks of Foreign Minister Maurice Schumann in the National Assembly debate, 9 June 1971, in *Politique étrangère de la France: Textes et Documents*, 1er semestre 1971, p. 231.

33. Quoted in *L'Année politique 1968*, p. 272.

Soames had requested an audience with President de Gaulle. De Gaulle finally responded by inviting him to a private meeting at the Elysée Palace on 4 February 1969. According to Soames's account[34], de Gaulle ranged broadly over the history of the postwar period before zeroing in on the substance of what he had to say. The European ideal had been profoundly compromised by the pro-American sentiments both of the states of Western Europe and of Great Britain. But Europe must be independent. There is some disagreement over whether, as the British claimed, de Gaulle went on to say that if Europe were truly independent, there would be no need for the Atlantic Alliance. Michel Debré rejects this interpretation, maintaining that de Gaulle asserted simply that a new situation would arise, should Europe become truly independent. If Britain entered the EEC, de Gaulle went on, the Community would perforce change in the direction of a free-trade zone, with the widening of the Community to all of Britain's EFTA partners. De Gaulle had no objection to that change, and was willing to move in that direction in exchange for tangible progress toward European political co-operation. 'He would be quite prepared to discuss with us what should take the place of the Common Market as an enlarged European Economic Association.'[35] Secret exploratory talks between France and Great Britain could establish whether there were sufficient views in common to justify proceeding further. If so, de Gaulle suggested a political directorate – 'un Conseil restreint d'association politique' – comprising Great Britain, France, West Germany and Italy could be set up. If the British Government were interested, he would welcome their taking the initiative in proposing such talks, which he would then welcome.

The upshot of the Soames conversation was, unfortunately, *l'affaire Soames*. The British Foreign Office, suspicious of de Gaulle's motives, and attaching great importance to de Gaulle's words, feared that de Gaulle might use his conversation with Soames to discredit Great Britain in the eyes of France's EEC partners. The Foreign Office, therefore, recommended insistently that Prime Minister Wilson inform Chancellor Kiesinger of the

34. A Foreign Office account of the meeting was leaked to the London *Times*, 22 February 1969, and was picked up by *Le Monde*, 23–4 February 1969.

35. Harold Wilson, *The Labour Government 1964–70: A Personal Record*, London, Weidenfeld, 1971, Boston, Little, Brown, 1971, p. 610.

conversation during their forthcoming meeting in Bonn. They further circulated, without Wilson's approval, a full report on the Soames conversation to all relevant diplomatic posts. In his memoirs, Wilson goes to great pains to make clear his opposition to, and anger at, the Foreign Office handling of the affair, pointing out the extent to which they resisted his lead and forced the situation; whereas his own view was that de Gaulle's proposals should be considered much more seriously before acting.[36] He himself did not see much that had not been said before in what de Gaulle had said.

The French were infuriated as they began gleaning reports back from European capitals of the British action in informing their partners of the Soames conversation, and eventually brought the matter to a head by boycotting meetings of the Western European Union, and announcing that they would play no further role within the organization. Accounts of the Soames conversation began to appear in French newspapers. Finally, the Foreign Office leaked to the London *Times* the full report that had been sent to British diplomatic posts, and that, in turn, was picked up by *Le Monde*. *L'Affaire Soames* exploded. French–British relations had reached an all-time low, and probably would have taken far longer to recover, were it not for the departure of de Gaulle from office at the end of April over a referendum on regional reform, on whose success he had engaged his continuation in office.[37]

Whatever the exact terms of the Soames–de Gaulle conversation were – and the British account was subsequently challenged on several points by Foreign Minister Michel Debré and Bernard Tricot, Secretary-General of the Elysée – the gist of de Gaulle's proposals is revealing. In the first place, de Gaulle did believe that the British entry would profoundly alter the existing Common Market structures. He had already expressed that reservation to Macmillan at Rambouillet in 1962.[38] In the second place, he was now less concerned by that prospect than he was interested

36. Wilson, *The Labour Government 1964–70*, p. 611.

37. The defeat over regional reform mobilized both the opponents of de Gaulle and the opponents of the proposed constitutional changes. Former Prime Minister Pompidou had won respect in his resolute handling of the May 1968 student uprising; consequently, de Gaulle was no longer the only political figure who could guarantee public order and the stability of state institutions. In these circumstances, he was defeated in the referendum and resigned. Pompidou was elected President in June, with a strong second-ballot majority.

38. See Macmillan, *At the End of the Day*, pp. 349 ff.

in the possible political role of Great Britain in Europe. He was eager to enlist British co-operation in building a political Europe, independent of the United States, and he had in mind an institutional form for that objective, once he had established that there was enough common ground between France and Great Britain to warrant proceeding. The Fouchet Plan had failed, despite the agreement of France, West Germany and Italy, because of small-power opposition. The quadripartite directorate de Gaulle proposed to Soames bypassed them altogether.

De Gaulle retired in the spring of 1969, before the government of Chancellor Willy Brandt, which succeeded the Grand Coalition in September 1969, set out on a path of establishing contacts with the Soviet Union and Poland which would eventually result in the recognition of the Oder–Neisse Line, in treaties with Poland and between the two German states, in the unilateral repudiation of the Munich Pact, and the re-establishment of relations with Czechoslovakia. It was the kind of *grande politique* that might eventually pave the way for the realization of *l'Europe européenne*. . . .

Sans doute, ces conditions paraissent-elles très complexes et ces détails semblent-ils bien longs. Mais quoi! La solution d'un problème aussi vaste que celui de l'Allemagne ne peut avoir que de grandes dimensions et de grandes conséquences.[39]

39. Press conference of 4 February 1965, in *L'Année politique 1965*, p. 430. 'Doubtless, these conditions do appear very complex and these delays do seem long indeed. But what else! The solution of so vast a problem as that of Germany can only have great dimensions and great consequences.'

CHAPTER TEN

Conclusion: The Contingencies of Change

Life is a combat during which there is never a victory that is decisively won. Even on the day of an Austerlitz, the sun does not shine on the battle-field.

De Gaulle, *Mémoires d'espoir*, p. 174

It is tempting, in assessing de Gaulle's European policy over the period since the close of World War II, to stress the continuities over the new directions – or to view the latter as merely dressed-up versions of the same old ambitions. In this view, de Gaulle's policies may all be reduced to one over-arching goal: promoting the *grandeur* of France, her pre-eminence and predominance in world affairs in the twilight of her power. One begins with the convenient quotation from his memoirs in which he depicts France as a fairy princess, and goes on to show how his irrational delusions of grandeur shine through all his policies, from the Nato Directorate scheme to the *force de frappe*, while viewing his European policy simply as an escalator designed to procure an enlarged power base for his nationalist ambitions in the name of France. *Grandeur* and *éclat* thus furnish the window-dressings for what is essentially old-style French nationalism in a modern setting. This interpretation has had a long career in American official circles, and, alas, in only slightly more attenuated form, in academic circles as well. There is little doubt that the *grandeur* and *éclat* of de Gaulle's brilliant rhetoric and brusque gesture went far toward perpetrating this view of his policies – to that extent, he was the first victim of his own mystique, in that his failure to win others over to his views often resulted from the antagonism provoked by his rhetoric and manner. But beneath the *mise-en-scène* of *grandeur*, de Gaulle was a shrewd observer of international politics and an accomplished master of the interplay of old issues and new opportunities.

The rhetoric of *grandeur* in fact constituted a kind of national cement, joining together in determination and sentimental longing a morally disillusioned and internally torn nation. Boiled down to a more commonplace reality, *grandeur* translated the on-going desire to play a role of major responsibility, to exert an effective influence on the direction of international politics, rather than surrendering responsibility, then settling for passive acquiescence to an American policy which was often in real conflict with French interests.[1] The rhetoric also served to divert attention from the complete withdrawal of France back to her continental borders – the end of a process in which successively Indo-China, Tunisia and Morocco, the former French Empire in Africa, and eventually Algeria as well, were surrendered, leaving in their aftermath bitter internal violence and defeat. It provided an outlet for the reaffirmation of France's determination to carry on, in the face of apparent decline and despair. The rhetoric was, however, certainly more than a calculated gesture – it was a style altogether natural to de Gaulle, and its vitality was undoubtedly due to the conviction he brought to it. In that sense, the *grand homme* de Gaulle corresponded remarkably to the need for renewed self-affirmation of France. He personified in many ways the ambition the nation required to avoid the despair of internal collapse.[2] He both understood that, and played on it. Only a leader of the moral stature of de Gaulle could compensate for the disillusionment of defeat sufficiently to rescue France from the threat of social and political disintegration brought on by its resistance to decolonization, coupled with its wartime collapse and occupation. On the other hand, the practical realities – the concrete ambitions, the retreats, the bargains and trades that are the stuff of politics – these, too, were essential ingredients of de Gaulle's policies.

1. 'Independence without renunciation but without arrogance, with a concern for honour and dignity; the determination to be neither self-effacing nor non-autonomous – which does not in the least exclude a keen awareness of possibilities – isn't this, after all, that policy of *grandeur* on which so much ink has been spilled? Does it really mean more than the desire to be and to remain oneself?' Couve de Murville, *Une Politique étrangère*, p. 482.

2. See Stanley and Inge Hoffmann, 'The Will to Grandeur: de Gaulle as Political Artist', *Daedalus* (summer 1968), pp. 829–87.

When de Gaulle returned to power in 1958, very little remained of his early postwar European policy. The division of the continent at Yalta had hardened as the cold war pitted the two superpowers against one another in a dramatic contest for Europe. The new international system based on bipolar confrontation had resulted in an uneasy stalemate symbolized by the continued division of Germany, the emergence of two rearmed German client-states, and the isolation of its divided former capital. European civilization knew no such artificial demarcation line between West and East. French and Germans both viewed the political legacy of the war as a provisional arrangement, to be suffered but not accepted as permanent. The intensity of their revisionism depended above all on the degree of interpenetration of issues of international politics and domestic politics. For the Bonn Government, whose whole constitutional order was presumably provisional, the issue of reunification, the question of Germany's eastern frontiers, and the future of Berlin were the primary concerns both of domestic and foreign policy.[3] The 'Provisorium' of the Bonn Government, in effect, made possible a *modus vivendi* in which revisionist goals could be acceptably postponed so long as domestic politics continued to acknowledge their ultimate validity. But this, in turn, meant that domestic politics were riveted on the Government's foreign policy behaviour; for the ultimate security of the West German state hinged on the international context.

For the French, too, the international context was a critical factor in internal politics. The French Government's commitment to *détente* included the important domestic fringe benefit of neutralizing the opposition of a strong Communist Party, which continued to win the support of 20–25 per cent of the French electorate. But *détente* was, beyond that, a worthy goal in itself. *Détente* promised, in the first place, freedom from an always reluctant dependence on Washington; and secondly, the resumption of 'normal' relations with the countries of central Europe, and with Soviet Russia, traditional focuses of French continental policy.

The desire to escape subordination to Washington reflected a chronic divergence in perceived interests between Paris and

3. See Karl Kaiser, *German Foreign Policy in Transition*, London, Oxford University Press for the Royal Institute of International Affairs, 1968.

Washington, both in conception and in the event. The persistent conflict over goals and the frustrations of subordination are evident enough, to cite just a few examples, in the German occupation policy of the immediate postwar period, in the hassle over German rearmament, in the humiliation of the Suez episode, and throughout the Algerian affair. In addition, the French Government was less wont than Washington to view the European policy of the Soviet Union as expansionist-communism-in-action, i.e. as an aggressive ideological crusade buttressed by military power. As de Gaulle put it to Eisenhower, 'After what has happened to Russia during the two world wars, do you really think that a Peter the Great would have handled the question of borders and territorial claims differently than Stalin did?'[4] Whereas the urgent need for military security during the cold war had coerced French policy into alignment with Washington – including rapprochement with Germany – the West German Government, owing its very creation to the cold war, found a total identity between its interests and the stated goals of American policy.

So long as the military and ideological confrontation between the United States and the Soviet Union continued in the form of Soviet efforts to alter the *status quo* by threat of force or by blackmail, there was, objectively, little leeway for French policy. De Gaulle sought, none the less, to improve France's position in Alliance diplomacy, to temper its passive dependence on Washington, and to enlarge the scope of the Alliance to win support for French policy in Algeria through the proposed Nato Directorate scheme. When that failed, as he expected it would, he turned to the West European forum.

The Fouchet Plan was clearly the prototype for de Gaulle's vision of future pan-European co-operation. In its proposed form, it promised at least a beginning, in the West, of the formulation of an independent concerted policy among the Six, which might set the example and eventually pave the way for a broader association. It would serve to anchor West Germany securely to the West, while forging in the West a union capable of dealings with the communist bloc in the East. The Fouchet Plan met its doom in an atmosphere of distrust and confusion, engendered in part by the fear of Franco-German domination of the proposed

4. De Gaulle, *War Memoirs*, p. 224.

union, and buttressed in the end by conflicting arguments in favour of both supranationalism and the prior inclusion of Great Britain.

The return to favour of supranationalism was, to say the least, intriguing, in that the Treaty of Rome, establishing the Common Market (which was signed before de Gaulle's return to power), actually represented a very substantial setback to supranationalism, when compared with the earlier treaty establishing the Coal and Steel Community. De Gaulle's rejection of the federalist path to union (essentially, majority vote) was well known. Paradoxically, had there been majority vote during the Fouchet negotiations, the Dutch opposition would have been in a minority and the Union would have been achieved. In practice, the Dutch were unwilling to go ahead with any political union until British membership guaranteed them a powerful defender of their interests against the Franco-German *entente* they feared.

The issue of the British entry was complex. For France, there was not merely the question of Britain's equivocal political commitment, but, more critically still, the question of what British membership would mean in the impending struggle over agricultural policy. It was not, after all, so clear that the British application for membership represented a very substantial change of direction. Quite the contrary. Macmillan had tried repeatedly in private conversations to urge de Gaulle to torpedo the Rome treaty in favour of a free trade area,[5] and, only when this had failed, had turned toward the Common Market – moreover, with uncommon promotion on the part of Washington. If de Gaulle had rejected Macmillan's appeals to jettison the Common Market, it was because, by his own account, he saw its advantage as an economic instrument, and his own 'conversion' was strictly limited to its economic utility: to spur the urgently required modernization of French industry and, still more, to spread out the cost of modernization and support of French agriculture.

> I must say that if in resuming responsibility for policy, I adopted the Common Market from the outset, it was because of our situation as an agricultural country, as well as the progress to be imposed on our industry. To be sure, I was not unaware that in order to include agriculture effectively within the Community we would have to act vigorously *vis-à-vis* our partners, whose interests are not the same as

5. See de Gaulle, *Mémoires d'espoir*, pp. 230 ff.

ours in this domain. But I insisted that this matter was for France a condition *sine qua non* of her participation.[6]

The inclusion of Britain in the Common Market before the agricultural agreements had been concluded was certain to undermine the French Government's chances of success in pressuring its reluctant partners to make the concessions which it considered absolutely crucial. That in itself was reason enough for delaying over the issue of British entry,[7] quite apart from the more publicized misgivings de Gaulle entertained about Britain's Atlanticist heresy – which, in any event, was shared to a greater or lesser degree by all her EEC partners. Britain was perhaps prepared to contract a *mariage de raison* in joining Europe for the commercial benefits she would obtain as an industrial nation, but she was by no means prepared at that juncture to commit herself fully to forgoing the advantages of low food prices and Commonwealth preferences in order to purchase French surpluses at much higher prices within a community-supported agricultural market.[8] Secondly, de Gaulle reasoned, British membership would perforce entail the entry of all Britain's EFTA partners, diluting still further the cohesiveness of the EEC as the economic instrument the French Government required.[9] In 1962, de Gaulle was not willing to run that risk. Finally, Britain's military–political commitment was not to the continent, but to her special relationship with Washington, as was made amply clear during the Skybolt–Polaris episode. But even while continuing to bar the way to British membership in the Common Market, de Gaulle continued to court the British discreetly behind the scenes on the possibility of political–military co-operation, as evidenced in his pre-Nassau conversations with Macmillan at Rambouillet, as well as much later on in the Soames affair.[10]

The Soames conversation was not out of keeping with the feelers de Gaulle put out to Macmillan at several turns – at Rambouillet in December 1962, for one. At that point, de Gaulle

6. De Gaulle, *Mémoires d'espoir*, p. 167.

7. This conclusion is, moreover, clearly borne out in Macmillan's account of the Rambouillet meeting with de Gaulle. See Macmillan, *At the End of the Day*, p. 349.

8. On the importance of the agricultural question for the outcome of negotiations with Britain, see Couve de Murville, *Une Politique étrangère*, pp. 397–410.

9. De Gaulle expressed this reservation openly to Macmillan in their conversations at Rambouillet in 1962. See also above, p. 134.

10. See above, pp. 173 ff.

was promoting Anglo-French nuclear co-operation, and was eager to enlist Macmillan's support in a British–French programme to serve as the nucleus for a European nuclear defence effort which could eventually supplant Nato. While de Gaulle would never have proceeded on such a venture with the West Germans, he saw the Franco–British combination as the logic of the future, if Europe were to be responsible for its own security. It was clear to him, as it has been to multiple writers on the subject, that only Europe with Great Britain 'may hope to attain the degree of independence of the superpowers that many Europeans wish her to achieve'.[11] But, at the very least, Great Britain had to be wholly committed to that goal: such was the political litmus-paper test to which de Gaulle repeatedly subjected the British over the question of Common Market entry – it was not so simply that, in petty nationalist terms, British entry would challenge French leadership – which, of course, was true. It was rather that the direction of whatever leadership Great Britain would exert had to be congenial to French interests. If Great Britain were to serve as the American Trojan Horse,[12] her contribution to leadership was unacceptable; whereas if she was prepared to embark on a common cause with France, the marriage was welcome. West European political co-operation, thus, continued to interest de Gaulle.

The hapless Fouchet Plan had represented de Gaulle's initial framework for West European political co-operation. The failure of the Fouchet negotiations was a bitter personal disappointment and a substantial setback for one of his highest foreign policy priorities,[13] even though he himself had contributed to its failure through his mishandling of the negotiations. The Franco-German substitute was a second best. This time, de Gaulle paid very careful attention to the political–psychological atmosphere attending the preferential relations the two countries were committed to establishing. Not one ingredient of the historical drama of reconciliation went unexploited. France and

11. Curt Gasteyger, *Europe in the Seventies*, London, Institute for Strategic Studies, Adelphi Papers, no. 37, June 1967, p. 12.

12. It has often been pointed out that West Germany was in fact still more of a Trojan Horse for US policy in Europe, but that conclusion neglects the fact that West Germany could not have exercised diplomatic leadership, despite her economic power, because the moral component of influence was lacking.

13. See Couve de Murville, *Une Politique étrangère*, p. 362.

Germany were to set an example for the others, to form a nucleus through which wider European political co-operation might yet be realized along the lines of the Fouchet Plan. This policy failed in the short run[14] for three reasons: (1) the wavering of the West German commitment to preferential relations with France as a result of shifts within the domestic political context, (2) the intrusion of an assertive US policy whose stated purpose was to deter Bonn from making common cause with de Gaulle's France, and (3) the primacy of security in West German politics and the impossibility of France's substituting for the US guarantee, once the issue of Franco-German co-operation came under direct fire from Washington.

By the end of 1962, the positions of Adenauer and de Gaulle within their respective domestic political systems were very different. De Gaulle, secure as *de facto* leader of a relatively cohesive parliamentary majority party, the UNR, enjoyed the assured backing, in a showdown, of the only domestic challenger to his foreign policy. His control over foreign policy was further reinforced by the effective transfer of decision-making from the Quai d'Orsay to the Elysée. As leader of an internally divided Christian Democratic Party, and chancellor in a governmental coalition deeply shaken by the removal of Franz-Josef Strauss, CSU leader and Adenauer's surest supporter in his French policy, Adenauer's leadership in foreign policy was increasingly challenged from within his own party ranks. With Adenauer's forced retirement and the emergence of Erhard and Schröder as CDU leaders, the West German political balance shifted away from Paris and toward Washington. The so-called 'Gaullist' faction within the CDU–CSU thereafter became an obstreperous fifth column within the Bundestag and the Foreign Office as well, leaking damaging reports to the press and waging internal war against the official government policy at every turn. A prime symbol of their effort to discredit the Schröder–Erhard policy

14. While it is true that the reconciliation begun under the Fourth Republic continued, and that de Gaulle can be credited with rallying the traditional Right to the Franco-German cause; and while the economic interpenetration that has made France and Germany each other's first-ranking trade partner has continued to grow, de Gaulle's policy must none the less be viewed as a failure in that the political co-operation and convergence which were the goals of his policy failed to materialize. What remained was a framework, which is facilitative, but no substitute for common policy.

was a sensational 1966 best-seller exposé by a former official at the Auswärtiges Amt, which characterized West German policy as a dead-end road to isolation.[15]

Not least of the paradoxes in the German domestic disarray was the fact that while the Christian Democratic coalition was bitterly divided between its so-called Gaullist and Atlanticist wings, there was actually very little resemblance between de Gaulle's policies and those advocated by the German *Gaullisten*. The German Gaullists, as typified by Strauss and Gutenberg, were, like de Gaulle, 'continentalists' rather than Atlanticists in their orientation, but they combined their belief in the solution to the German question through a European confederation in which national frontiers had ceased to exist, with a dogmatic anti-communism which opposed in practice all contacts between the two German regimes. They were fervently committed to support of the Hallstein Doctrine, thus effectively precluding improvement in relations with the countries of Eastern Europe and the wider *détente* de Gaulle had espoused. In addition, while they opposed the MLF, they nurtured the fond hope of an active role for Germany within a West European nuclear force, and they therefore favoured the French *force de frappe* as the symbol, in widened form, of their own nuclear aspirations. Thus, beneath their rhetoric of priority to relations with France, the kind of common policy they desired to pursue was hardly the one de Gaulle had repeatedly proclaimed in his public statements. They adopted the Gaullist banner as a rallying point for their resistance to American policy within Nato – particularly in that they saw in the MLF the instrument for assuring Germany's permanent nuclear discrimination – but their so-called 'Gaullism' was, beyond their superficial attachment to Catholic, continental France, purely opportunistic.[16] The American effort to checkmate de Gaulle's European policy was, thus, very substantially aided by conflicts in the West German domestic political context.

De Gaulle offered West Germany the attractive but non-specific prospect of a future based on co-operation, and, in the present, a kind of public absolution that marked the culmination

15. See Hans Graf Huyn, *Die Sackgasse: Deutschlands Weg in die Isolierung*, Stuttgart, Seewald Verlag, 1966.

16. For Strauss's views, see his *The Grand Design*. It was the German Socialist Party which in fact proved most receptive to de Gaulle's policy of improvement on the German question in a framework of *détente, entente, et coopération.*

of Bonn's efforts to win international respectability through good relations. In practice, the West Germans proved somewhat wont to perceive the Franco-German Treaty more as the culmination of a route of reconciliation than as the instrument of future policy which de Gaulle intended. Washington's ploy was to play the trump card of national security, and thereby to re-emphasize the political–military dimension which bound West Germany to its US protector. Did de Gaulle tour the Ruhr, the Rhineland and Bavaria? Kennedy went to Berlin, symbol of cold war tensions. De Gaulle proposed economic and cultural interpenetration, and co-operation in arms development and research. The US offered nuclear participation through the multilateral force, and supported Bonn's official catechism on the German question by pledging itself at every turn to promote the future reunification of Germany through free elections. At the same time, Washington stepped up its pressure on the Bonn Government to increase its purchase of US arms in order to offset the burdensome cost of maintaining US forces in West Germany. This made the proposed Franco-German co-operation on arms development the victim of the most elementary quandary of resource allocation from the outset.

It is puzzling, in retrospect, to appreciate precisely what aspect of de Gaulle's German policy appeared so threatening to US interests as to warrant the whole-hog American effort during the Kennedy and Johnson Administrations to thwart the Franco-German enterprise. What de Gaulle was preaching to the Germans was hardly a gospel designed to threaten peace and security in Europe. Quite the contrary. De Gaulle confronted squarely the contradictions involved in the official Deutschlandpolitik of the West German Government. As early as 1959, at his first press conference, he spelled out in candid detail the policy the West German Government should follow if it was truly committed to ending the artificial division of Germany and to reaching a postwar settlement:

> The reunification of the two parts into a single Germany which would be entirely free seems to us the normal destiny of the German people, provided they do not reopen the question of their present frontiers to the west, the east, the north and the south, and that they move toward integrating themselves one day in a contractual organization of all Europe for co-operation, liberty and peace.

But, pending the time when this ideal can be achieved, we believe that the two separated sections of the German people should be able to multiply the ties and relations between themselves in all practical fields. Transport, communications, economic activity, literature, science, the arts, the goings and comings of peoples, etc., would be the subject of arrangements which would bring together the Germans within and for the benefit of that which I would call 'Germanness' and which after all is common to them, in spite of the differences in regimes and conditions.[17]

De Gaulle's 1959 proposal was virtually a charter for the Brandt Administration's Ostpolitik one decade later. He advocated no less than scrapping the cornerstone of Bonn's official policy, the Hallstein Doctrine, which maintained an effective *cordon sanitaire* around the East German frontiers; abandoning the hope of forcing the Pankow regime to capitulate at 'free elections' as the route to reunification. In this respect, the revisionist mood of French European policy differed markedly from that of Bonn. The French policy was indeed a policy of movement, but it proceeded from an acknowledgment of the present 'realities' in order to bring about improvement. French policy sought improvement through practical measures of *détente*, while refusing adamantly to yield to Soviet threats by unilateral concessions.[18]

De Gaulle's pronouncements on Germany's future were, none the less, always prefaced by a short refrain, which contains implicitly both an affirmation and a revealing reservation: 'Germany, *as she is*, in no way threatens us.'[19] That Germany should no longer present a threat to the peace of Europe was both the essential condition for France's support, and what must be guaranteed through present and future policies:

Henceforth, all precautions must be taken to prevent the return in force of the evil Germanic demons. But . . . how can one imagine establishing true and enduring peace on a basis which this great people could not resign itself to, or a real union of the continent without its participation. . . .[20]

French support for German national aspirations hinged in practice on two non-negotiable requirements: (1) German

17. Press conference of 25 March 1959, *Major Addresses*, p. 43.

18. See de Gaulle, *Mémoires d'espoir*, pp. 270–1 on the difference between *détente* and appeasement.

19. *Major Addresses*, p. 42. Emphasis added.

20. De Gaulle, *Mémoires d'espoir*, p. 183.

acceptance of the postwar frontiers, and (2) permanent renunciation of both the possession and production of nuclear weapons:

> The Oder–Neisse Line, which separates her from Poland, is her definitive limit; nothing must remain of her former claims on Czechoslovakia; another Anschluss in any form whatsoever is excluded. Furthermore, at no cost is she to gain the right to the production or possession of atomic weapons – which, moreover, she has formally renounced.... Thus, security between the Atlantic and the Urals would be guaranteed for all....[21]

The unresolved question of Germany's place and limits in Europe, which had haunted European history for a century, would thus find a solution within the framework of the pan-European system which de Gaulle saw as the long-range destiny of the continent. In the meantime, nothing must be done to compromise that hope, or to enable the Germans to threaten the security of Europe. Whence the importance of tying West Germany firmly to the West and to France, both through the mechanisms of the EEC and through establishing preferential political relations with Bonn.[22] Whence, also, de Gaulle's vigorous intervention against the MLF in the autumn of 1964, when it began to appear as a bilateral American–German arrangement affording nuclear access to Bonn. And whence finally, the importance of good relations between Paris and Moscow. The lesson of 1939 was not that far behind. Might not a West Germany, disenchanted with the West, fearing her isolation, and buoyed by her remarkable economic prowess, take up the initiative for her own destiny and turn ultimately to Moscow to obtain the national satisfactions which the West could not provide?[23] The alternative was for France to espouse the German cause, albeit to dissuade Kennedy and Macmillan from their temptation to make concessions on Berlin in response to Khrushchev's threat,[24] and to cut a public figure as defender of Bonn's interests in dealings with the Russians. The final guarantee was the *force de frappe*, which

21. De Gaulle, *Mémoires d'espoir*, p. 183.

22. See Couve de Murville, *Une Politique étrangère*, p. 396.

23. Couve de Murville sees this as one of the most unfortunate outcomes of the failure to construct a framework for West European political co-operation, and cites the bilateral German–Soviet treaty of 1970 as an example: 'The emancipation of German policy marked in 1970 by the conclusion of a treaty with the Soviet Union – alas! outside any European framework since none existed....' *Une Politique étrangère*, p. 383.

24. See de Gaulle, *Mémoires d'espoir*, pp. 270 ff.

secured, in the military sphere, the permanent superiority of France over either a divided or a reunited-but-non-nuclear Germany, both in the present and in the event of a less harmonious future. The constant possibility of change was never far from the thoughts of de Gaulle-the-disciple-of-Bergson.

De Gaulle's policy toward Germany and his wider European policy thus served both in the short term and in the long run to guarantee French national security through a combination of political–psychological and military elements. This reflected his view that there was an essential link between French interests – indeed, French security – and the settlement of outstanding political claims on the continent, principally the future of Germany. His policy of *détente* aimed at creating the atmosphere within which a permanent European settlement could be reached. To be sure, his policy of *détente* could not have been implemented without a shift in mood in Moscow in the aftermath of the Cuban missile crisis and the period of tense confrontation over Berlin. The practical *détente* between the two superpowers provided increased leeway for French policy just at the time when whatever hopes de Gaulle had held out for the Franco-German Treaty as the motor of West European political co-operation were at an all-time low, and when he was engaged on the West European front in the last stages of the showdown over agriculture.

Détente as normalization, of course, represented a traditional reflex of a country historically committed to a policy of *équilibre continental*. De Gaulle's Eastern policy went beyond that in that he saw in his version of a 'concert of European states' the possibility of co-operation evolving toward common policies in a Europe whose peoples no longer entertained claims at one another's expense: 'My policy aims, thus, at establishing a concert of European states, so that by developing links of all sorts between them, their solidarity will grow. Nothing prevents us from believing that in beginning thus . . . they may evolve toward confederation.'[25] The old system of balance of power sought to counterbalance German expansionist designs by a French–Russian, or French–British guarantee, or other variations thereof. De Gaulle's long-range vision was of a Europe beyond hegemonial designs, based on a community of shared values and

25. De Gaulle, *Mémoires d'espoir*, p. 182.

interests, which might gradually, through interpenetration, evolve toward a community of destiny. Dante, Goethe, Dostoevsky, Shakespeare, Chateaubriand – and even Karl Marx – were, after all, all Europeans, whose influence constituted a common European patrimony, he was fond of pointing out. If the seesaw of past history could be left behind, even as the bitter antagonisms which during his own youth had pitted French against Germans over the destiny of Alsace and Lorraine had been forgotten one generation later, then the future held out great hope for the accomplishing of the age-old dream of European unity. What stood in the way were the vestiges of the cold war and the persistent unresolved status of Germany.

The success or failure of de Gaulle's European policy must, on balance, be weighed in the context of the two focuses of that policy: Western Europe, and the wider pan-European framework. Within Western Europe, he accorded highest priority to the creation of a framework for political co-operation, which would both anchor West Germany securely to the West and forge a West European entity capable of dealings with the communist bloc in the East. He was successful in obtaining the constant support of the Bonn Government under Adenauer in pursuit of that objective. When the Fouchet Plan failed, de Gaulle agreed to pursue the proposal, in reduced form, bilaterally with West Germany. In the short run, this policy, based on the establishment of preferential relations between France and West Germany, as the model and motor of European co-operation, failed for a convergence of three reasons: (1) an overwhelming US opposition operating within its own domestic constituency in West Germany; (2) the lack of political will in Bonn, which was reinforced opportunely by US policy; and (3) Bonn's ultimate reliance on the US for security. The West German Government was caught partially in the crossfire between Paris and Washington – in what Couve de Murville correctly labels the crisis in Franco-American relations – and partially in the contradictions implicit in its own lack of coherent direction.

The policy of bilateral co-operation with France was thwarted from the outset by the West German obsession with security, and the impossibility of France's substituting for the US defender in Bonn's eyes, once the issue had been posed by Washington's obstruction. But it must, in fairness, be emphasized that Bonn's policy demonstrated no imagination at all in contributing to its own stated foreign policy goals – particularly in regard to the German question, where it contented itself with a mixture of wishful thinking and illusion, which in the long run was as potentially destabilizing internally as it was provocative externally. Bonn clung instead to its old security blanket of unwavering reliance on Washington as a substitute for policy. The United States Government continued to support Bonn's *combat d'arrière-garde*[26] until 1976, when the Bonn Government, dragged along by events and abandoned by Washington, finally reviewed its foreign policy.

De Gaulle's wider policy of resolving the 'German anomalies' within the pan-European framework which he affirmed both as a political goal and the historical destiny of the continent, cannot yet be evaluated in terms of final success or failure, because the long-term returns are not yet in. One aspect of that policy was certainly to preach realism to the West Germans in an effort to urge them to assume responsibility in improving their own situation through recognition of the postwar borders, definitive renunciation of nuclear weapons, and improving their relations with both their East German and East European neighbours. This much has been and is being accomplished. Whether the policy of *détente* which de Gaulle both preached and practised will result in the ultimate emergence of the European political confederation he dreamed of, the integration of the German people in a Europe at last purged of hegemonial ambitions, is the subject of future history. In 1977, one is struck by the proliferation of dissident movements within the communist bloc, challenging their states on issues of human rights. Whether such fruits of *détente* policy will result in political liberalization or further repression remains unclear.

There is doubtless little common ground between the lofty visions Charles de Gaulle required for France and those of his critics whose implicit advice to middle-level powers like France was to stay out of 'high policy' affairs and to cultivate their own backyards in the form of domestic welfare and economic prosperity. For, beyond the horizon of the policies he pursued in the name of France and which were indeed calculated to defend French interests as defined by his government, de Gaulle enter-

26. Couve de Murville, *Une Politique étrangère*, p. 273.

tained a haunting dream, whose inspiration was anything but the parochial, old-style nationalism he was so often accused of:

When two-thirds of the earth's inhabitants lead a miserable existence, while certain peoples have at their disposal what is necessary to ensure the progress of all – what is the use of the dangerous wrangling over West Berlin, the German Democratic Republic and German disengagement?

For, in our time, the only quarrel worth-while is that of mankind. It is mankind that must be saved, made to live and enabled to advance.

We, who live between the Atlantic and the Urals; we, who are Europe, possessing with Europe's daughter America the principal sources and resources of civilization; we, who have the means to feed, clothe and house ourselves and to keep warm; we who have mines and factories operating full blast, trains, roads choked with cars, ports filled with ships, airports full of aircraft; we, all of whose children learn to read, who build universities and laboratories, who form armies of engineers and technicians, who can see hear, read what is made to satisfy the mind; we who have enough doctors, hospitals, medicines to ease suffering, to care for the sick, to ensure the life of newborn infants – why do we not erect, all together, the fraternal organization which will lend its hand to others? Why do we not pool a percentage of our raw materials, our manufactured goods, our food products; some of our scientists, technologists, economists; some of our trucks, ships, aircraft in order to vanquish misery, develop resources and help in the work of the less-developed peoples? Let us do this - not that they may be the pawns of our policies, but to improve the chances of life and peace. How much more worth-while that would be than territorial demands, ideological claims, imperialist ambitions which are leading the world to its death.[27]

27. First press conference held by General de Gaulle as President of the Fifth Republic, 25 March 1959, in *Major Addresses*, pp. 44–5. Translation adapted.

APPENDIX 1

Letter from President Eisenhower to General de Gaulle, dated 20 October, 1958[1]

Dear General de Gaulle:

I have given considerable thought to the views expressed in your letter of September 17. You have posed serious questions which require earnest thinking and careful study.

The central problem you raise – the organization of the Free World's defense – is very much on my mind also. I agree that we should constantly seek means for making that organization more effective.

We are, I believe, in full agreement that the threat we face is global and that our policies should be adapted to deal with the world-wide nature of the threat. Although recognizing that more needs to be done, we believe that our policies have to an extent already been adapted to this end. It is in recognition of the need to deal with the world-wide threat that the United States has joined with its Allies in establishing elements of strength throughout the world. The United States and France are closely associated in certain of these groupings, such as NATO and SEATO. The United States has also associated itself with many other countries, in both multilateral and bilateral arrangements, all directed toward the same general purpose. We have also sought to give recognition to the fact that the threat is more than military through our economic, financial and technical assistance programs designed to aid nations throughout the world to resist subversion.

As for the Atlantic Alliance itself, I believe there has been a significant evolution in NATO over the past two years. Consultation in NATO has in fact been extended well beyond the confines of the European area. We, for example, have sought to use the NATO Council to inform or consult with our Allies on the threat facing the Free World in the Far East and the Middle East. We have also sought to use the Council to develop common policies toward the Soviet bloc. We feel that this 'habit of consultation' among the NATO nations must be still further broadened but that this cannot be forced. I do not believe that we can afford to lose any of this developing intimacy among all the members of NATO and the closer bonds it forges.

1. Source: *Atlantic Community Quarterly*, no. 3 (Fall 1966), pp. 457–8.

As for the means for dealing with the problems which you propose, our present procedures for organizing the defense of the Free World clearly require the willing cooperation of many other nations, both within and outside NATO. We cannot afford to adopt any system which would give to our other Allies, or other Free World countries, the impression that basic decisions affecting their own vital interests are being made without their participation. As regards NATO itself, I must in all frankness say that I see very serious problems, both within and outside NATO, in any effort to amend the North Atlantic Treaty so as to extend its coverage beyond the areas presently covered.

All this having been said, I must add that I recognize that a community association to live must constantly evolve and find means to make itself more useful in the face of changing conditions. I am quite prepared to explore this aspect of the matter in appropriate ways.

With best personal wishes,

Sincerely,

DWIGHT D. EISENHOWER

APPENDIX 2

The first Fouchet draft, submitted on 2 November, 1961[1]

The High Contracting Parties,

convinced that the organization of Europe in a spirit of freedom that respects its diversity will enable their civilization to develop still further, protect their common spiritual heritage from any threats to which it may be exposed and in this way contribute to the maintenance of peaceful relations in the world;

resolved jointly to safeguard the fundamental dignity, freedom and equality of men, regardless of their status, race or creed, and to work for the advent of a better world in which these values would permanently prevail;

affirming their attachment to the principles of democracy, to human rights and to justice in every sphere of social life;

desirous of welcoming to their ranks the other countries of Europe that are prepared to accept the same responsibilities and the same obligations;

resolved to pursue the task of reconciling their essential interests, already the objective, in their respective fields, of the European Coal and Steel Community, the European Economic Community and the European Atomic Energy Community, in order to lay the foundation for a destiny to be henceforth irrevocably shared;

resolved, to this end, to give statutory form to the union of their peoples, in accordance with the declaration adopted in Bonn on 18 July 1961 by the Heads of State or Government. . . .

TITLE I – UNION OF THE EUROPEAN PEOPLES

Article 1

By the present Treaty, a union of States, hereafter called 'the Union,' is established.

The Union is based on respect for the individuality of the peoples and of the Member States and for equality of rights and obligations. It is indissoluble.

1. Source: Silj, *Europe's Political Puzzle*, pp. 141–8.

Article 2

It shall be the aim of the Union:
– to bring about the adoption of a common foreign policy in matters that are of common interest to Member States;
– to ensure, through close co-operation between Member States in the scientific and cultural field, the continued development of their common heritage and the protection of the values on which their civilization rests;
– to contribute thus in the Member States to the defence of human rights, the fundamental freedoms and democracy;
– to strengthen, in co-operation with the other free nations, the security of Member States against any aggression by adopting a common defence policy.

Article 3

The Union shall have legal personality.

The Union shall enjoy in each of the Member States the most extensive legal capacity accorded to legal persons under their domestic law. It may, in particular, acquire or dispose of movable or immovable property and may go to law.

TITLE II – INSTITUTIONS OF THE UNION

Article 4

The Institutions of the Union shall be as follows:
– the Council;
– the European Parliament;
– the European Political Commission.

Article 5

The Council shall meet every four months at Head of State or Government level, and at least once in the intervening period at Foreign Minister level. It may, moreover, at any time hold extraordinary sessions at either level at the request of one or more Member States.

At each of these meetings at Head of State or Government level, the Council shall appoint a President who shall take up his duties two months before the subsequent meeting and continue to exercise them for two months after the meeting.

Meetings of the Council held at Foreign Minister level shall be presided over by the Foreign Minister of the State whose representative presides over meetings at Head of State or Government level.

The President in office shall preside over extraordinary meetings that may be held during his term of office.

The Council shall choose the place for its meetings.

Article 6

The Council shall deliberate on all questions whose inclusion on its agenda is requested by one or more Member States. It shall adopt decisions necessary for achieving the aims of the Union unanimously. The absence or abstention of one or of two members shall not prevent a decision from being taken.

The decisions of the Council shall be binding on Member States that have participated in their adoption. Member States on which a decision is not binding, by reason of their absence or abstention, may endorse it at any time. From the moment they endorse it, the decision will be binding on them.

Article 7

The European Parliament provided for under Article 1 of the Convention relating to certain institutions common to the European Communities signed in Rome on 25 March 1957, shall deliberate on matters concerning the aims of the Union.

It may address oral or written questions to the Council.

It may submit recommendations to the Council.

Article 8

The Council, on receipt of a recommendation addressed to it by the European Parliament, shall give its reply to the Parliament within a period of four months.

The Council, on receipt of a recommendation addressed to it by the European Parliament, shall inform the Parliament of the action it has taken thereon within a period of six months.

The Council shall each year submit to the European Parliament a report on its activities.

Article 9

The European Political Commission shall consist of senior officials of the Foreign Affairs departments of each Member State. Its seat shall be in Paris. It shall be presided over by the representative of the Member State that presides over the Council, and for the same period.

The European Political Commission shall set up such working bodies as it considers necessary.

The European Political Commission shall have at its disposal the staff and departments it requires to carry out its duties.

Article 10

The European Political Commission shall assist the Council. It shall prepare its deliberations and carry out its decisions. It shall perform the duties that the Council decides to entrust to it.

. . . .[2]

TITLE III – OBLIGATIONS OF MEMBER STATES

Article 11

There shall be solidarity, mutual confidence and reciprocal assistance as between Member States. They undertake to abstain from any step or decision that might hinder or delay the achievement of the aims of the Union. They shall loyally co-operate in any consultations proposed to them and respond to requests for information addressed to them by the Council or, in compliance with the instructions of the Council, by the European Political Commission.

TITLE IV – FINANCES OF THE UNION

Article 12

The budget of the Union shall be drawn up by the Council each year and shall include all revenues and expenditures.

Article 13

The revenues of the Union shall be derived from contributions by the Member States calculated according to the following scale:

Belgium	7·9
France	28
Federal Republic of Germany	28
Italy	28
Luxembourg	0.2
Netherlands	7·9
	100·0

Article 14

The budget shall be implemented by the European Political Commission which may delegate to its chairman all or part of the powers necessary for the purpose.

2. The provisions relating to cultural co-operation should, if necessary, be inserted here.

TITLE V – GENERAL PROVISIONS

Article 15

The present Treaty may be reviewed. Draft amendments shall be submitted to the Council by Member States. The Council shall pronounce on such drafts and decide whether or not they should be passed on for an opinion to the European Parliament.

Draft amendments adopted unanimously by the Council shall be submitted for ratification by the Member States, after the European Parliament, where appropriate, has expressed its opinion. They shall come into force once all the Member States have ratified them.

Article 16

Three years after this Treaty comes into force, it shall be subjected to a general review with a view to considering suitable measures for strengthening the Union in the light of the progress already made.

The main objects of such a review shall be the introduction of a unified foreign policy and the gradual establishment of an organization centralizing, within the Union, the European Communities referred to in the Preamble to the present Treaty.

The amendments arising from this review shall be adopted in accordance with the procedure outlined in Article 15 above.

Article 17

The Union shall be open for membership to Member States of the Council of Europe that accept the aims set out in Article 2 above and that have previously acceded to the European Communities referred to in the Preamble to this Treaty.

The admission of a new Member State shall be decided unanimously by the Council after an additional Act has been drawn up to this Treaty. This Act shall contain the necessary adjustments to the Treaty. It shall come into force once the State concerned has submitted its instrument of ratification.

Article 18

This Treaty, drawn up in a single original in the Dutch, French, German and Italian languages, all four texts being equally authentic, shall be deposited in the archives of the Government of . . . which shall transmit a certified copy to each of the Governments of the other signatory States.

This Treaty shall be ratified. The instruments of ratification shall be deposited with . . . which shall notify the Governments of the other Member States that this has been done.

This Treaty shall come into force on the day when the instrument of ratification is deposited by the last signatory State to do so.

In witness whereof, the undersigned Plenipotentiaries have affixed their signatures below this Treaty under their common seal.

APPENDIX 3

The revised draft of the Fouchet Plan, dated 15 March, 1962, with proposed alterations

[The left-hand column represents the text proposed by the French delegation; the right-hand column represents the text proposed by the other delegations. The articles for which only one text is given were agreed upon by all delegations.[1]]

TITLE I – UNION OF THE EUROPEAN PEOPLES

Article 1

By the present Treaty, a union of States [and of European peoples], hereafter called 'the European Union,' is established.

The European Union is based on the principle of the equality of the rights and obligations of its members.

Article 2

It shall be the aim of the Union to reconcile, co-ordinate and unify the policy of Member States in spheres of common interest: foreign policy, economics, cultural affairs and defence.

Article 2

1. It shall be the task of the European Union to promote the unity of Europe by reconciling, co-ordinating and unifying the policy of Member States.

2. For the purpose of accomplishing this task, the objectives of the Union shall be:

– the adoption of a common foreign policy;

– the adoption of a common defence policy [within the framework of the Atlantic Alliance] [as a contribution towards strengthening the Atlantic Alliance];

1. Source: Silj, *Europe's Political Puzzle*, pp. 149–64.

– close co-operation in the educational, scientific and cultural fields;
– the harmonization and unification of the laws of Member States;
– the settlement, in a spirit of mutual understanding and constructive co-operation, of any differences that may arise in relations between Member States.

3. Objectives other than those laid down in the preceding paragraph may be defined by the Council after consultation with the European Parliament.

4. This Treaty shall not derogate from the competence of the European Communities.

Article 3

There shall be solidarity and reciprocal assistance as between Member States. They undertake to co-operate to the full in pursuing the objectives of the European Union and in facilitating the accomplishment of its task.

Draft Treaty for the establishment of a union of States	Draft Treaty for the establishment of a union of States and of European peoples
PREAMBLE	PREAMBLE

The High Contracting Parties,

convinced that the union of Europe in freedom and respect for its diversity will permit its civilization to develop, add to the prestige of its spiritual heritage, increase its capacity to defend itself against external threats, facilitate the contribution it makes to the progress of other peoples and contribute [in keeping with the principles of the United Nations Charter] to world peace;

affirming their attachment to the principles of democracy, to respect for law and to social justice;

resolved jointly to safeguard the dignity, freedom and equality of men, regardless of their status, race or creed;

resolved to pursue the task of reconciling their essential interests already initiated, in their respective fields, by the European Coal and Steel Community, the European Economic Community and the European Atomic Energy Community;	resolved to pursue the task of reconciling their essential interests, already the objective, in their respective fields, of the European Coal and Steel Community, the European Economic Community and the European Atomic Energy Community, in order to lay the foundation for a destiny to be irrevocably shared;

[desirous of welcoming] [ready to welcome] to their ranks other countries of Europe that are prepared to accept in every sphere the same responsibilities and the same obligations [and conscious of thus forming the nucleus of a union, membership of which will be open to other peoples of Europe that are as yet unable to take such a decision];[2]

resolved, to this end, to give statutory form to the union of their peoples, in accordance with the declaration of 18 July 1961 by the Heads of State or Government;

Have Appointed as Their Plenipotentiaries:

. . . .

who, having exchanged their Full Powers, found in good and due form, have agreed as follows:

Article 4

The European Union shall have legal personality.

The Union shall enjoy in each of the Member States the most extensive legal capacity accorded to legal persons under their domestic law.

TITLE II INSTITUTIONS OF THE UNION	TITLE II INSTITUTIONS OF THE UNION
Article 5	*Article 5*
The Institutions of the Union shall be as follows: – the Council; – the Committees of Ministers – the Political Commission; – the European Parliament	1. The Institutions of the European Union shall be as follows: – the Council and the Committees of Ministers; – the European Parliament; – the Court of Justice. 2. The Council and the Committees of Ministers shall be assisted by a Political Commission and a Secretary-General.

2. The square brackets in this text enclose phrases regarding which the various delegations failed to agree.

Article 6

The Council shall consist of the Heads of State or Government of Member States. It shall meet in principle every four months and not less than three times a year.

Article 6

1. The Council shall consist of the representatives of the Member States. Member States shall be represented on the Council, in accordance with the constitutional requirements and the usage prevailing in each country, by the Heads of State or Government and, where appropriate, by the Foreign Ministers.

2. The Council shall meet in ordinary session three times a year and in principle every four months. Extraordinary sessions of the Council may be convened at any time by its President on his own initiative or at the request of one or more Member States of the European Union.

3. The office of the President shall be exercised in rotation by each member of the Council for a term of [six months] [one year].

4. The Council shall lay down its own rules of procedure.

Article 7

The Council shall deliberate on questions whose inclusion on its agenda is requested by one or more Member States. The agenda shall be drawn up by the President. The Council shall adopt decisions necessary for achieving the aims of the Union unanimously. The Council's decisions shall be binding on Member States. The abstention of one or of two members shall not prevent a decision from being taken.

The decisions of the Council shall be implemented by Member

Article 7

1. The Council shall deliberate on all questions whose inclusion on the agenda is requested by one or more Member States or by the Secretary-General under the terms of Article 2. The agenda shall be drawn up by the President.

The meetings of the Council shall be prepared by the Committee of Foreign Ministers. Decisions necessary for achieving the aims of the European Union shall be passed by the Council unanimously.

2. The decisions of the Council

States that have participated in their adoption. Member States that are not bound by a decision, by reason of their absence or abstention, may endorse it at any time. From the moment they endorse it, the decision shall be binding on them.

shall be carried out in accordance with the constitutional requirements in force in each Member State. The Council may, by a unanimous decision, waive the principle of unanimity in specific cases. The abstention of one or of two members shall not prevent decisions requiring unanimity from being taken.

3. If a decision that requires unanimity cannot be adopted because it is opposed by one Member State, the Council shall adjourn the deliberation to a later date to be specified by it. Before this second deliberation takes place, the Council may decide to obtain the opinion of the European Parliament.

Article 8

1. The Council may conclude agreements on behalf of the European Union with Member States, third countries or international organizations. It shall lay down the methods to be followed in its rules of procedure.

2. The agreements shall be submitted to the Parliament for an opinion. They shall not come into force until they have been approved in all Member States by the bodies that, under the respective constitutional requirements, must, where appropriate, approve such agreements concluded by these States.

3. Agreements concluded in accordance with the preceding provisions shall be binding on the institutions of the European Union and on Member States.

Article 8	*Article 9*
1. The following committees shall be set up: – a Committee of Foreign Ministers; – a Committee of Ministers of Defence and for the Armed Forces; – a Committee of Ministers of Education or of Ministers responsible for international cultural relations. The competence of this Committee shall be governed, without prejudice to the provisions of this Treaty, by the Convention embodying the Statute of the European Cultural Council and the annexed Conventions which as a whole are to be regarded as an integral part of this Treaty.	
The Council may decide to set up other Committees of Ministers.	2. The Council may set up other Committees of Ministers. 3. The Committees enumerated above shall meet not less than four times a year and report to the Council.
Article 9	*Article 10*
The Political Commission shall consist of representatives appointed by each Member State. It shall prepare the deliberations of the Council and ensure that its decisions are carried out. It shall perform such other duties as the Council decides to entrust to it. It shall have at its disposal the necessary staff and departments.	The Political Commission shall consist of senior officials appointed by each State. This Commission shall prepare the deliberations of the Council and of the Committees of Ministers and perform the duties which the Council decides to entrust to it.
	Article 11
	1. The Council shall appoint for a period of . . . a Secretary-General who shall be independent of the Governments of the Member States of the European Union. His term of office shall be renewable. 2. He shall be assisted in the performance of his duties by a staff appointed by him in accordance with a procedure to be laid

down, on his proposal, by the Council.

3. The functions of the Secretary-General and of members of the Secretariat shall be deemed to be incompatible with the exercise of any other office.

4. In the performance of their duties, the Secretary-General and the members of the Secretariat shall neither solicit nor accept instructions from any government. They shall abstain from any act that is incompatible with the nature of their functions.

5. The Member States undertake to respect the independence of the Secretary-General and of his staff and to refrain from influencing them in the accomplishment of their task.

Article 10

Article 12

1. The parliamentary institution of the European Union shall be the Parliament provided for under Article 1 of the Convention relating to certain institutions common to the European Communities signed in Rome on 25 March 1957.

2. In fields that relate to the aims of the European Union, the Parliament [or its members] may address questions to the Council.

3. In the same fields, the Parliament may submit recommendations to the Council.

4. The Council, on receipt of a question or of a recommendation from the European Parliament, shall make known at its next meeting what action it has taken in respect thereof.

Article 11

Article 13

The Council shall each year submit to the European Parliament [a report] [a communication] on its activities.

The Council shall be represented at the debates held on [its report] [its communication].

The Council and the European Parliament shall jointly lay down the procedure for their collaboration.

Article 14

1. The Court of Justice of the European Communities shall be competent to decide on any dispute between Member States connected with the interpretation or application of this Treaty.

Member States undertake not to subject such disputes to any other form of settlement.

2. The Court of Justice of the European Communities shall be competent:

a) to decide on any dispute between Member States where the said dispute is submitted to the Court under a special agreement between them;

b) to give a decision pursuant to any arbitration clause contained in a contract, whether governed by public law or private law, concluded by or on behalf of the European Union.

TITLE IV

FINANCES OF THE EUROPEAN UNION

Article 12

TITLE IV

FINANCES OF THE EUROPEAN UNION

Article 15

1. The budget of the European Union shall be drawn up annually. The financial year shall run from 1 January to 31 December inclusive.

2. The Council shall lay down the financial regulations of the European Union.

3. The draft budget, drawn up by the Political Commission, shall be adopted by the Council which may, where appropriate, make such amendments as it considers necessary.

3. The draft budget, drawn up by the Secretary-General with the assistance of the Political Commission, shall be adopted by the Council, after obtaining the Parliament's opinion.

Article 13 — *Article 16*

1. The administrative expenditure of the European Union shall be met from contributions by the Member States calculated according to the following scale:

[Belgium	7.9
France	28
Federal Republic of Germany	28
Italy	28
Luxembourg	0.2
Netherlands	7.9]

2. In the event of the accession of a further State, this scale shall be adjusted by decision of the Council.

3. A study shall be made, within the framework of the general review referred to in Article 20, of the conditions under which the contributions of Member States could be replaced or supplemented by the European Union's own resources.

Article 14

The budget shall be implemented by the Political Commission.

Article 17

The budget shall be implemented by the Secretary-General.

TITLE V
GENERAL PROVISIONS

Article 18

The European Union shall enjoy on the territory of Member States such privileges and immunities as are necessary for it to accomplish its task under the conditions stipulated in a separate protocol which forms part of this Treaty. This shall also define the contractual and non-contractual liability of the European Union and the principles which shall govern its relations with its staff.

Article 15

This Treaty may be reviewed. Draft amendments shall be submitted to the Council by the

Article 19

1. This Treaty may be reviewed, without prejudice to the general review referred to in Article 20.

Governments of the Member States.

Draft amendments adopted unanimously by the Council shall be submitted for ratification to the Member States, after the European Parliament, where appropriate, has expressed its opinion. They shall come into force once all the Member States have ratified them.

Article 16

Three years after this Treaty comes into force, it shall be subjected to a review in order to consider suitable measures either for strengthening the Union in general in the light of progress already made or, in particular, for simplifying, rationalizing and co-ordinating the ways in which Member States co-operate.

2. Draft amendments shall be submitted to the Council either by the Member States or by the Parliament. If the Council, after having consulted the Parliament where a draft is proposed by one of the Member States, unanimously adopts such a draft amendment, this shall be submitted to Member States for ratification.

Such draft amendment shall come into force when all the Member States have ratified it in accordance with their respective constitutional requirements.

Article 20

1. At the time fixed for the transition from the second to the third stage laid down in the Treaty establishing the European Economic Community, the present Treaty shall be subjected to a general review. This shall aim at determining suitable measures for strengthening the European Union and the powers of its institutions in the light of the progress already made.

With this end in view, a draft constitution of the European Union shall be drawn up by the Council before expiry of the time-limit specified above, and submitted to the European Parliament for its opinion.

2. The general review shall in particular have the following objectives:

a) To associate the European Parliament more closely with the work of defining the common policy and carrying out the provisions of Article 138 of the Treaty establishing the European Economic Community relating to the election of the Parliament by direct universal suffrage;

b) To gradually introduce the majority principle in decisions of the Council of the Union.

3. At the time of the general review, the conditions shall be fixed under which, at the end of the transition period of the Common Market, the European Union and the European Communities will be incorporated in an organic institutional framework, without prejudice to the machinery provided for in the Treaties of Paris and Rome. To facilitate this process, reforms shall be undertaken, in accordance with the procedures laid down in the Treaties of Paris and Rome and before the general review is carried out, with a view to simplifying and rationalizing the machinery provided for in those Treaties.

4. The competence of the Court of Justice shall be extended in the light of reforms introduced by the general review.

Article 17 *Article 21*

The Union shall be open for membership to States that have acceded to the European Communities referred to in the Preamble to this Treaty.

Article 18 *Article 22*

The rules governing the languages of the European Union shall, without prejudice to the rules of procedure of the European Parliament and of the Court, be determined by unanimous decision of the Council.

Article 19 *Article 23*

This Treaty shall be ratified. The instruments of ratification shall be deposited with . . . which shall notify the Governments of the other Member States that this has been done.

This Treaty shall come into force on the day when the instrument of ratification is deposited by the last signatory State to do so.

Article 20 *Article 24*

1. This Treaty is drawn up in a single original in Dutch, French, German and Italian, which shall be the official working languages of the Institutions of the European Union. All four texts, which are equally authentic, shall be deposited in the archives of the Government of . . . which shall transmit a certified copy of each of the Governments of the other signatory States.

APPENDIX 4

The Common Declaration and the Treaty between the French Republic and the Federal Republic of Germany, dated 22 January, 1963[1]

COMMON DECLARATION

General Charles de Gaulle, President of the French Republic, and Dr. Konrad Adenauer, Chancellor of the Federal Republic of Germany.

At the close of the conference which was held in Paris on January 21 and 22, 1963 and which was attended, on the French side, by the Premier, the Minister of Foreign Affairs, the Minister of the Armed Forces, and the Minister of National Education and, on the German side, by the Minister of Foreign Affairs, the Minister of Defense, and the Minister of Family and Youth Affairs.

Convinced that the reconciliation of the German people and the French people, bringing an end to the age-old rivalries, constitutes a historic event which profoundly transforms the relations of the two peoples,

Conscious of the solidarity which unites the two peoples both with respect to their security and with respect to their economic and cultural development,

Observing particularly that young people have become aware of this solidarity and find themselves called upon to play the determinant role in the consolidation of Franco-German friendship,

Recognizing that a strengthening of the cooperation between the two countries constitutes a vital stage along the road to a united Europe, which is the goal of the two peoples,

Have agreed to the organization and to the principles of the cooperation between the two States as they are stated in the Treaty signed this day.

THE TREATY

Following the Common Declaration of the President of the French Republic and the Chancellor of the Federal Republic of Germany, dated January 22, 1963, on the organization and the principles of the coopera-

1. Ambassade de France, Service de Presse et d'Information, New York, 1963.

tion between the two States, the following provisions have been agreed upon:

I Organization

1. The Heads of State and of Government will give whenever required the necessary directives and will follow regularly the implementation of the program set hereinunder. They will meet for this purpose whenever this is necessary and, in principle, at least twice a year.

2. The Ministers of Foreign Affairs will see to the implementation of the program as a whole. They will meet at least once every three months. Without prejudice to the contacts normally established through the channels of the embassies, high officials of the two Ministries of Foreign Affairs, responsible respectively for political, economic and cultural affairs, will meet each month in Paris and Bonn alternately to survey current problems and to prepare the Ministers' meeting. In addition, the diplomatic missions and the consulates of the two countries, and also the permanent missions to the international organizations, will make all the necessary contacts on problems of common interest.

3. Regular meetings will take place between the responsible authorities of the two countries in the fields of defense, education and youth. These meetings will not in any way affect the functioning of the already existing bodies – Franco-German Cultural Commission, Permanent General Staff Group – whose activities will on the contrary be extended. Both the Ministers of Foreign Affairs will be represented at these meetings in order to ensure the overall coordination of the cooperation.

(a) The Ministers of the Armed Forces or of Defense will meet at least once every three months. Similarly, the French Minister of National Education will meet, at the same intervals, with the person who will be designated by Germany to follow up the program of cooperation on the cultural level.

(b) The Chiefs of Staff of the two countries will meet at least once every two months; in the event of their being unable to meet, they will be replaced by their responsible representatives.

(c) The French High Commissioner for Youth and Sports will meet, at least once every two months, with the Federal Minister for Family and Youth Affairs of his representative.

4. In each of the countries, an interministerial commission will be charged with following problems of cooperation. It will be presided over by a high Foreign Ministry official and it will include representatives of all the administrations concerned. Its role will be to coordinate the action of the Ministries concerned and to report periodically to its Government on the state of Franco-German cooperation. It will also have the task of presenting all useful suggestions with a view to imple-

menting the program of cooperation and to its ultimate extension to new domains.

II Program

A – Foreign Affairs

1. The two Governments will consult each other, prior to any decision, on all important questions of foreign policy, and in the first place on questions of common interest, with a view to arriving, insofar as possible, at a similar position.

This consultation will cover, among other subjects, the following:

– Problems relative to the European Communities and to European political cooperation;

– East–West relations, both on the political and economic levels;

– Subjects dealt with in the North Atlantic Treaty Organization and the various international organizations in which the two Governments are interested, notably the Council of Europe, Western European Union, the Organization for Economic Cooperation and Development, the United Nations and its specialized agencies.

2. The cooperation already established in the area of information will be continued and developed between the services concerned in Paris and Bonn and between the [diplomatic] missions in other countries.

3. With regard to aid to the emergent countries, both Governments will systematically compare their programs with a view to maintaining close cooperation. They will study the possibility of engaging in joint undertakings. Since several Ministerial departments are responsible for these matters in both France and Germany, it will be the duty of the two Ministries of Foreign Affairs to determine together the practical bases for this cooperation.

4. The two Governments will study together the means for strengthening their cooperation in other important sectors of economic policy, such as agricultural and forest policy; energy policy; communications and transportation problems and industrial development, within the framework of the Common Market; as well as export credits policy.

B – Defense

1. The following objectives will be pursued in this domain:

(a) On the level of strategy and tactics, the competent authorities of both countries will endeavor to harmonize their doctrines with a view to arriving at mutual concepts. Franco-German Institutes for operational research will be created.

(b) Exchanges of personnel between the armed forces will be increased. These particularly concern professors and students from the general staff schools. They may include temporary detachments of entire units. In order to facilitate these exchanges, an effort will be made on both sides to give the trainees practical language instruction.

(c) With regard to armaments, both Governments will endeavor to organize a joint program from the time of drafting appropriate armaments projects and formulating financing plans.

To this end, joint committees will study the research being conducted on these projects in both countries and will carry out a comparative study. They will submit proposals to the Ministers, who will examine them during their quarterly meetings and will give the necessary directives for implementation.

2. The Governments will make a study of the conditions in which Franco-German cooperation could be established in the area of civil defense.

C – Education and Youth

With regard to education and youth, the proposals contained in the French and German memoranda of September 19 and November 8, 1962 will be studied, in accordance with the procedures indicated hereinabove.

1. In the field of education, the effort will chiefly concern the following points:

(a) Language instruction:

The two Governments recognize the essential importance that the knowledge in each of the two countries of the other's language holds for Franco-German cooperation. They will endeavor, to this end, to take concrete measures with a view to increasing the number of German students learning the French language and that of French students learning the German language.

The Federal Government will examine, with the governments of the Länder competent in this matter, how it is possible to introduce regulations making it possible to achieve this objective.

In all the establishments for higher education, practical courses in French will be organized in Germany and practical courses in German will be organized in France, which will be open to all students.

(b) The problem of equivalences:

The competent authorities of both countries will be asked to accelerate the adoption of provisions concerning the equivalence of academic periods, examinations and university degrees and diplomas.

(c) Cooperation in scientific research:

Research bodies and scientific institutes will increase their contacts, beginning with more extensive reciprocal information. Concerted research programs will be established in the areas in which it will appear possible.

2. All opportunities will be offered to the young people of both countries in order to draw closer the ties that unite them and to strengthen their mutual cooperation. Collective exchanges, particularly, will be increased.

A body whose purpose will be to develop these possibilities and to promote exchanges will be created by the two countries with an autonomous administrative council at its head. This body will have at its disposal a joint Franco-German fund for the exchange between the two countries of pupils, students, young artists, and workers.

III – Final Provisions

1. The necessary directives will be given in each country for the immediate enactment of the above. The Ministers of Foreign Affairs will examine the progress made at each of their meetings.

2. The two Governments will keep the Governments of the member States of the European Communities informed on the development of Franco-German cooperation.

3. With the exception of the provisions concerning defense, the present Treaty will also be applied to the Land of Berlin, barring a contrary declaration made by the Government of the Federal Republic of Germany to the Government of the French Republic in the three months following the entry into force of the present Treaty.

4. The two Governments may make any improvements which might appear desirable for the implementation of the present Treaty.

5. The present Treaty will enter into force as soon as each of the two Governments will have made known to the other that, on the domestic level, the necessary conditions for its implementation have been fulfilled.

Bibliography

Ailleret, (General), 'Conférence prononcée le 26 juin 1964 devant les anciens auditeurs du Collège de l'OTAN', *Revue de Défense Nationale*, XX (août 1964), pp. 1823–40.

L'Année politique, économique, sociale et diplomatique en France, Paris, Presses Universitaires de France, published annually.

Apel, Hans, 'Les Nouveaux Aspects de la politique étrangère allemande', *Politique Etrangère*, XXXII, no. 1 (1967), pp. 5–21.

Aron, Raymond, *The Great Debate*, New York, Doubleday, 1965.

Aron, Raymond, and Daniel Lerner (eds), *La Querelle de la CED*, Paris, A. Colin, 1956.

Aron, Robert, *Charles de Gaulle*, Paris, Librairie Académique Perrin, 1964.

Augstein, Rudolf, 'Ein Neues Rapallo? Lehren aus de Gaulles Ostpolitik', *Der Spiegel*, XX (25 April 1966).

Bainville, Jacques, *L'Histoire de deux peuples*, Paris, Arthème Fayard, 1933.

Barzel, Rainer, 'The German Question Remains Paramount', *Atlantic Community Quarterly*, IV, no. 3 (Fall 1966), pp. 366–76.

Barzel, Rainer, 'Pour un projet de Réunification', *Documents*, XXII, no. 1 (janvier–février 1967), pp. 36–50.

Beaufre, (General) André, 'The Sharing of Nuclear Responsibilities – a Problem in Need of a Solution', *Foreign Affairs*, XLII, no. 3 (July 1961), pp. 411–19.

Beaufre, (General) André, *NATO and Europe*, Joseph Green, trans., New York, Vintage Books, 1966.

Bechtoldt, H., 'Das Malaise der deutschen Frankreich-Politik', *Aussenpolitik*, XV, no. 10 (October 1964), pp. 659–62.

Beck, Robert H., *et al.*, *The Changing Structure of Europe: Economic, Political, and Social Trends*, Minneapolis, University of Minnesota Press, 1970.

Birrenbach, Kurt, *Die Zukunft der atlantischen Gemeinschaft*, Freiburg, Rombach Verlag, 1962.

Birrenbach, Kurt, 'Partnership and Consultation in NATO', *Atlantic Community Quarterly*, II (Spring 1964).

Blanc, Ulrich, 'Une Démocratie relevée', *Documents*, IX, no. 3 (mai–juin 1964), pp. 16–21.

Bloes, Robert, *Le 'Plan Fouchet' et le problème de l'Europe politique*, Bruges, Collège d'Europe, 1970.

Bodenheimer, Suzanne, *Political Union, A Microcosmos of European Politics 1960–66*, Leyden, A.W. Sijthoff, 1967.

Bondy, François, 'La Fin des Tabous en Allemagne', *Preuves*, XVII, no. 191 (janvier 1967), pp. 3–7.

Bonnefous, Edward, *L'Europe en face de son destin*, Paris, Presses Universitaires de France, 1955.

Bourel de la Roncière, Philippe, 'La Doctrine Hallstein', *Documents*, XXII, no. 2 (mars–avril 1967), pp. 39–49.

Bracher, Karl Dietrich (ed.), *Nach 25 Jahren*, Munich, Kindler Verlag, 1970.

Buchan, Alistair, *The Multilateral Force: an Historical Perspective*, Institute for Strategic Studies, Adelphi Papers, no. 13 (October 1964).

Buchan, Alistair, *NATO in the 1960's*, London, Weidenfeld & Nicolson, 1960.

Bulletin Mensuel du Comité Français pour l'Union Paneuropéenne.

Camps, Miriam, *Division in Europe*, PEP Occasional Paper no. 8 (June 1960).

Camps, Miriam, *European Unification in the Sixties*, London, Oxford University Press, 1967.

Carmoy, Guy de, 'L'Europe et l'Allemagne après le voyage de Moscou', *Revue Politique et Parlementaire*, no. 770 (September 1966), pp. 7–19.

Carmoy, Guy de, *Les Politiques extérieures de la France: 1944–1966*, Paris, La Table Ronde, 1967.

Chace, James and Earl Ravenal (eds), *Atlantis Lost: U.S.–European Relations after the Cold War*, New York University Press, 1976.

Chapsal, Jacques, *La Vie Politique en France depuis 1940*, Paris, Presses Universitaires de France, 1966.

Combaux, (General) E., 'Armes atomiques et non-atomiques dans la défense de l'Europe', *Revue de Défense Nationale* (janvier 1958).

Comité d'Etudes des relations franco-allemandes, 'Modèles de sécurité européenne', *Politique Etrangère*, XXXII, no. 6 (1967), pp. 519–41.

'Commentaires sur la crise de l'OTAN', *Documents*, XXI, no. 3 (mai–juin 1966), pp. 6–17.

Courtin, René, *L'Europe de l'Atlantique à l'Oural*, Paris, Editions l'Esprit Nouveau, 1963.

Couve de Murville, Maurice, 'La Politique étrangère de la France', *Entreprise*, no. 584 (17 novembre 1966), pp. 19–51.

Couve de Murville, Maurice, *Une Politique étrangère: 1958–1969*, Paris, Librairie Plon, 1971.

Cromwell, William C. (ed.), and N. Forman and J. Joffe, *Political Problems of Atlantic Partnership*, Bruges, College of Europe, Studies in Contemporary European Issues, no. 3, 1969.

Curtis, Michael, *Western European Integration*, New York, Harper & Row, 1965.

Debré, Michel, 'Contre l'intégration', *Tour d'Horizon*, no. 71 (octobre 1964), pp. 7–16.

Delmas, Claude, *L'OTAN*, Paris, Presses Universitaires de France, Collection 'Que Sais-je?', 3e édition, 1965.

De Porte, A.W., *De Gaulle's Foreign Policy: 1944–46*, Cambridge, Harvard University Press, 1968.

Destler, Irving, *Political Union in Europe: 1960–1962*, Washington, DC, Woodrow Wilson School of Public Affairs, 1964.

Deutsch, Karl W., and Lewis J. Edinger, Roy C. Macridis, and Richard L. Merrit, *France, Germany and the Western Alliance*, New York, Charles Scribner's Sons, 1967.

'Dix Années de Gaullisme', *La Nef*, XXV, no. 33 (février–avril 1968). Special issue with contributions by P. Bauchard, J. Ferniot, P.-M. de la Gorce, C. Krief, J. Planchais, R. Stéphane, J.-R. Tournoux, and P. Viansson-Ponté.

Erhard, Ludwig, 'La Société façonnée', *Documents*, XXI, no. 2 (mars–avril 1966), pp. 31–42.

Erler, Fritz, 'Die Deutsche Aussenpolitik nach dem Abkommen von Nassau', *Europa Archiv*, XVIII, 24 Folge, 1963.

Erler, Fritz, 'The Basis of Partnership', *Foreign Affairs*, XLII, no. 1 (October 1963).

Erler, Fritz, 'The Alliance and the Future of Germany', *Foreign Affairs*, XLIII, no. 3 (April 1965), pp. 436–46.

Fauvet, Jacques, *La IVe République*, Paris, Fayard, 1959.

Fontaine, André, 'Histoire de la Force multilatérale', series of articles in *Le Monde*, 15–20 novembre 1964.

Fontaine, André, 'What is French Policy?' *Foreign Affairs*, XLV, no. 1 (October 1966), pp. 58–76.

Fontaine, André, *Histoire de la Guerre Froide*, 2 vols, Paris, Arthème Fayard, 1967.

Frisch, Alfred, 'L'Allemand moyen et la politique étrangère', *Revue de Défense Nationale*, XIX (juin 1963), pp. 966–76.

Furniss, Edgar S., *France, Troubled Ally*, New York, Praeger, 1960.

Gallois, Pierre, 'L'Alliance entre deux stratégies', *Politique Etrangère*, no. 3 (1966), pp. 217–36.

Gallois, Pierre, 'New Teeth for NATO', *Foreign Affairs*, XXXIX, no. 1 (October 1960), pp. 67–70.

Gallois, Pierre, 'La Nouvelle politique extérieure des Etats-Unis et la sécurité de l'Europe', *Revue de Défense Nationale*, XIX (avril 1963), pp. 566–93.

Gallois, Pierre, *Paradoxes de la paix*, Paris, Presses du Temps Présent, 1967.

de Gaulle, Charles, *Vers l'armée de métier*, Paris, Presses Pocket, [n.d.], [text written in 1934].

de Gaulle, Charles, *Mémoires de Guerre*, 3 vols. ('Le Salut', 'L'Appel', 'L'Unité'), Paris, Librairie Plon, 1959.

de Gaulle, Charles, *The Edge of the Sword*, Gerard Hopkins, trans., London, Faber & Faber Ltd; New York, Criterion Books, 1960.

de Gaulle, Charles, *The Complete War Memoirs of Charles de Gaulle*, Jonathan Griffin and Richard Howard, trans., London, Weidenfeld & Nicolson; New York, Simon & Schuster, 1967.

de Gaulle, Charles, *Major Addresses, Statements and Press Conferences of General Charles de Gaulle: May 19, 1958–May 16, 1967*, 2 vols, New York, French Embassy, Press and Information Division.

de Gaulle, Charles, *The Army of the Future*, [trans. not indicated], London, Hutchinson & Co.; New York, J.B. Lippincott Co., [n.d.]

de Gaulle, Charles, *Discours et messages*, 5 vols, Paris, Librairie Plon, 1970.

de Gaulle, Charles, *Mémoires d'espoir: le renouveau 1958–1962*, Paris, Librairie Plon, 1970. Translated as *Memoirs of Hope: Renewal and Endeavour*, London, Weidenfeld & Nicolson; New York, Simon & Schuster, 1971.

'De Gaulle's 1958 Tripartite Proposal and U.S. Response', *Atlantic Community Quarterly*, IV, no. 3 (Fall 1966), pp. 455–8.

Genevey, Pierre, 'Détente en Europe', *Politique Etrangère*, XXXII, no. 6 (1957), pp. 507–17.

Gerbet, Pierre, 'La Genèse du Plan Schuman', *Revue Française de Science Politique*, VI, no. 3 (juillet–septembre 1956).

Gerbet, Pierre, *La Politique d'unification européenne*, Paris, Amicale des Elèves de l'Institut d'Etudes Politiques de Paris, mimeographed, 1965.

Gladwyn, Lord, (Hubert Miles Gladwyn Jebb, Baron), *De Gaulle's Europe or Why the General says No*, London, Secker & Warburg, 1969.

Gladwyn, Lord, *Europe After de Gaulle*, New York, Taplinger, 1969.

Gladwyn, Lord, *The Memoirs of Lord Gladwyn*, London, Weidenfeld & Nicolson, 1972.

Goodman, Elliot, 'De Gaulle's NATO Policy in Perspective', *Atlantic Community Quarterly*, IV, no. 3 (Fall 1966), pp. 349–57.

Gorce, Paul-Marie de la, *De Gaulle entre deux mondes: une vie et une époque*, Paris, Fayard, 1964.

Graubard, Stephen, ed., *A New Europe?*, Boston, Beacon Press, 1967.

Grewe, Wilhelm, 'L'Avenir de l'Alliance atlantique', *Documents*, XX, no. 2 (mars–avril 1965), pp. 7–25.

Griffith, William, 'The German Problem and American Policy', *Survey*, no 61 (October–November 1966), pp. 105–17.

Grosser, Alfred, *Die Bonner Demokratie*, Düsseldorf, 1960.

Grosser, Alfred, *La IVe République et sa politique extérieure*, Paris, Armand Colin, 1961.

Grosser, Alfred, 'Divergences franco-allemandes', *Revue de Défense Nationale*, XXI (janvier 1965), pp. 13–20.

Grosser, Alfred, 'France and Germany: Divergent Outlooks', *Foreign Affairs*, XLIV, no. 1 (October 1965), pp. 26–36.

Grosser, Alfred, *La Politique extérieure de la Ve République*, Paris, Editions du Seuil, 1965.

Grosser, Alfred, 'An Washington scheiden die Geister', *Die Zeit*, XXII, 13 January 1967, p. 3.

Grosser, Alfred, *French Foreign Policy under de Gaulle*, Lois A. Pattison, trans., Boston, Little, Brown & Co., 1967.

Hanrieder, Wolfram F., *West German Foreign Policy 1949–1963*, Stanford, Stanford University Press, 1967.

Harcourt, R. d', 'De Gaulle et l'opinion allemande', *Revue des Deux Mondes*, XIX (1er mai 1963), pp. 3–15.

Harcourt, R. d', 'Gaullisme et antigaullisme en Allemagne', *Revue des Deux Mondes*, XX (15 octobre 1964), pp. 481–91.

Hassel, Kai-Uwe von, 'Détente through Firmness, *Foreign Affairs*, XLII, no. 2 (January 1964), pp. 184–94.

Hassel, Kai-Uwe von, 'Propos sur la défense', *Documents*, XVIII, no. 2 (mars–avril 1963).

Hassel, Kai-Uwe von, 'Organizing Western Defense', *Foreign Affairs*, XLIII, no. 2 (January 1965), pp. 209–16.

Hassner, Pierre, 'German and European Unification: Two Problems or One?' *Survey*, no. 61 (October 1966), pp. 14–37.

Hassner, Pierre, 'L'Europe entre le statu quo et l'anarchie', *Preuves*, XVII, no. 191 (janvier 1967), pp. 18–37.

Hassner, Pierre, 'From Napoleon III to de Gaulle', *Interplay*, I, no. 7 (February 1968), pp. 12–19.

Heck, Bruno, 'L'Europe a-t-elle encore un avenir?' *Documents*, XX, no. 2 (mars–avril 1965), pp. 26–36.

Heck, Bruno, 'De l'Office franco-allemand pour la jeunesse', *Documents*, IX, no. 2 (mars–avril 1964), pp. 20–28.

Hinterhoff, E., 'Le Spectre de Rapallo', *Revue de Défense Nationale*, XIX (juin 1963), pp. 1019–34.

Hoffmann, Stanley, 'De Gaulle, l'Europe, l'Alliance', *La Caravelle* (publication of l'Association Française de la Nouvelle Angleterre), no. 15 (printemps 1963), pp. 3–10.

Hoffmann, Stanley, *et al.*, *In Search of France*, Cambridge, Harvard University Press for the Harvard University Center for International Affairs, 1963.

Hoffmann, Stanley, 'De Gaulle, Europe and the Atlantic Alliance', *International Organization*, XVIII, no. 1 (Winter 1964), pp. 1–28.

Hoffmann, Stanley, *Gulliver's Troubles*, New York, McGraw-Hill for the Council on Foreign Relations, Atlantic Policy Studies Series, 1968.

Hoffmann, Stanley, and Inge Hoffmann, 'The Will to Grandeur: de Gaulle as Political Artist', *Daedalus* (Summer 1968), pp. 829–87.

Huyn, Hans Graf, *Die Sackgasse: Deutschlands Weg in die Isolierung*, Stuttgart, Seewald Verlag, 1966.

Ivernel, P., 'La Diplomatie gaulliste dans le miroir allemand', *Esprit*, XXXIII, no. 2 (février 1965), pp. 385–9.

Jacquier-Bruère (pseudonym for Michel Debré and Emmanuel Monick), *Demain la paix – esquisse d'un ordre international*, Paris, Librairie Plon, 1945.

Jouve, Edmond, *Le Général de Gaulle et la construction européenne (1940–1966)*, Paris, Librairie Générale de Droit et de Jurisprudence, 2 vols, 1967.

Lippmann, Walter, *Western Unity and the Common Market*, Boston, Little, Brown & Co., 1962.

Macmillan, Harold, *At the End of the Day, 1961–1963*, London, Macmillan; New York, Harper & Row, 1973.

Macridis, Roy, *De Gaulle, Implacable Ally*, New York, Harper & Row, 1966.

Malraux, André, *Felled Oaks: Conversation with De Gaulle*, Irene Clephane, trans., New York, Holt, Rinehart & Winston, 1971.

Massip, Roger, *De Gaulle et l'Europe*, Paris, Flammarion, 1963.

Merchant, Livingston, 'Evolving United States Relations with the Atlantic Community', *International Organization* (Summer 1963).

Monnet, Jean, 'Des Partenaires égaux', *La Nef* (février 1966).

Monnet, Jean, *Mémoires*, Paris, Arthème Fayard, 1976.

Murphy, Robert, *Diplomat among Warriors*, New York, Doubleday, 1964.

Neustadt, Richard, *Alliance Politics*, New York, Columbia University Press, 1970.

Newhouse, John, *Collision in Brussels: the Crisis of June 30*, New York, Norton, The Twentieth Century Fund, Tocqueville Series, no. 2, 1967.

Newhouse, John, *De Gaulle and the Anglo-Saxons*, London, Deutsch; New York, Viking, 1970.

Osgood, Robert, *NATO, the Entangling Alliance*, University of Chicago Press, 1962.

Passeron, André, *De Gaulle parle: 1958–1962*, Paris, Librairie Plon, 1962.

Passeron, André, *De Gaulle parle: 1962–1966*, Paris, Fayard, 1966.

Pinder, John, *Europe against de Gaulle*, New York, Praeger, 1963.

Pompidou, Georges, 'France: the Real Europe', *Atlantic Community Quarterly*, III, no. 3 (Fall 1965), pp. 326–31.

Popper, D. H., 'The United States, France and NATO: a Comparison of Two Approaches', *Department of State Bulletin,* LII (8 February 1965), pp. 180–7.

'Le Problème allemand', *Cahiers de la Nef*, no. 1, Paris, Editions Julliard, 1965.

'Problèmes de l'Allemagne occidentale', special issue of *Revue Economique* (mai 1962).

Reynaud, Paul, *The Foreign Policy of Charles de Gaulle*, M. Saville, trans., New York, Odyssey Press, 1964.

Richardson, James L., *Germany and the Atlantic Alliance*, Cambridge, Harvard University Press, 1966.

Rivau, (SJ), Jean de, 'La Dégradation des rapports franco-allemands', *Etudes* (mars 1966), pp. 291–305.

Rolin, H., and R. Delcour, 'Les Relations franco-allemandes', *Le Monde Diplomatique*, XI, no. 118 (février 1964), p. 7.

Rovan, Joseph, 'Le Danger allemand', *Esprit*, XXXV, no. 1 (janvier 1967), pp. 10–14.

Schlesinger, Arthur, Jr, *A Thousand Days: John F. Kennedy in the White House*, London, Deutsch; Boston, Houghton Mifflin Co., 1965.

Schneider, (Col.) F., 'Perspectives ouest-allemandes: après Nassau et Bruxelles', *Revue de Défense Nationale*, XIX (avril 1963), pp. 622–31.

Schoenbrun, David, *The Three Lives of Charles de Gaulle*, New York, Athenaeum, 1966.

Schwarz, S., 'Veränderungen in den Beziehungen Bonn–Paris', *Deutsche Aussenpolitik*, no. 9 (September 1965), pp. 1051–60.

Serfaty, Simon, *France, de Gaulle and Europe: The Policy of the Fourth and Fifth Republic toward the Continent*, Baltimore, The Johns Hopkins Press, 1968.

Seydoux, François, 'Le Traité allemand', *Politique Etrangère*, XXVIII, no. 6 (1963), pp. 449–58.

Sherwood, Robert, *Roosevelt and Hopkins*, New York, Harper, 1948.

Silj, Alessandro, *Europe's Political Puzzle: a Study of the Fouchet Negotiations and the 1963 Veto*, Cambridge, Harvard University Center for International Affairs, Occasional Paper no. 17 (December 1967).

Sorenson, Theodore C., *Kennedy*, New York, Harper & Row, 1965.

Strauss, Franz-Josef, 'Pour une Communauté atlantique', *Documents*, XVII, no. 1 (1962).

Strauss, Franz-Josef, 'La France et l'Allemagne devraient élaborer un programme politique commun', *Le Monde Diplomatique*, September 1964, p. 1.

Strauss, Franz-Josef, 'An Alliance of Continents', *International Affairs*, XLI, no. 2 (April 1965), pp. 191–203.

Strauss, Franz-Josef, *Entwurf für Europa*, Stuttgart, Seewald Verlag, 1966.

Strauss, Franz-Josef, *The Grand Design: A European Solution to German Reunification*, London, Weidenfeld & Nicolson Ltd; New York, Praeger, 1966.

Strauss, Franz-Josef, 'Tuchfühling mit de Gaulle', *Die Zeit*, XXI, no. 47 (18 November 1966), pp. 9–10.

Taylor, Maxwell, *The Uncertain Trumpet*, London, Stevens & Sons, 1960; New York, Harper Bros, 1959.

Tournoux, J.-R., *La Tragédie du Général*, Paris, Librairie Plon, 1967.

'Le Traité de coopération franco-allemand', *Chroniques Etrangères: Allemagne*, no. 63 (février 1963), pp. 13–16.

Vernant, Jacques, 'L'Allemagne au creux de la vague', *Revue de Défense Nationale*, XX (août–septembre 1964), pp. 1453–8.

Vernant, Jacques, 'Paris, Bonn und Europa', *Europa Archiv*, XX, no. 1 (1965).

Vernant, Jacques, 'Perspectives franco-allemandes', *Politique Etrangère*, XXXII, no. 1 (1967), pp. 22–34.

Wilcox, Francis O. (ed.), *The Atlantic Community*, New York, Praeger, 1963.

Willis, F. Roy, *France, Germany and the New Europe, 1945–1967*, Stanford, Stanford University Press, 2nd edition, 1968.

Wilson, Harold, *The Labour Government 1964–70: A Personal Record*, London, Weidenfeld & Nicolson; Boston, Little, Brown & Co., 1971.

Index

Index